Anne

with much love and gratitude

from

TH

Christmas 1980.

THE WAY TO BLESSEDNESS

also by Thomas Traherne

CENTURIES

THE WAY TO BLESSEDNESS

THOMAS TRAHERNE's *Christian Ethicks*

THE SPELLING AND PUNCTUATION
MODERNIZED BY
MARGARET BOTTRALL

PUBLISHERS
A. R. Mowbray & Co. Ltd
Saint Thomas House, Becket Street
Oxford, OX1 1SJ
ISBN 0 264 66592 9

PRINTED IN GREAT BRITAIN
in 10 point Garamond type
BY THE FAITH PRESS LTD.
LEIGHTON BUZZARD

INTRODUCTION

In 1675, a few months after the death of Thomas Traherne, the book appeared which he had intended to be the public expression of his vision of the good life. It was entitled *Christian Ethicks.* Its sub-title, *The Way to Blessedness,* seems today a more accurate descriptive label; for though Traherne was certainly both Christian and moralist, he was pre-eminently mystic and poet. What makes the book relevant in the twentieth century is not so much its handling of conduct and motives as its concern with happiness. Because it is the testimony of one who speaks from 'the actual knowledge of true felicity,' it is worth our attention; all the more because nowadays felicity has become an almost meaningless concept. Moments of unexpected joy come and go, desires may be temporarily assuaged; but happiness, at best, seems a by-product. We can neither compass the ethical notion that it is the crown of a wise and noble life, nor the religious notion that it is the fulfilment of the soul's desire for union with the divine. But this book of Traherne's springs from the assurance that felicity can be found, if we set about the quest in the right spirit. It is a plea for a new evaluation of virtues, by one who saw this mortal life irradiated by the light of eternity.

The work which we know as *Centuries of Meditations* was never intended for publication, nor did Traherne ever publish his poems; but *Christian Ethicks* appeared with the ascription, 'By Tho. Traherne, B.D., Author of *The Roman Forgeries,*' and undoubtedly it represents his considered message to his contemporaries. His own preface makes his intentions beautifully clear. The message, however, seems to have fallen on barren ground, for the book was not reprinted, and the 1675 edition is something of a rarity.

For the very reason that it was designed for the general public, this is a far less intimate and directly autobiographical book than the *Centuries,* yet it bears the stamp of Traherne's personality from beginning to end. One of the few authentic anecdotes we have about him tells of his habit of launching off into discourses about felicity in season and out of season; and here we find, as in the poems and meditations, an eager, evangelistic fervour to communicate his secret of happiness.

As we discover in the *Centuries,* particularly in the fourth section, many indications of Traherne's interest in morals, so here in his treatise on ethics we find constant evidence of his absorption in the glories of the divine and infinite. It is this preoccupation with the beauty of holiness that is Traherne's peculiar hallmark as a moralist. Merely prudential morality he naturally despises, but he is just as remote from the penitential and the restrictive. It is in terms of recovery of vision, rather than conquest of sin, that he discusses the restoration of man to spiritual wholeness.

Underlying the whole arrangement of *The Way to Blessedness* is Traherne's division of the virtues into three categories; those pertaining to the estate of innocence, those that belong to our present estate of trial and grace, and those proper to the estate of glory. He undertakes to discuss divine attributes as well as human qualities, and this accounts for the apparently unpractical tone of some of his chapters; but since his central thesis is that man was originally made in the divine image, and is capable of being restored to the likeness of God, it is quite essential to his purpose that the limitless possibilities of wisdom, love and justice should be established. No reader of Traherne's poems or meditations needs to be reminded of his impassioned interest in the yet unfallen Adam. In this treatise on ethics, too, we find that his estimate of man's moral potentialities is determined by the consideration of what man was meant to be—a free, joyous, worshipping intelligence. Therefore he gives extraordinary prominence to the glorious qualities which, though beyond the actual attainment of fallen man, are not beyond his contemplation; qualities which, indeed, he must reckon with if he is to be redeemed from spiritual torpor and blindness.

Although Traherne can give, within the limits of a chapter, the impression of logical orderliness, the treatment of his material is not particularly systematic. The plan of the book can, however, be roughly outlined as follows. The first four chapters form an introduction, in which he discusses the nature of happiness, giving great weight to Aristotle's definition, but pointing out the divergences between pagan and Christian conceptions of the true end of man. If, without the special revelation of Christianity, the ancients could see that the practice of virtue was the best means to the conquest of happiness, how needful it is for Christians to reaffirm this, in the context of immortality and redemption! What Traherne calls 'the harsh and sour virtues'—repentance, patience and the like—are indeed necessary in our present condition, but they should not, he thinks, be over-emphasized at the expense of wisdom, love, righteousness; qualities which are not restricted to the state of trial and grace, but belong in fullest measure to the states of innocence and glory.

After this introduction, Traherne deals in chapters V–XIII with the divine virtues, on which the Christian philosopher and moralist should especially meditate. Chapters XIV–XIX are concerned with the essentials for a fully Christian life, and chapters XX–XXX with the virtues requisite for the good life that is less specifically Christian. In this section, however, there are additions and digressions. It may also be noted that several poems, salvaged, it would appear, from an earlier period, have been incorporated by Traherne in this latter part of *The Way to Blessedness*. The final section deals with Magnificence in God, and with Gratitude, to which he characteristically devotes two chapters. The reader has thus been led from innocence, through experience, to felicity. Finally there is an appendix, in which, after the ecstatic flights of his last section, Traherne brings us back to the conditions of this mortal life, not without some regrettable jolts. His ultimate exhortation, however, is in his finest vein; gratitude, we are reminded once again, is the surest of incentives to the practice of all the virtues.

The optimism of Traherne's approach is discernible even in such a brief summary as this. He explicitly refuses to discuss the vices, regarding this as a waste of the time that could be better spent in the consideration of what is true, good and beautiful. Although the general tenor of his writing is so positively happy that we credit him with an unusual capacity for rejoicing, it should be recognized that there is much more behind his raptures than a naturally cheerful disposition. His attitude to the potentialities of human nature can be paralleled in other religious writers of his epoch.

Traherne belongs with those whom the Abbé Brémond has called the Devout Humanists. In seventeenth century England, as in seventeenth century France, theocentric humanism flourished alongside the gloomier creeds that stressed man's natural depravity. The Cambridge Platonists, in particular, were notable for their repudiation of the black doctrine of absolute reprobation, and for their insistence that human beings, though estranged from God, do yet possess a divine spark which raises them above the rest of created natures and makes them gravitate towards truth and felicity. The alienation of mankind from God they did not attribute to our inherent predisposition to sin so much as to a voluntary blindness, a willing absorption in self-centred delusions, by which we shut ourselves off from the divine light and hamper the growth of our true selves. They dwelt constantly on the dignity of man as *capax Dei,* and proclaimed the infinite goodness of God, as expressed in the creation and redemption of this world. There are passages in John Smith's *Selected Discourses* (1659) which are as exalted as anything in the *Centuries,* and Traherne's kinship with these thinkers is quite unmistakable.

In *The Way to Blessedness* a particular link with the Cambridge Platonists can be observed, for they explicitly opposed their Christian philosophy of idealism to the materialism of their alarming contemporary, Thomas Hobbes; and the spectre of *Leviathan* haunts this book of Traherne's. In his first chapter he affirms the *summum bonum,* which Hobbes had denied; there are frequent sallies, and a direct frontal attack in chapter XXXII. Moreover, his whole polemical method makes it clear that Traherne was writing for educated, sophisticated men who, in a scientific and profligate age, might well be inclined to religious scepticism and near-sighted morals. The scholastic turn of some of his arguments and his constant appeals to reason remind us that, for all his soarings into enthusiasm, he was convinced (like the Cambridge Platonists again) that faith in revelation was fully compatible with confidence in the validity of human reason.

A further link with this group is, of course, Traherne's intense interest in Neoplatonism, whether as interpreted by the Florentine commentators of the Renaissance or as transmitted in the writings attributed to Hermes Trismegistus. There are pages on end borrowed from Pico della Mirandola in the *Centuries,* summaries of Ficino in his notebooks; and in this book one of the key chapters, that on Magnanimity, contains lengthy extracts from Dr. John Everard's 1650 translation of *The Divine Pymander.* It is largely from such sources that Traherne derives his immense confidence in the 'interior excellence of the soul of man,' and in the gloriously liberating power of the imagination. But though he sometimes lets himself be seduced into a disregard for the finite nature of mortal man, he steadfastly rejects the magical elements in the Hermetic writings, and their esoteric notion of spiritual wisdom as something available only to initiates. His interpretation of the Bible is coloured by his reading of the Neoplatonists, but he firmly adheres to the central doctrines of Christianity, borrowing only such ideas as he reckons can be harmonized with the truths revealed in Holy Scriptures. There is, besides, a strongly Hebraic element in his delight in all the works of the Creator.

Traherne in his treatise on the way to blessedness is certainly not aiming to provide a 'plain man's pathway to heaven.' In his preface, he gives due praise to *The Whole Duty of Man,* an admirably practical and pastoral book that had been published just before the Restoration, while the Anglican Church was still in eclipse. Within the capacity of the humblest practising Christian, it was deservedly popular, and he does not propose to emulate it. Rather, he addresses himself to 'the curious and unbelieving soul.' But if he assumes a certain scepticism, necessitating a great deal of argument, he also assumes that his ideal reader will be entirely at home with the orthodox doctrines of Christianity and extremely familiar with the Bible. He will also be well grounded in ancient philosophy, an heir to the whole tradition of renaissance learning, a man alive to the rapid progress of science, and fascinated by the almost boundless capacities of the human mind.

Though a well-disposed reader of the twentieth century may

measure up to some of these requirements, it is unlikely that he will meet them all. Why, then, disinter this book? Has it really anything significant to say to us? Does it add anything to what we already know of Traherne?

The second question concerns those whose interest in him may be primarily literary, and the answer must surely be 'yes.' *The Way to Blessedness* reveals aspects of Traherne scarcely apparent in his poems and meditations. It shows him as the learned divine, rather than the mystical recluse. It suggests why he left his Herefordshire parish of Credenhill for London, and why Sir Orlando Bridgeman, Lord Keeper of the Great Seal, employed him for several years as his chaplain; for here, alongside the rhapsodies on divine love and wisdom, are reasoned argument and good shrewd advice. We see here Traherne's methods of public persuasion, whereas the poems and *Centuries* are communings with a friend, with himself, or with God.

The more important question, however, is the first one, about the relevance of this book to our present spiritual needs. The answer to that depends upon the importance that the reader attaches to the quest for happiness. We can sympathize nowadays with the pursuit of truth, but we do not seriously expect intelligent men and women to devote themselves to the search for felicity. Dead sea fruit is a metaphor more intelligible than the apples of the Hesperides. Yet in other ages than our own, thinking people have normally admitted that we come into this world with a natural capacity for happiness, which it is the business of our whole lifetime's education to develop wisely. This persistent conviction, common to pagans and Christians, cannot be dismissed as illusory just because we live in a world threatened by terrors undreamed of a hundred years ago. Most epochs seem catastrophic to those who have to live through them. Traherne himself grew up in an England where battle, murder and sudden death were commonplaces; where plague, syphilis and madness claimed thousands of helpless victims; where more babies died than survived, and where witches were burnt alive. For the most part, the fear of eternal damnation was a haunting threat to righteous and sinners alike, although it was not an age of simple, unquestioning faith. Yet happiness was earnestly pursued by thoughtful men; and Traherne claimed to have found it.

We can neither doubt the authenticity of his experience, revealed most fully in the *Centuries,* nor the vigour of his intellect, manifested just as clearly in *The Way to Blessedness.* Always he writes with impassioned urgency. He is a man with good news to impart. Having pondered his message, we can either dismiss him as a freakish enthusiast, or recognize that he has indeed something to say to those who, whether professing Christians or not, are aware in their daily lives of the dimension of eternity.

It is a sensitiveness to the non-temporal that distinguishes the religious from the merely moral man. Sometimes the attention is so intensely directed to the eternal that time and place appear illusory, and whatever is finite, particularly the human body, becomes of little value. Mystics of whatever creed naturally tend to underestimate the temporal; and the weight of evidence, eastern as well as western, suggests that for the attainment of pure contemplation a strict ascetic discipline is necessary. But there are a great many men and women, certainly not adapted or attracted to the cloister, who do have intimations of eternity. Though the glimpses may be intermittent and fleeting, they are powerful enough to affect the whole quality of the inner life of those who experience them, so that their terms of reference include eternity and their standards of value differ from those of the non-religious. Imaginative artists—poets, painters, musicians—may have these intimations of an order transcending, though interpenetrating, time and place. And there are masses of quite ordinary people going about their daily affairs who are aware of this other dimension as giving to everyday doings a richer significance. These people live 'in the world.' It is their vocation to work, play, love, marry, rear children; they cannot hope, they do not wish, to advance by paths of asceticism to the heights of mystical achievement. But, on the other hand, they cannot easily subsist without some kind of spiritual help that will strengthen their apprehensions of the unseen order. They have no intention of relinquishing the good insights of humanism, yet they know that their lives are ultimately God-centred. To such people, Traherne has much to say.

He does not urge the renunciation of 'wealth and honour, beauty and wit . . . for, as a man may be happy without all these, so may he make a happy use of them.' It may be recalled that the first of his *Thanksgivings* is for the body; and in chapter XIV of *The Way to Blessedness* he writes: 'Man seems to be the head of all things visible and invisible, and the golden clasp whereby things material and spiritual are united. He alone is able to beget the divine image . . .' Many will find this a welcome change from the almost manichean precepts of some of the religious ascetics (whose counsels, to do them justice, were seldom intended for lay folk). Traherne, though a man much given to meditation, and one who chose for many years a retired and simple life, would have thought it ingratitude to underestimate any of the opportunities for happiness which God affords to man.

He may also commend himself to sceptics of to-day because his appeal is primarily to the intelligence. Right thinking is, for him, the essential preliminary to any religious or moral achievement. Whereas many preachers begin by urging a change of heart or a conversion of the will, Traherne declares that a change of mind, a new mental outlook, can revolutionize one's whole conception of the possibilities, purpose and obligations of life. Happiness, he insists, lies within the grasp of any one who will make the effort to adjust his scale of values from the false to the true. Such an adjustment can only be made if the imagination is given full play; ratiocination alone will not accomplish it.

All Traherne's writings insist that it is only the man who possesses imaginative discernment who is able to reach full human stature. As a creature, he can render thanks to his Maker for the gift of life and the treasures of the phenomenal world; and, as made in the divine image, he can do something still more distinctively human. As Traherne puts it in the second *Century*: 'God hath made you able to create worlds in your own mind, which are more precious to him than those which he created; and to give and offer up the world to him, which is very delightful in flowing from him, but much more in returning to him.' His contention is that man's greatest privilege consists in this capacity to re-present the divine pattern of creation, by bringing his own shaping intelligence into action, together with the emotion of loving wonder. The material on which his senses play is given; there are given truths on which his mind may ponder; but not all the giving comes from the divine initiative. There must be a human response. Without a proper enjoyment of God's creation, man cannot make this due return; without a proper conception of the marvellous range of his own mental and spiritual faculties, man cannot rise to the heights of praise, thanksgiving and self-offering that God has a right to expect of him. That human beings are capable of apprehending the mysteries of religion and perceiving the wonders of the world is the most cogent reason why they should transcend the limits of self-absorption.

Unless we realize that this is the heart of Traherne's doctrine of felicity, we may find his treatment of Christian ethics pointlessly eccentric. He is so ready to forsake the discussion of human predicaments for speculations about the divine activity; he is so inattentive to the limitations imposed by mortal infirmity. But he is trying to communicate a vision of life as a sustained act of worship. He never tires of reiterating that man, as a redeemed and intelligent creature, has only to reach out and take and enjoy the happiness for which he was destined—the happiness of being in a right relation to God and his fellow men and the entire creation.

As a moralist, Traherne has some obvious deficiencies. An imperfect apprehension of the power of evil characterizes all his writings. He underestimates the human propensity to make wrong decisions, and minimizes the sheer weight of pain in the world. Occasionally, as in the appendix to this book, he can be convicted of a shallow complacency. But, on the whole, *The Way to Blessedness* is less stamped with other-worldliness than the rest of his writings. He does here acknowledge the difficulties that beset any one attempting to find happiness and peace of mind through the practice of virtue in a much disordered world. He shows a warm-hearted compassion for the distressed, and a deep desire to be of service to his fellows.

There is nothing so profoundly devotional in this book as the meditations on the Cross in the first *Century*, but it is perhaps even more explicitly Christian than the *Centuries* as a whole; permeated by the certainty that our present felicity, in its fullness, does depend on the recognition that this world has truly been redeemed through the saving action of Christ. In chapter XIV, where Mercy is his subject, Traherne argues that man forgiven and reclaimed has far profounder reasons for loving God than any innocent being could have; and the act of redemption he sees as perpetually being accomplished, for he makes no sharp distinction between past, present and future. He lays hold upon the gospel story, on the myth of Eden, on the revelations of the prophets and psalmists, to illuminate the significance of Now. Though man's mortal body is subject to the action of time, he has access through his imagination to what is infinite, and can begin even in this life to enjoy the glorious liberty of the sons of God, by an 'act of the understanding.'

All these ideas are set out in the *Centuries,* sometimes less cumbrously than in *The Way to Blessedness;* yet the emphasis falls differently in the two books, and it seems only belated justice that the treatise which Traherne himself planned to offer to the public should at last be reprinted. Often we are very conscious that a voice from the seventeenth century is speaking. The chapter on Courage has quite a Restoration air; the little essay on Modesty could almost be by Owen Felltham; the arguments used in the chapter on Faith seem to us ill-based and deficient. Sometimes the archaism is pleasing, sometimes we feel that for modern tastes the book could be improved by some harsh pruning. But despite its various shortcomings, it does communicate the last message of a wise and happy man; a man to whom many today are already disposed to listen.

The phraseology, in this version, has not been altered at all. Traherne's mastery of the familiar style is particularly evident in the chapters that deal with the more down-to-earth virtues, and there are passages of splendid exaltation too, scattered throughout the book. The few words no longer in current usage, or changed in their significance, have been glossed in footnotes. The spelling has been modernized, and so has the punctuation—in the original so erratic as to involve occasional obscurity. Printers' errors, fairly frequent in the 1675 edition, have been emended without comment.

MARGARET BOTTRALL

Cambridge, 1962

CONTENTS

TO THE READER

THE design of this treatise is not to stroke and tickle the fancy but to elevate the soul and refine its apprehensions, to inform the judgment and polish it for conversation, to purify and enflame the heart, to enrich the mind, and guide men that stand in need of help in the way of virtue; to excite their desire, to encourage them to travel, to comfort them in the journey, and so at last to lead them to true felicity, both here and hereafter.

I need not treat of virtues in the ordinary way, as they are duties enjoined by the law of God; that the author of *The Whole Duty of Man* hath excellently done: nor as they are prudential expedients and means for a man's peace and honour on earth; that is in some measure done by the French Charron, *Of Wisdom.* My purpose is to satisfy the curious and unbelieving soul concerning the reality, force and efficacy of virtue. And having some advantages from the knowledge I gained in the nature of felicity (by many years' earnest and diligent study) my business is to make as visible as it is possible for me the lustre of its beauty, dignity and glory; by showing what a necessary means virtue is, how sweet, how full of reason, how desirable in itself, how just and amiable, how delightful, and how powerfully conducive also to glory; how naturally virtue carries us to the temple of bliss, and how immeasurably transcendent it is in all kinds of excellency.

And, if I may speak freely, my office is to carry and enhance virtue to its utmost height, to open the beauty of all the prospect, and to make the glory of God appear in the blessedness of man, by setting forth its infinite excellency; taking out of the treasures of humanity those arguments that will discover the great perfection of the end of man, which he may achieve by the capacity of his nature; as also by opening the nature of virtue itself, thereby to display the marvellous beauty of religion, and light the soul to the sight of its perfection.

I do not speak much of vice, which is far the more easy theme, because I am entirely taken up with the abundance of worth and beauty in virtue, and have so much to say of the positive and intrinsic goodness of its nature. But besides, since a straight line is the measure both of itself and of a crooked one, I conclude that the very glory of virtue, well understood, will make all vice appear like dirt before a jewel, when they are compared together. Nay, vice as soon as it is named in the presence of these virtues will look like poison and a contagion or, if you will, as black as malice and ingratitude; so that there will need no other exposition of its nature, to dehort [1] men from the love of it, than the illustration of its contrary.

Virtues are listed in the rank of invisible things, of which kind some are so blind as to deny there are any existent in nature; but yet it may, and will, be made easily apparent that all the peace and beauty in the world proceedeth from them, all honour and security is founded in them, all glory and esteem is acquired by them. For the prosperity of all kingdoms is laid in the goodness of God and of men. Were there nothing in the world but the works of amity, which proceed from the highest virtue, they alone would testify of its excellency. For there can be no safety where there is any treachery. But were all truth and courtesy exercised with fidelity and love, there could be no injustice or complaint in the world, no strife nor violence, but all bounty, joy and complacency. Were there no blindness, every soul would be full of light, and the face of felicity be seen, and the earth turned into heaven.

The things we treat of are great and mighty. They touch the essence of every soul, and are of infinite concernment, because the felicity is eternal that is acquired by them. I do not mean immortal only, but worthy to be eternal; and it is impossible to be happy without them. We treat of man's great and sovereign end, of the nature of blessedness, of the means to attain it: of knowledge and love, of wisdom and goodness, of righteousness and holiness, of justice and mercy, of prudence and courage, of temperance and patience, of meekness and humility, of contentment, of magnanimity and modesty, of liberality and magnificence, of the ways by which love is begotten in the soul, of gratitude, of faith, hope and charity, of repentance, devotion, fidelity and godliness. In all which we show what sublime and mysterious

[1] Dissuade.

creatures they are, which depend upon the operations of man's soul: their great extent, their use and value, their original and their end, their objects and their times: what virtues belong to the estate of innocency, what to the estate of misery and grace, and what to the estate of glory: which are the food of the soul and the works of nature; which were occasioned by sin, as medicines and expedients only; which are essential to felicity, and which accidental; which temporal, and which eternal: with the true reason of their imposition, why they all are commanded, and how wise and gracious God is in enjoining them. By which means all atheism is put to flight, and all infidelity. The soul is reconciled to the Lawgiver of the world, and taught to delight in His commandments. All enmity and discontentment must vanish as clouds and darkness before the sun, when the beauty of virtue appeareth in its brightness and glory. It is impossible that the splendour of its nature should be seen, but all religion and felicity will be manifest.

Perhaps you will meet some new notions; but yet when they are examined the author hopes that it will appear to the reader that it was the actual knowledge of true felicity that taught him to speak of virtue; and, moreover, that there is not the least tittle pertaining to the catholic faith contradicted or altered in his papers. For he firmly retains all that was established in the ancient Councils, nay, and sees cause to do so, even in the highest and most transcendent mysteries; only he enriches all, by farther opening the grandeur and glory of religion, with the interior depths and beauties of faith.

Yet indeed it is not he, but God that hath enriched the nature of it; he only brings the wealth of virtue to light, which the infinite wisdom and power of God have seated there; which though learned men know perhaps far better than he, yet he humbly craves pardon for casting in his mite to the vulgar exchequer. He hath nothing more to say, but that the glory of God and the sublime perfection of human nature are united in virtue. By virtue the creation is made useful and the universe delightful. All the works of God are crowned with their end, by the glory of virtue. For whatever is good and profitable for men is made sacred, because it is delightful and well-pleasing to God; who, being Love by nature, delighteth in His creatures' welfare.

There are two sorts of concurrent actions necessary to bliss; actions in God, and actions in men; nay, and actions too in all the creatures. The sun must warm, but it must not burn; the earth must bring forth, but not swallow up; the air must cool without starving, and the sea moisten without drowning; meats must feed, but not poison; rain must fall, but not oppress. Thus in the inferior creatures you see actions are of several kinds. But these may be reduced to the actions of God, from whom they spring; for He prepares all these creatures for us. And it is necessary to the felicity of His sons that He should make all things healing and amiable, not odious and destructive; that He should love and not hate. And the actions of men must concur aright with these of God and His creatures. They must not despise blessings because they are given, but esteem them; not trample them under foot, because they have the benefit of them, but magnify and extol them. They too must love and not hate. They must not kill and murder, but serve and pleasure one another. They must not scorn great and inestimable gifts, because they are common, for so the angels would lose all the happiness of heaven. If God should do the most great and glorious things that infinite wisdom could devise, if men will resolve to be blind and perverse and senseless, all will be in vain; the most high and sacred things will increase their misery. This may give you some little glimpse of the excellency of virtue.

You may easily discern that my design is to reconcile men to God, and make them fit to delight in Him; and that my last end is to celebrate His praises, in communion with the angels. Wherein I beg the concurrence of the reader, for we can never praise Him enough, nor be fit to praise Him. No other man, at least, can make us so, without our own willingness and endeavour to do it.

Above all, pray to be sensible of the excellency of the Creation, for upon the due sense of its excellency the life of felicity wholly dependeth. Pray to be sensible of the excellency of divine laws, and of all the goodness which your soul comprehendeth. Covet a lively sense of all you know of the excellency of God and of Eternal Love, of your own excellency, and of the worth and value of all objects whatsoever. For to feel is as necessary as to see their glory.

CHAPTER I

Of the end, for the sake of which virtue is desired

It is the prerogative of human nature to understand itself, and guide its operations to a known end; which he doth wholly forfeit that lives at random, without considering what is worthy of his endeavours or fit for his desires.

The end is that which crowns the work; that which inspires the soul with desire, and desire with a quick and vigorous industry. It is last attained but first intended in every operation. All means which can be used in the acquisition of it derive their value from its excellency, and we are encouraged to use them only on account of that end which is attained by them.

It is the office of morality to teach men the nature of virtue, and to encourage them in the practice of it, by explaining its use and efficacy.

The excellence of virtue is the necessity and efficacy thereof in the way to felicity. It consisteth in this; virtue is the only means by which happiness can be obtained.

Since the consideration of the end is that alone which does animate a man to the use of the means, they that treat of virtue do worthily propose the end in the beginning, and first show the excellency of bliss before they open the nature of virtue. For it is a vain thing to discover the means, unless the end be desired by those to whom the nature and use of them, in their tendency to that end, is taught and commended; for if the end be despised, all endeavours are but fruitless which instruct us in the means; and the knowledge of them vain, if they never be used or improved.

That Reason whereby man is able to contemplate his end is a singular advantage, wherein he is privileged above a beast. It enables him not only to examine the nature and perfection of his end, but the equity and fitness of the means in order thereunto;

and the singular excellency of his First Cause, as its glory and goodness appeareth in the design and contrivance; especially in making man's happiness so complete and perfect.

The heathens, who invented the name of Ethics, were very short in the knowledge of man's end; but they are worse than heathens, that never consider it.

The more excellent the end is, the more prone by nature we are to pursue it; and all the means conducive thereunto are the more desirable.

Reason, which is the formal essence of the soul of man, guides him to desire those things which are absolutely supreme. For it is an eternal property in reason to prefer the better above the worse. He that prefers the worse above the better acts against nature, and swerves from the rule of right reason.

Whatever varieties of opinion there are concerning happiness, all coincide and agree in this, that man's last end is his perfect happiness; and the more excellent his happiness is, the more ought his soul to be enflamed with the desire of it, and inspired with the greater industry.

The more perfect his bliss is, the greater the crime of despising it. To pursue an infinite and eternal happiness is divine and angelical; to pursue a terrene and sensual felicity is brutish; but to place felicity in anger and envy is diabolical, the pleasures of malice being bitter and destructive.

To live by accident, and never to pursue any felicity at all, is neither angelical, nor brutish, nor diabolical, but worse than anything, in some respect in the world. It is to act against our own principles, and to wage war with our very selves. They that place their ease in such a carelessness are of all others the greatest enemies and disturbers of themselves.

It is madness and folly to pursue the first object that presents itself, under notion of felicity; and it is base to content one's self in the enjoyment of a mean estate, upon a suspicion there is no true happiness, because the nature thereof is so much doubted in the world. The disputations concerning its nature argue its existence. And we must cease to be men before we can extinguish the desire of being happy. He only is truly generous that aspires to the most perfect blessedness of which God and Nature have made him capable.

By how much greater the uncertainty is, by so much the more heedful ought we to be, lest we should be seduced and deceived in the choice of happiness, for the danger is the greater. And by how much the more eager men are in their disputations concerning it, by so much the more weighty is the nature of the theme to be presumed.

Hastiness in catching at an unexamined felicity is the great occasion of all the error about it, among the vulgar; who are led, like beasts, by their sense and appetite, without discerning or improving any other faculty. The lip of the cup is anointed with honey which, as soon as they taste, they drink it up, though the liquor be nothing but gall and poison. Being deluded with a show instead of pleasure, they rush hand over head on their own destruction.

It is as natural to man to desire happiness as to live and breathe. Sense and instinct carry him to happiness, as well as reason; only reason should rectify and direct his instinct, inform his sense, and complete his essence, by inducing those perfections of which it is capable.

Things good in themselves, when they stand in competition with those that are better, have the notion of evil; better things are evil, if compared with the best; especially where the choice of the one hinders the acquisition of the other. For where good, better and best are subservient to each other, the one is better for the other's sake; but where they interfere and oppose each other, the good are bad in comparison with the better, and the better worse than the best of all. This is the cause why reason cannot acquiesce in any felicity less than the supreme; which must needs be infinite, because Almighty Power, which made reason active, is illimited in its operations, and never rests but in the production of a glorious act, that is infinite in perfection.

If felicity be infinite, the loss is as great that attends our miscarriage, and the misery intolerable that follows our loss. For, our eyes being open, a loss that is incomprehensible must needs produce a grief immeasurable, an anguish as infinite as our damage.

All inferior felicities are but miseries compared with the highest. A farthing is good and pleaseth a beggar in time of distress; but a piece of gold is better. An estate of a thousand pounds a year is better than a piece of gold; but our ambition carries us to principalities and empires. An empire is more desirable than a province; and the wider, the richer, the better it is, the more desirable. But the empire of all the earth is a bubble compared to the heavens; and the heavens themselves less than nothing to an infinite dominion.

Perfect felicity is not dominion, nor pleasure, nor riches alone; nor learning, nor virtue, nor honour; but all in perfection. It requires that every soul should be capable of infinite dominion, pleasure, learning and honour for the full and perfect attainment of it.

If all these be infinite and eternal in that felicity which is prepared for man, those actions are of inestimable value by virtue of which his felicity is gained; and it becomes his wisdom and courage to suffer many things for so noble an end; especially if in this life it may in any measure be thereby acquired and enjoyed.

The great reason why God has concealed felicity from the knowledge of man is the enhancement of its nature and value; but that which most conceals it is the corruption of nature. For as we have corrupted, so have we blinded ourselves. Yet are we led by instinct eagerly to thirst after things unknown, remote and forbidden. The truth is, our palates are vitiated and our digestion so corrupted that, till our nature be purified by a little industry, to make felicity known is but to expose it to contempt and censure. It is too great and pure for perverted nature.

The concealment of an object whets our appetite, and puts an edge upon our endeavours, and this carries something of a mystery in it; for whereas the maxim is, *Ignoti nulla Cupido, All Love comes in at the eye,* we affect an object to which we are blind, and the more blind we are, the more restless. We are touched with an unknown beauty which we never saw, and in the midst of our ignorance are actuated with a tendency which does not abate the value of our virtues but puts life and energy into our actions.

Though felicity cannot perfectly be understood, because it is incomprehensible to men on earth, yet so much of it may be discerned as will serve to meet our instinct and feed our capacity, animate our endeavour, encourage our expectation to hope for more than we enjoy, enable us to subdue our lusts, support us in temptations, and assist us in overcoming all obstacles whatsoever.

Infinite honours and pleasures, were there no more in felicity, are enough to allure us; but the fruition of all in the best of manners, in communion with God, being full of life and beauty and perfection in Himself, and having the certain assurance that all shall be included in His bliss that can be thought on; it is a thing so divine that the very hope of it fills us with comfort here, and the attainment with satisfaction hereafter.

He that can enjoy all things in the image of God need not covet their fruition in a baser manner. Man was made in God's image that he might live in His similitude.

I am not so stoical as to make all felicity consist in a mere apathy, or freedom from passion; nor yet so dissolute as to give the passions all their liberty. Neither do I persuade you to renounce the advantages of wealth and honour, any more than those of beauty and wit; for as a man may be happy without all these, so may he make a happy use of them when he has them. He may be happy with difficulty without them, but easily with them. If not in heaven, yet certainly on earth, the goods of Fortune concur to the completing of temporal felicity, and therefore where they are freely given are not to be despised.

That which I desire to teach a man is, how to make a good use of all the advantages of his birth and breeding; how in the increase of riches and honours to be happy in their enjoyment; how to secure himself in the temptations of affluence, and to make a man glorious in himself and delightful to others in abundance; or else, if affliction should arise and the state of affairs change, how to triumph over adverse fortune, and to be happy notwithstanding his calamities; how to govern himself in all estates so as to turn them to his own advantage.

For though felicity be not absolutely perfect in this world, nor so complete in poverty as in a great and plentiful estate, you are not to believe that wealth is absolutely necessary; because sometimes it is requisite to forfeit all for the sake of felicity. Nothing is absolutely necessary to bliss but grace and virtue, though to perfect bliss ease and honour be absolutely necessary.

There are many degrees of blessedness beneath the most

supreme, that are transcendentally sweet and delightful; and it sometimes happens that what is most bitter to sense is pleasant to reason.

Rather than make shipwreck of a good conscience, we must do as mariners in a storm, cast our riches overboard for our own preservation. It is better losing them than ourselves.

Virtue is desirable and glorious, because it teacheth us through many difficulties in this tempestuous world to sail smoothly and attain the haven.

CHAPTER II

Of the nature of Felicity, its excellence and perfection

THE Peripatetics, so far forth as they contemplated the nature and estate of man in this world, were wise in defining the goods of the body, soul and fortune to concur to man's perfect happiness. For difficulties and conflicts are not essential to the nature of bliss, nor consistent with the fruition of its fullness and perfection.

There is the Way, and the Journey's End.

In the Way to Felicity, many things are to be endured that are not to be desired. And therefore is it necessary to make a distinction between the Way to felicity and the Rest which we attain in the end of our journey.

The goods of the soul are absolutely necessary in the Way to happiness; the goods of the body are very convenient, and those of fortune commodious enough. But the latter of these are not with too much eagerness to be pursued.

The goods of the soul are wisdom, knowledge, courage, all the virtues, all the passions, affections, powers and faculties. And these you know are absolutely necessary.

The goods of the body are health, agility, beauty, vivacity, strength and liberty; and these shall in heaven itself, together with those of the soul, be enjoyed; by which you may discern that the goods of the body are real parts and ingredients of happiness.

The goods of fortune are food and raiment, houses and lands, riches, honours, relations and friends, with all those convenient circumstances without the body that are subject to chance; by which virtue is assisted, and of which a noble use may be made, in works of justice, hospitality, courtesy and charity, which may redound to our greater felicity here and in heaven.

The more honour and pleasure we enjoy, the greater and more perfect is our present happiness; though many times in the way to felicity we are forced to quit all these, for the preservation of our innocence.

Gallant behaviour in slighting all transitory things for the preservation of our virtue is more conducive to our future perfection than the greatest ease imaginable in our present condition.

It is incumbent upon us, as a special part of our care, to take heed that we be not ensnared by the easiness of prosperity, and that we do not set up our rest in the Way to happiness; nor deceive ourselves in thinking the goods of fortune essential, nor discourage ourselves by thinking it impossible to be happy without them. Our thoughts and affections must be always disentangled, that we may run with alacrity the race set before us, and close with the sublimest perfection of bliss as our only portion and desire.

Felicity is rightly defined to be *the perfect fruition of a perfect soul, acting in perfect life by perfect virtue;* for the attainment of which perfection we must, in the way to felicity, endure all afflictions that can befall us. For though they are not parts of felicity themselves, yet we may acknowledge them great advantages for the exercise of virtue, and reckon our calamities among our joys, when we bear and overcome them in a virtuous manner, because they add to our honour and contribute much to our perfection, both here and hereafter.

For this purpose we are to remember that our present estate is not that of reward, but labour; it is an estate of trial, not of fruition; a condition wherein we are to toil and sweat and travail hard for the promised wages; an appointed seed-time for a future harvest; a real warfare, in order to a glorious victory; in which we must expect some blows, and delight in the hazards and encounters we meet with, because they will be crowned with a glorious and joyful triumph, and attended with ornaments and trophies far surpassing the bare tranquillity of peace.

When we can cheerfully look on an army of misfortunes without amazement, we may then freely and delightfully contemplate the nature of the highest felicity.

Aristotle never heard of our ascension into heaven, nor of sitting down on the throne of God, yet by a lucky hit (if I may so say) fell in point blank upon the nature of blessedness. For a perfect fruition by perfect virtue is all that can be thought of; it implies our objective, and our formal, happiness.

Objective happiness is all the goodness that is fit to be enjoyed either in God or in His creatures; while formal happiness is an active enjoyment of all objects by contemplation and love, attended with full complacency in all their perfections.

Perfect fruition implies the perfection of all its objects; among which God Himself is one, angels and saints are next, the world also with all the variety of creatures in it, the laws of God and His ways in all ages, His eternal counsels and divine attributes, are other objects of our content and pleasure. Unless all these be perfect in their nature, variety, number, extent, relation, use and value, our fruition cannot be simply perfect, because a greater and more perfect fruition might, upon the production of better objects, be contrived; and no fruition can be truly perfect that is not conversant about the highest things. The more beautiful the object is, the more pleasant is the enjoyment; but where delight may be increased, the fruition is imperfect.

A perfect soul is a transcendent mystery. As God could not be perfect, were it possible that there could be any better essence than He, so neither would the soul be perfect, could any more perfect soul be created.

It is a soul in which no defect or blemish can be discerned; perfect in the variety and number of its powers, in the fitness and measure of every power, in the use and value of every endowment. A perfect soul is that whereunto nothing can be added to please our desire. As all its objects are perfect, so is itself. It is able to see all that is to be seen, to love all that is lovely, to hate all that is hateful, to desire all that is desirable, to honour all that is honourable, to esteem all that can be valued, to delight in all that is delightful, and to enjoy all that is good and fit to be enjoyed. If its power did fall short of any one object, or of any one perfection, in any object, or of any degree in any perfection, it would be imperfect; it would not be the masterpiece of eternal power.

Perfect life is the full exertion of perfect power. It implies two things: perfection of vigour, and perfection of intelligence; an activity of life, reaching through all immensity to all objects whatsoever; and a freedom from dullness in apprehending; an exquisite tenderness of perception in feeling the least object, and a sphere of activity that runs parallel with the omnipresence of the Godhead. For if any soul lives so imperfectly as to see and know but some objects, or to love them remissly and less than they deserve, its life is imperfect; because either it is remiss or, if never so fervent, confined.

Perfect fruition, as it implies the perfection of all objects, more nearly imports the intrinsic perfection of its own operations. For if its objects be never so many, and perfect in themselves, a blemish lies upon the enjoyment if it does not reach unto all their excellence. If the enjoyment of one object be lost, or one degree of the enjoyment abated, it is imperfect.

Perfect virtue may best be understood by a consideration of its particulars. Perfect knowledge is a thorough, complete understanding of all that may be known. Perfect righteousness is a full and adequate esteem of all the value that is in things. It is a kind of spiritual justice, whereby we do right to ourselves and to all other beings. If we render to any object less than it deserves, we are not just thereunto. Perfect wisdom is that whereby we choose a most perfect end, actually pursue it by the most perfect means, acquire and enjoy it in most perfect manner. If we pitch upon an inferior end, our wisdom is imperfect; and so it is if we pursue it by feeble and inferior means, or neglect any one of those advantages whereby we may attain it. And the same may be said of all the virtues.

Now if all objects be infinitely glorious, and all worlds fit to be enjoyed; if God has filled heaven and earth and all the spaces above the heavens with innumerable pleasures; if His infinite wisdom, goodness and power be fully glorified in every being, and the soul be created to enjoy all these in most perfect manner; we may well conclude with the holy apostle, that we are *the children of God, and if children, then heirs—heirs of God, and joint heirs with Christ, if so be that we suffer with Him, that we may also be glorified together. That our light affliction, that is but for a moment, worketh out for us a far more exceeding and eternal weight of glory. That beholding as in a glass the glory of the Lord, we shall at last be transformed into the same image from glory to glory, even as by the Spirit of the Lord.* For all His works, of which the psalmist saith, *They are worthy to be had in remembrance, and are sought out of all them that have pleasure therein, are like a mirror, wherein His glory appeareth, as the face of the sun doth in a clear fountain.* We may conclude further that virtue, by force of which we attain so great a kingdom, is infinitely better than rubies. All the things thou canst desire are not to be compared to her. So that with unspeakable comfort we may take courage to go on, not only in the study but the practice of all kind of virtues, concerning which we are to treat in the ensuing pages. For as the Apostle Peter telleth us, *He hath given to us all things that pertain to life and godliness, through the knowledge of Him that hath called us to glory and virtue; whereby are given unto us exceeding great and precious promises; that by these you might be partakers of the divine nature, having escaped the corruption that is in the world through lust. And besides this,* saith he, *giving all diligence, add to your faith virtue; and to virtue, knowledge; and to knowledge, temperance; and to temperance, patience; and to patience, godliness; and to godliness, brotherly kindness; and to brotherly kindness, charity. For so an entrance shall be ministered to you abundantly into the everlasting kingdom of our Lord and Saviour Jesus Christ. Which kingdom being so divine and glorious as it is, we have need to bow our knees to the God and Father of our Lord Jesus Christ, of whom the whole family in heaven and earth is named; that He would grant us according to the riches of His glory to be strengthened with might by His Spirit in the inward man, that Christ may dwell in our hearts by faith; that we being rooted and grounded in love, may be able to comprehend with all saints what is the breadth and length and depth and height, and to know the love of Christ which passeth knowledge, that we may be filled with all the fullness of God.*

To be partaker of the divine nature, to be filled with all the fullness of God, to enter into His kingdom and glory, to be transformed into His image and made an heir of God and a joint heir with Christ; to live in union and communion with God, and to be made a temple of the Holy Ghost; these are divine and transcendent things that accompany our souls in the perfection of their bliss and happiness—the hope and belief of all which is justified and made apparent by the explanation of the very nature of the soul, its inclinations and capacities, the reality and greatness of those virtues of which we are capable, and all those objects which the universe affordeth to our contemplation.

CHAPTER III

Of virtue in general: the distribution of it into its several kinds, its definition

BEFORE we come to treat of particular virtues, it is very fit that we speak something of Virtue in general.

Virtue is a comprehensive word, by explaining which we shall make the way more easy to the right understanding of all those particular virtues into which it is divided; forasmuch as the nature of virtue enters into knowledge, faith, hope, charity, prudence, courage, meekness, humility, temperance, justice, liberality, etc. Every one of these hath its essence opened in part by the explication of that which entereth its nature, which is virtue in general.

The predicament of quality contains within it either natural dispositions or habits. Habits may be either virtuous or vicious. Virtuous habits are either theological, intellectual, moral or divine; and these are branched into so many kinds of virtue, as followeth.

The theological virtues are generally divided into three—faith, hope and charity; which are called theological because they have God for their principal object and are, in a peculiar manner, taught by His word among the mysteries of religion. To which we may add repentance; forasmuch as this virtue, though it be occasioned by sin, is chiefly taught by the Word of God, and respects God as its principal object; for which reason we shall account the theological virtues to be four—faith, hope, charity and repentance, to which, if we are making them more, we may add obedience, devotion, godliness.

The intellectual virtues are generally reckoned to be five—intelligence, wisdom, science, prudence, art; which, inasmuch as the distinction between them is over-nice and curious (at least too obscure for vulgar apprehensions) we shall reduce them perhaps to a fewer number.

Intelligence is the knowledge of principles; science the knowledge of conclusions; wisdom, that knowledge which results from the union of both prudence and art, has been more darkly explained. The objects of wisdom are always stable. Prudence is that knowledge by which we guide ourselves in thorny and uncertain affairs. Art is that habit by which we are assisted in composing tracts and systems, rather than in regulating our lives, and more frequently appears in fiddling and dancing than in noble deeds. Were it not useful in teachers for the instruction of others, we should scarce reckon it in the number of virtues.

All these are called intellectual virtues, because they are seated in the understanding and chiefly exercised in contemplation. The virtues that are brought down into action are called practical, and at other times moral, because they help us in perfecting our manners, as they relate to our conversation with men.

The moral virtues are either principal or less principal. The principal are four—prudence, justice, temperance and fortitude; which, because they are the hinges upon which our whole lives do turn, are called cardinal,[1] and are commonly known by the name of the four Cardinal Virtues. They are called principal not only because they are the chief of all moral virtues, but because they enter into every virtue, as the four elements of which it is compounded.

The less principal virtues are magnificence and liberality, modesty and magnanimity, gentleness of behaviour, affability, courtesy, truth and urbanity. All these are called less principal, not because they are indifferent or may be accounted useless, for then they would not be virtues; but because, though their practice be of extraordinary importance in their place, they are more remote, and less avail in the way to felicity, and are more confined in their operations.

Divine virtues, which we put instead of the heathenish Heroical, are such as have not only God for their object and end but their pattern and example. They are virtues which are seen in His eternal life, by practising which we also are changed into the same image and are made partakers of the divine nature. Wisdom, knowledge and truth in the sublimest height we confess to be three; but we shall chiefly insist upon goodness and righteousness and holiness (all which will appear in divine love, in more peculiar manner to be handled).

Besides all these, there are some virtues which may more properly be called Christian; because they are nowhere else taught but in the Christian religion, are founded on the love of Christ, and the only virtues distinguishing a Christian from the rest of the world; of which sort are love to enemies, meekness and humility.

All these virtues are shut up under one common head, because they meet in one common nature, which bears the name of virtue; the essence of which being well understood will conduce much to the clear knowledge of every one in particular.

Virtue, in general, is that habit of soul by force of which we attain our happiness. Or, if you please, it is a right and well ordered habit of mind, which facilitates the soul in all its operations, in order to its blessedness.

These terms are to be unfolded.

Virtue is a habit. All habits are either acquired or infused.

[1] Note, 1675: *Cardo* is a hinge.

By calling it a habit, we distinguish it from a natural disposition, or power of the soul. For a natural disposition is an inbred inclination, which attended our birth and began with our beings; not chosen by our wills, nor acquired by industry. These dispositions, because they do not flow from our choice and industry, cannot be accounted virtues. 'Tis true indeed that virtuous habits are sometimes infused in a miraculous manner, but then they are rather called graces than virtues; and are ours only as they are consented to by our wills, not ours by improvement and exercise. Though they agree with virtues in their matter and their end, yet they differ in their original and form. For as all human actions flow from the will and the understanding, so do all virtues, when they are rightly understood; whereas we are passive in the reception of these, and they flow immediately from heaven.

And it is far more conducive to our felicity that we should conquer difficulties in the attainment of virtue—study, choose, desire, pursue and labour after it, acquire it finally by our own care and industry, with God's blessing upon it—than that we should be dead and idle, while virtue is given us in our sleep. For which cause God ordered our state and condition so, that by our own labour we should seek after it; that we might be as well pleasing in His eyes, and as honourable and admirable in the acquisition of virtue, as in the exercise and practice of it. And for these reasons God doth not so often infuse it, and is more desirous that we should by many repeated actions of our own attain it.

God does sometimes upon the general sloth of mankind inspire it, raising up some persons thereby to be like salt among corrupted men, lest all should putrefy and perish; yet is there little reason why He should delight in that way, without some such uncouth and ungrateful necessity to compel Him thereunto.

For any man to expect that God should break the general order and course of nature, to make him virtuous without his own endeavours, is to tempt God by a presumptuous carelessness, and by a slothful abuse of his faculties to fulfil the parable of the unprofitable servant.

The powers of the soul are not virtues themselves, but when they are clothed with virtuous operations they are transformed into virtues; for powers are in the soul, just as limbs and members in the body, which may be indifferently applied to virtues and vices, alike to be busied and exercised in either.

As the members are capable of various motions, either comely or deformed, and are one thing when they are naked, another when attired, and capable of being modified with several habits; so are the powers and faculties of the soul. As they are in the nature of man without exercise, they are void and naked; but by many acts of vice or virtue they put on a habit, which seems chiefly to consist in an inclination and tendency to such actions, a facility of working, an acquaintance with them, a love to them and a delight in them. For by long custom it turns to a second nature, and becomes at last as necessary as life itself; a confirmed habit being taken in and incorporated with the powers of the soul by frequent exercise.

In the second definition we add that *Virtue is a right and well ordered habit.* A habit is something added to that which wears it, and every power of the soul is naked, without the quality wherewith long custom clothes it. Much of the formal reason of virtue is shut up in those words, *Right and well ordered.* For confused, irregular and careless habits will be always erroneous and deformed, and must consequently end in dishonour and miseries. He must aim at the mark that hits it, for only those actions which are well guided produce right and well ordered habits; which right and well ordered habits alone can carry us to our sovereign end.

A mind in frame is a soul clothed with right apprehensions; thoughts and affections well ordered, principles and contrivances well proposed, means and ends rationally consulted, all considered and the best chosen. Long custom, inuring us to the benefit and excellence of these, disposes the soul into a right and well ordered habit or frame of spirit, which regards that glorious end for which we were created.

By force of which we attain our happiness. Idleness and virtue are as destructive to each other as fire and water. In all virtue there is some force, and in all force much action. A virtuous habit ceaseth to be virtuous unless it actually incline us to virtuous operations. As the powers of the soul when they are well exercised turn into virtues, so is it by that exertion that we attain our happiness. *Virtue is that right and well ordered habit by force of which we attain our happiness.*

Its force is never expressed but in exercise and operation. Yet even when we are asleep, it may tacitly incline us and make us ready, when we awake, to be virtuous. Perhaps the habit sleeps and awakes with the body; but if the habit and its energy be the same thing, it still sleepeth when its energy ceaseth; if they be diverse, the habit may continue for some time without the force of its operation.

But not to divert into blind and obscure corners; whether the soul of a man asleep may be styled virtuous or no; whether the habits continue in him at that time without their acts, is nothing to our purpose. It is sufficient that, when he is awake, he that hath a virtuous habit is in all his actions inclined and carried to his own felicity, unless he falls into an oblivion worse than sleep; because, without some such damnable and vicious lethargy, he is always mindful of his last end, and tends towards it in a direct line.

All his actions derive a tincture from the first principle, that habit of the soul by which he is carried toward his own felicity. All those actions that spring from that habit tend to bliss, and by force of that habit are made virtuous and with facility performed.

All the difficulty is in the beginning. Virtues in the beginning are like green fruits, sour and imperfect; but their maturity is accompanied with sweetness and delight. It is hard to acquire a virtuous habit at first, but when it is once gotten, it makes all virtue exceeding easy; and not easy alone, but happy and delightful. For a virtuous habit as certainly acts according to its own nature as the sun shines, which is light by constitution. It acts freely, yet when it does act, it must needs act virtuously, and can do nothing else; for it is not virtuous habit, but some other principle, that exerteth vicious and bad operations.

Happiness is with so much necessity the end of virtue that we cannot take a due estimate of the excellence of virtue without considering the tendency which it has to felicity. For as the means are extravagant (and indeed no means) that have no relation nor proportion to their end; so would all the virtues be inept and worthless (no virtues) if they did not in some sort conduce to our happiness. For happiness is the adequate end, which by nature we seek. Whether it be glory or pleasure or honour that we design, or wealth or learning; all that is delightful and grateful to our reason is comprehended in our happiness. If we desire to glorify God, or to please the angels, or be grateful[1] to men, it is because we love ourselves and delight in our own happiness, and conceit[2] all those actions whereby we so do either a means or a part of it. So that in the partition and distribution of virtues, we must take another courage to display their glory, by exhibiting them in such a prospect as that is, wherein their place and office will appear in their tendency towards man's last end, his blessedness and glory.

CHAPTER IV

Of the powers and affections of the soul: what virtues pertain to the estate of innocency; what to the estate of grace; what to the estate of glory

Two things in felicity are apparent to the eye, glory and treasure; and the faculties of the soul do in a several manner affect both. The understanding was made to see the value of our treasure, and the freedom of the will to achieve glory to our actions; anger, to stir us up against all difficulty and opposition that might stand in our way; appetite, to pursue the pleasure in either; fear, to heighten our concernment, that we might more dread the danger of losing that happiness, wherein no less than glory and treasure

[1] Pleasing.
[2] Conceive.

are infinitely united; reason itself, to compare felicities and weigh which is the most perfect; desire, to covet it; hope, to encourage us in the pursuit of it; aversion, for the avoiding of all temptations and impediments; love, to the goodness of it; joy, for its fruition; hatred, to keep us from the misery which is contrary thereunto; boldness, to attempt it; sorrow and despair, to punish and torment us if we fail to attain it. For these two, being unpleasant affections, serve to engage us in the pursuit of happiness because we are loath to experience the sense of such troublesome passions.

Ambition and covetousness are inclinations of the soul, by the one of which we are carried to glory, by the other to treasure. And as all the rest, so may these be made either virtues or vices; virtues when they are means conducive to the highest end; vices when they distract and entangle us with inferior objects.

The inclinations and affections of the soul may be defective or excessive in their exercise towards objects. In relation to the highest object there is no danger of excess. We can never too violently either love or desire our supreme happiness. Our hope can never exceed its greatness, we can never too much rejoice in the fruition of it. Nor can we exceed in anger or hatred against those things that would bereave us of it; or too much fear the misery of that life which will be ever without it; or be affected with too much sorrow and despair at the loss of it. But if we look upon inferior things, which are merely accidental to the nature of felicity, such as the favour of men, injuries, crosses, temporal successes, the beauty of the body, the goods of fortune and such like, our affections and passions may be too excessive, because the good or evil of these is but finite; whereas the good of sovereign bliss is altogether infinite, and so is the evil of eternal misery.

When our own actions are regular, there is nothing in the world but may be made conducive to our highest happiness; nor is there any value in any object or creature in the world but as it is subservient to our bliss. No member of the body, no sense or endowment of any member, no inclination or faculty of the soul, no passion or affection, no virtue, no grace, no spiritual gift, no assistance, no means of grace, nothing how great or precious soever can be of any value, but in order to felicity. In real truth, nothing without this can be great or estimable. Every virtue therefore must have this in common with all the laws and ordinances and works of God—they must all directly or obliquely tend to our supreme happiness; upon this dependeth all their excellency.

Some virtues are necessary in the estate of innocency, some in the estate of grace, some in the estate of glory.

Without seeing, it is impossible to enjoy our happiness or find out the way unto it. Therefore is Knowledge necessary in all estates. Without Loving it is impossible to delight in its goodness. The office of Righteousness is to render to everything a due esteem, and without this it is apparent that no treasure can be to us (though in itself never so great) of any value. Holiness is the conscience that we make of discharging our duty, and the zeal wherewith we avoid the profaneness of its contrary. Goodness is necessary, because we ourselves cannot without that be amiable, nor, unless we be delightful to others, enjoy ourselves or acquire glory. The office of Wisdom is to choose and pursue the highest end, by the best of all means that can be chosen.

These are transcendent virtues, whereby even God Himself doth enjoy His felicity. They are incumbent on us by the law of nature, and so essentially united to our formal happiness that no blessedness or glory can be enjoyed without them. Therefore are we to look upon them as the life and soul of religion, as eternal duties in all estates for ever to be exercised. They are all exercised in the very fruition itself, as will more apparently be seen when we come to every one of these virtues in particular. They were enjoined in the estate of innocency, without any need of a positive law, by the very nature of God and the soul and of things themselves; and must be exercised in the state of grace, and will abide for ever in the state of glory.

That virtues might be ours, in being wrought by ourselves; and be virtues indeed, in being wrought with difficulty; that we might be so much the more laudable and glorious in our eternal condition, God gave us liberty, in the beginning, that we might choose what we would; and placed us in such an estate that, having in us only the seeds and principles of all virtue, we might exercise our natural powers of our own accord, for the attainment of that actual knowledge, wisdom and righteousness wherein the perfection of our soul consisteth, and by which the perfection of our bliss is to be enjoyed. That being naked by nature, though pure and clean, we might clothe ourselves with our own habits, attain the glory of those ornaments, in our own acts, for which we were created, and work our own righteousness in such a way as God had appointed.

For the glory which we were to attain is that goodness which we are to show in our voluntary care and obedience; and that goodness is chiefly expressed in the kind and genuine exercise of our own liberty, while we are tender of displeasing Him to whom we are obliged, and so good as to gratify His desires, though we had no restraint upon us.

To make ourselves amiable and beautiful by the exercise of our own power produces another kind of beauty and glory than if we were compelled to be good by all His preventing [1] power. All goodness is spoiled by compulsion. Our own actions, springing from an interior fountain, deep within the soul, when voluntarily and freely exerted, are more acceptable; and the will, whence they spring, is more excellent and perfect. This I would have you to note well, for the intrinsic goodness and glory of the soul consists in the perfection of an excellent will, and without this it might be a piece of dirt surrounded with gold, but no imputed or annexed virtue could make it a jewel.

The actions of God or of the angels or of other men towards it add no value to the soul, if it will do nothing of itself. If it be idle or unactive, the more excellent the action of God and of all other creatures are towards it, so much the more deformed and perverse is the soul; nor will all the glory of its powers and inclinations excuse it, but the more great and divine they are, the more abominable will it make itself by abusing them, in frustrating their inclinations.

For the removing of all constraint and the infusing of greater excellency and beauty into these holy actions which He required from them, it pleased God to make men obnoxious [2] to temptations, that having obstacles to overcome and disadvantages to

[1] Predisposing.
[2] Liable.

struggle with, man's righteousness might be more full of virtue, and himself made capable of victory and triumph. For this end, He seated him in a low estate, even in an estate of trial; wherein was the occasion of exercising faith and hope, because his felicity was distant from him; faith in believing the promises of God, and hope in waiting for the accomplishment of his bliss. He had occasions for fear also, in relation to God's power and justice, who was able to remove his happiness upon the least offence, and to bring upon him that misery that was denounced for his transgressions. In this estate of trial, prudence, which is conversant in nice [1] affairs, was to watch and consider and direct his behaviour, in the midst of those dangers and temptations that might possibly be expected. His temperance was to be exercised in the government of his appetite, so that all inferior satisfactions and sensual pleasures might be limited and ordered as it most consists with his highest happiness; humility, in the acknowledgment of his own unworthiness, who was taken out of nothing; and gratitude in a kind of just retribution to his benefactor, for all the glory to which he was advanced.

All these virtues are in themselves delightful, and easy in their exercise. They immediately respect felicity, and are by nature necessary to man's enjoyment of it. They are consonant to reason, and agreeable to the circumstances of his happy condition. His fear and humility, which were in Paradise the severest, were aided and comforted with a transcendent hope and assurance that upon his diligent care he might be eternally blessed; and with the sweet sense of his happy change, and a glorious admiration [2] resulting from the comparison between his present estate and the estate to which by his Creator he was to be exalted.

I will not say but that there were more virtues than these to be exercised in Eden; but by these you may discern of what nature they all are, and conjecture they must be such as obedience to God and charity to one another.

All harsh and sour virtues came in by sin; and we are to look upon them not as virtues intended by God and nature, but occasioned afterwards, because their use and existence is accidental.

[1] Subtle. [2] Wonder.

When we fell into sin, we let death and misery into the world, contracted shame and guilt upon ourselves, defiled our nature with deformities and diseases, and made many things upon that occasion necessary to our happiness that before were not so. And whereas they have a mixture of bitterness and advantage in them, we may thank ourselves for the bitterness and God for the advantage. For as we by sin forfeited our happiness, so a new obedience, consisting in the practice of proper virtues, was necessary to recover it—virtues, whose names and natures were of another kind, and never heard of before. All which we must look upon not as food, but physic; and considering them under the notion of remedies, not admire [1] that there should be something in them distasteful to sense; though they are now, when their occasions are known, infinitely agreeable to reason.

They are but an equivocal offspring of the Fall. Sin could never beget such beautiful children as meekness, repentance, patience, alms-deeds, self-denial, submission and resignation to the divine will, fortitude, contentment in all estates, etc.

While there was no sin, there was no need of penitence; while there was no pain or misery, no patience. Without wrongs and injuries, there is no use of meekness; no place for alms-deeds, where there is no poverty; no courage, where are no enemies. In Eden there was no ignorance, nor any supernatural verities to be confirmed by miracles. Apostles therefore and prophets, ministers and doctors were superfluous there; and so were tithes and temples, schools of learning, masters and tutors, together with the unsavoury duty incumbent on parents to chastise their children. For as all would have been instructed by the light of nature, so all had been innocent and just and regular; whereupon no magistrate had been needful to put any to shame, no courts of judicature, nor lawyers in the world; no buying or selling, and thereupon no commutative justice, because the blessed earth had naturally been fertile, and abounded with rich and glorious provisions. Nakedness had been the splendour and ornament of men, as it will be in heaven. The glorious universe had been their common house and temple; their bodies fitted for all seasons; no alien or stranger, no want, distress or war, but all peace and

[1] Wonder.

plenty and prosperity; all pleasure, and all fellow-citizens throughout the world. Masters and servants had been unknown, had we continued in that estate; all had enjoyed the liberty of kings, and there had been no dominion but that of husbands and fathers, a dominion as full of sweetness as so gentle and free a relation importeth. I can see no use that there had been of trades and occupations, only the pleasant diversion that Adam had in dressing the garden, and the consequent of that. I am sure there had been no funeral pomps, no sickness, physic or physician. There had been no faith in the Incarnation of the Son of God, because no occasion for that Incarnation; no ceremonial law of Moses, no Baptism, nor Lord's Supper, because there were no supernatural mysteries to be typified; but the clear light of a diviner reason, and a free communion with God in the right discharge of those virtues divine and moral, which naturally belong to the estate of innocency. All which original and primitive virtues ought now to continue, as it were the face of religion beneath that mask or vizor of ordinances and new duties, which sin and corruption hath put upon it; though we have forgotten the virtues of our first estate, and are apt now to terrify ourselves with that disguise wherewith we have concealed their beauty, by regarding only the virtues that were occasioned by sin and misery.

It is a great error to mistake the vizor for the face, and no less to stick in the outward kind and appearance of things, mistaking the alterations and additions that are made upon the Fall of Man for the whole business of religion. And yet this new constellation of virtues, that appeareth aboveboard, is almost the only thing talked of or understood in the world. Whence it is that the other duties, which are the soul of piety, being unknown, and the reason of these, together with their original and occasion, unseen, religion appears like a sour and ungrateful thing to the world, impertinent to bliss and void of reason; whereupon God is suspected and hated, enmity against God and atheism being brought into and entertained in the world.

For it is an idea connatural to the notion of God to conceive Him wise and good; and if we cannot see some reason in His ways, we are apt to suspect there is no Deity, or, if there be, that He is malevolent and tyrannical, which is worse than none.

For all wisdom and goodness are contained in Love; and if it be true that God is Love, He will show it in our beings, by making us great and excellent creatures; in His gifts and bounties, by surrounding us with real and serviceable treasures; in all His laws, as well as in all His works, by consulting our welfare in the one and in the other. And as He makes the world glorious and beautiful for us to dwell in, so will He make such actions and virtues only needful to be exercised by us as are excellent and divine; He will impose no duties but such as are full of reason, and lead us more advantageously to bliss and glory.

We are apt to charge our own faults on God, by confounding all things; and because we see not how penitence, and meekness, and acts of charity in relieving the poor, directly and immediately bring us into bliss, are apt to repine at their imposition. But when we see all these virtues in their several places and offices, their objects and their uses, the ends for which and the occasions on which they were introduced, all are delightful to the reason of man's soul, and highly eligible[1]; while God is adored and admired for the depth of His wisdom and goodness, and beloved for the equity and excellency of His proceedings. For all these occasional virtues are but temporary. When our life and this present world are past and gone as a dream, love and joy and gratitude will be all that will continue for ever; in which estate wisdom and knowledge, goodness and righteousness and true holiness shall abide, as the life and glory into which the souls of all that are blessed will be transformed. Repentance shall be gone and patience cease, faith and hope be swallowed up in fruition, right reason be extended to all objects in all worlds, and eternity in all its beauties and treasures seen, desired, esteemed, enjoyed.

Let it be your care to dive to the bottom of true religion, and not suffer your eyes to be dazzled with its superficial appearance. Rest not in the helps and remedies that it bringeth, but search for the hidden manna, the substantial food underneath, the satisfaction of all wishes and desires, the true and celestial pleasures, the causes of love and praise and thanksgiving, founded in the manifestations of God's eternal favour; especially in the ends, for the sake of which all helps and remedies are prepared. *For it is*

[1] Desirable.

exceeding true that His laws are sweeter than honey and the honey-comb, and far more precious than thousands of gold and silver.

CHAPTER V

Of the necessity, excellency and use of Knowledge; its depths and extents, its objects and its end

KNOWLEDGE and Love are so necessary to Felicity that there can be no enjoyment or delight without them. Heaven and earth would be dark and obscure, angels and men vain and unprofitable, all the creatures base and unserviceable, felicity impossible, were there no knowledge. Nay, God Himself, without knowledge and love, could not well exist; for His very essence is seated in infinite knowledge.

God is Light, and in Him is no darkness at all. He is Love by nature, and there is no hatred in His essence. His very Godhead is all perfection, by the infinite knowledge and love in His nature.

The original of our knowledge is in His Godhead; His essence and will are the fountain of it, and the stream so excellent that in all estates it is for ever to be continued, as the light and glory of the whole creation.

The understanding power, which is seated in the soul, is the matter of that act wherein the essence of knowledge consisteth. Its form is the act itself, whereby that power of knowledge apprehendeth its object.

Its nature is invisible, like that of all other spirits; so simple and uncompounded that its form and matter are the same; for all powers, when transformed into act, are acts themselves. And the faculty of understanding, in a complete and perfect act of knowledge, attains its perfection, and is power exerted, or an act in its exercise; for every act is power exerted.

The power of knowledge is vain if not reduced into act, and

the soul a melancholy and dreadful cave or dungeon of darkness, if void of knowledge. Had God Himself a power of knowing distinct from its operation, if He never exercised that power, it would be useless to Him. His glory and blessedness are seated in the light of that knowledge which to us upon earth appeareth inaccessible.

If we would be perfect, as our Father which is in heaven is perfect, our power of knowing must be transformed into act, and all objects appear in the interior light of our own understanding. For though all Eternity were full of treasures, and the whole world and all the creatures in it transformed into joys, and our interest to all never so perfect; yet if we are ignorant of them, we shall continue as poor and empty as if there were nothing but vacuity and space. For not to *be,* and not to *appear,* are the same thing to the understanding.

Were a man a seraphim by his essence, or something by nature more glorious and divine than the highest order of the most blessed angels, nay, the greatest creature that Almighty Power was able to produce, his soul and body would signify nothing, if he were unknown to himself and were not aware of his excellence.

If you would have a solid prospect of any virtue, you must understand that virtues are powers transformed into right, wise and regular acts, avoiding all extremes of remissness on the one hand and excess on the other. The extremes of knowledge are ignorance and error.

For aught you know, heaven and earth are as full of treasures as Almighty Power was able to create them, and you by nature the best and highest of all possible creatures, made like God, for the highest and best of all possible ends, and called to live in communion with Him, in all His fruitions; but being vilely corrupted, you have lost the sense of all these realities, and are ignorant of the excellences of your own estate and nature.

I am sure that God is infinite in wisdom, goodness and power, and nothing is wanting on His part to perfect your desires; but yet you may be blind, and idle, and ignorant, and dead in a manner, while you are wanting to yourself and have need of nothing but clear and perfect apprehensions; but because they are sottish and erroneous at present, they may make you miserable, and poor, and blind, and naked.

If Sin had been like Circe's cup, and changed the shape of man's body to that of a swine or dragon, the depravation of his nature had been plain and visible; yet without knowing what kind of form he had before, it would not appear, because we should be unsensible of his first form, and unable to compare the one with the other. But Sin is a moral obliquity, and the change it produceth in the soul is spiritual. It makes a man to differ far more from himself than any alteration of body can do; but withal so blinds his understanding that he does not remember what he was in his first parent. Though the first man, who had experience of both estates, was able to compare them, because in his corruption he might possibly retain a sense of that nature and life which he enjoyed in his integrity, yet all his posterity, that are born sinners, never were sensible of the light and glory of an innocent estate, and for that cause may be wholly ignorant both of God and themselves; utterly unable to conceive the glory of the world, or of that relation wherein they should by nature have stood towards all the creatures.

It is impossible to conceive how great a change a slight action may produce. It is but pressing the wick a little with one's finger, and a lamp is extinguished, and darkness immediately made to overspread the room. The glory and splendour of the whole world would vanish upon the extinction of the sun; and one instant's cessation from the emission of its beams would be its extinction. A soul is a more glorious thing than the sun; the sphere of its activity is far greater, and its light more precious. All the world may be filled with the splendour of its beams; Eternity itself was prepared for it. Were there but one soul to see and enjoy all the creatures, upon the suspension of its light all the creation would be rendered vain. Light itself is but darkness, without the understanding.

The existence of many souls is so far from abating the value of one, that it is by reason of their multitude more useful and excellent. For the value of the objects imputes a lustre and higher value to the light wherein they are enjoyed. And if souls themselves are more excellent than all the other creatures, and with and above all other to be enjoyed, that power whereby this soul is able to enjoy them is more to be esteemed upon the account of those souls than for all the other creatures which are made for the same. God Himself and His holy angels are objects of the understanding. Those felicities and glories which the sun cannot extend to the soul, can comprehend. All which, since their fruition depends upon that act of the understanding by which they are considered, reflect a lustre and add a value to that knowledge by which the soul doth attain them. Whereupon it follows that the infinite value of all these is seated in the intellect; and as the power, so the act of knowledge, on which their fruition depends, is of infinite use and excellency. As the loss is infinite when the soul is bereaved of them, so is the damage which it suffers by failing of its light, whether that defect be voluntary or imposed by some outward impediment.

As for the use of knowledge, it is apparent enough. For the relation between the use and excellency of things is so near and intimate that, as nothing useless can be at all excellent, so is every excellence in every being founded in its usefulness. The use of souls is as great as their excellency. The use of knowledge is as endless in variety as in extent and value.

Knowledge is that which does illuminate the soul, enkindle love, excite our care, inspire the mind with joy, inform the will, enlarge the heart, regulate the passions, unite all the powers of the soul to their objects, see their beauty, understand their goodness, discern our interest in them, form our apprehensions of them, consider and enjoy their excellences. All contentments, raptures and ecstasies are conceived in the soul and begotten by knowledge; all laws, obligations and rewards are understood by knowledge. All virtues and graces of the mind are framed by knowledge. All advantages are by it improved, all temptations discerned, all dangers avoided, all affairs ordered, all endowments acquired. All the ornaments of life, all the beauties of the inward man, all the works of piety are affected by knowledge. In the light of knowledge all pleasures arise, and as fruits and flowers are begotten in the earth by the beams of the sun, so do all kinds of joy spring from the creatures and are made ours, by the help of that knowledge that shineth on them; its last offspring are eternal thanksgivings and praises. The Divine Image and the perfection of bliss are founded in knowledge.

God Himself dwelleth in the soul, with all His attributes and perfections, by knowledge. By it we are made temples of the Holy Ghost, and partakers of the divine nature. And for this cause it is that St. Paul prayeth, *that we might be filled with the knowledge of His will, in all wisdom and spiritual understanding, that we might walk worthy of the Lord unto all pleasing; being fruitful in every good work, and increasing in the knowledge of God, strengthened with all might according to His glorious power, unto all patience and long-suffering; with joyfulness giving thanks to the Father, who hath made us meet to be partakers of the inheritance of the saints in light; who hath delivered us from the Power of Darkness, and translated us into the Kingdom of His dear Son.*

The Sun is a glorious creature, and its beams extend to the utmost stars. By shining on them it clothes them with light, and by its rays exciteth all their influences. It enlightens the eyes of all the creatures. It shineth on forty kingdoms at the same time, on seas and continents in a general manner; yet so particularly regardeth all, that every mote in the air, every grain of dust, every sand, every spire of grass, is wholly illuminated thereby, as if it did entirely shine upon that alone. Nor does it only illuminate all these objects in an idle manner; its beams are operative, enter in, fill the pores of things with spirits and impregnate them with powers, cause all their emanations, odours, virtues and operations. Springs, rivers, minerals and vegetables are all perfected by the sun; all the motion, life and sense of birds, beasts and fishes dependeth on the same. Yet the sun is but a little spark among all the creatures that are made for the soul. The soul, being the most high and noble of all, is capable of far higher perfections, far more full of life and vigour in its uses. The sphere of its activity is illimited; its energy is endless upon all its objects. It can exceed the heavens in its operations, and run out into infinite spaces. Such is the extent of knowledge that it seemeth to be the light of all eternity. All objects are equally near to the splendour of its beams. As innumerable millions may be conceived in its light, with a ready capacity for millions more, so can it penetrate all abysses, reach to the centre of all nature, converse with all beings—visible and invisible, corporeal and spiritual, temporal and eternal, created and uncreated, finite and infinite, substantial and accidental, actual and possible, imaginary and real. All the mysteries of bliss and misery, all the secrets of heaven and hell are objects of the soul's capacity here, and shall be actually seen and known hereafter.

Were almighty power magnified by filling eternity with created objects, and were all the omnipresence of God full of joys, it is able, when assisted by His divine knowledge, to look upon all; and though every one of them should have an infinite depth within, an endless variety of uses, a relation to all the rest of the world, the soul, as if it were able to contract all its strengths from all the expansions of eternity and space, and fix them upon this moment, or on this centre, entirely beholding this alone, in all its fullness, can see its original, its end, its operations, effects and properties; as if it had nothing to consider but this alone, in a most exquisite and perfect manner.

It is not to be denied that every being in all worlds is an object of the understanding. Nor can that of the psalmist be doubted. In His presence there is fullness of joy, and at His right hand there are pleasures for evermore; that is, His omnipresence is full of joys, and His eternity of riches and pleasures. Nor is it to be denied that the soul is by its creation intended for the throne of God. For it is made capable of His omnipresence and eternity and, as the Apostle speaketh, may be filled with all the fullness of God; which fullness is adequate to the immensity of His eternal power (of which you will see more in the virtues of love, wisdom, righteousness and holiness). This only is here to be noted; that nature never made any power in vain, but ever intendeth the perfection of what it produceth, and prepareth objects for the understanding, the perfection of which power is the actual attainment of that knowledge of which it is capable.

The principal objects of our knowledge are God, and a man's self. The Kingdom of God, His laws and works, His ways in all ages, His counsels and His attributes, man's interest and duty, transactions of the world, the thoughts and actions of angels and men are considerable; which though they may be styled less material objects of the understanding, yet in relation to God and a man's self are of great importance.

God as He is the life and fountain of all felicity, the end of all perfection, and the creator of our being; almighty in power, infinite in wisdom and goodness, author of the universe and Lord of all the creatures, is most fit to be known. Plato makes Him the very light of the understanding, and affirms that, as three things are necessary to vision—the eye rightly prepared, the object conveniently seated, and light to convey the idea to the eye—so there are three things required to complete and perfect intelligence; an understanding eye, an intelligible object, and a light intelligible in which to conceive it; which last is God. Nor is the royal psalmist and divine philosopher David far from the notion while he saith, In thy Light we shall see light. For God is the light of the understanding. His Nature is the light of all the creation. Therefore it is said by Christ Himself that the knowledge of God is life eternal. For His light is the life of men, and without Him we can do nothing. Till we know His nature, we cannot apprehend the excellency of His works; for all their goodness is derived from Him and ends in Him. His love moved Him to create the world, and the principal end for which it was made is the glory of the Creator in the felicity of His creatures. The glory of the creatures is seen in His. By His wisdom and goodness we are guided to the hope and investigation of their excellence. His infinite bounty made them all our treasures, that for the perfection of their beauty and worth we might celebrate His praises.

He that would not be a stranger to the universe, an alien to felicity and a foreigner to himself must know God to be an infinite benefactor, all eternity full of treasures, the world itself the beginning of gifts, and his own soul the possessor of all, in communion with the Deity; that the business of religion is complacency [1] in God, and that God never laid aside His wisdom in any operation of His power, never forgot to make the least of His works agreeable to His goodness. Nay rather, He is so perfect that His infinite goodness, wisdom and power are exerted wholly and are wholly conspicuous in every operation. It is the beauty of truth that maketh knowledge to be of such infinite value. For if all the treasures of wisdom and knowledge be

[1] Delight.

ordained for a wise and knowing man; if all objects in the clear light of heaven and eternity be laudable and glorious; if the divine wisdom hath so far obtained that the number and value of God's gifts is accurate and exactly answerable to the nature of its causes; if every soul that will live in His image may be the friend of God, and acquire the empire of the world, and be beloved of angels and admired of men; if fruition be the end of knowledge, and all things made that they may be enjoyed; knowledge is the only thing that enriches the soul, and the knowing man is the friend of God. The exercise and pleasure of this divine amity is the end of the creation and the perfection of the soul.

The knowledge of a man's self is highly conducive to his happiness; not only as it gives him power to rejoice in his excellences but as it shows him his end, for which he was created. For by knowing what inclinations and powers are in his soul, he discerns what is agreeable with and fit for his essence; what objects and what operations are conducive to his welfare; what means he is to use for the attainment of his end, and what that is wherein his perfection consisteth. If the powers of his soul are illimited, his desire infinite and his reach eternal; if he be able to see and enjoy all worlds, and all that is above all worlds, in the image of God; if his ambition carry him to be pleasing to all angels and men, and to be glorious in the eyes of all kingdoms and ages; if his abilities are indeficient [1] for the fruition of all that is excellent in eternity itself, it is a token that he is ordained for God and the enjoyment of His Kingdom; and a wicked folly to restrain himself to the miserable contentment of a cell or cottage, and to delight in nothing but some fragments of the creation, that in comparison of the whole are infinitely defective.

Of all other things I would have this most deeply engraven in the mind; that God hath exceeded all imagination in the works of His hands; that he that overcometh shall be the son of God and inherit all things; that there is an infinite end why the secrets of all hearts shall at last be revealed; that in heaven all thoughts and things shall be known; that the Kingdom of Heaven is so glorious that all the blessed are perfect sovereigns, every one the

[1] Sufficient.

possessor and end of it all; that all things, proceeding immediately from God, are the best that are possible; that the best and worst things, as ordered by Him, are perfectly amiable, and subservient to felicity; that He Himself alone hath a perfect right to all that is excellent; and that God is in everything to be enjoyed that He is enjoyed only when His essence and His works satisfy the desires of perfect reason, and exceed all wishes in filling and delighting the soul; that, having filled the soul with infinite wisdom, He has laid infinite obligations upon us, and set infinite rewards before us, made laws infinitely amiable and given us duties infinitely desirable; for which He deserves eternal adorations and thanksgivings.

CHAPTER VI

Of Love and Hatred. The necessity and sweetness of love. Its general use and efficacy. The several kinds of love. Of the power, inclination and act of love. Its extent and capacity.

BECAUSE Love is the most desirable employment of the soul, the power of loving is to be accounted the most high and noble of the faculties. It is not seated by itself in the mind, but attended with a mighty proneness and inclination.

There is no creature so unsociable and furious but it is capable of loving something or other. Wolves and tigers live at peace among themselves, lions have an inclination to their grim mistresses, and deformed bears a natural affection to their whelps, expressed in their rage when they are bereaved of them. Things must be absolutely dead, or live in misery, that are void of love. Whatsoever is endued with life and sense delights in easy and grateful operations. Love is a necessary affection of their souls, because it is impossible to apprehend anything delightful but it must be pleasing; and what is pleasing must be lovely. For to be pleased and to love are the same thing. If there be any difference, the pleasure we take in any object is the root of that desire which we call love; and the affection, whereby we pursue the pleasure that is apprehended in it, is part of the love that we bear unto it; the end of which is the completion of that pleasure which it first perceives. All is love, variously modified according to the circumstances wherein the object is represented.

As love is the only easy and delightful operation, so is hatred of all other the most troublesome and tormenting. Displeasure and enmity are the ingredients of its nature; and the fruits of it (allied to their root) as bitter as gall and wormwood. Murder and vexation and grief are the offspring of the one, with separation, contention and horror; peace and embraces are the fruit of the other, with praises and complacencies,[1] honours, services, benefits and pleasures. These are the little cupids that fly about this celestial Venus, when it is what it ought to be, the Mother of Felicity and the Daughter of God.

All creatures that are sensible of pain or pleasure must of necessity be addicted to love and hatred; to the love of what is pleasing, to the hatred of what is painful. And if any question be made, which of these twins is the first born, the answer is, that they may seem twins in respect of Time, but in Nature love is the first born, and the mother of hatred. For where nothing to be hated does at all appear, pleasant things are beloved for their own sake; whereas if there were no pleasant thing to be beloved, nothing could be hated, because nothing could be hurtful; which appeareth by this, because where there is no love, there is no interest; and where there is no concernment, there can be no affection, no fear or hope, or joy or sorrow.

As fire begets water by melting ice, so does love beget contrary passions in the soul of a living creature—anger, malice, envy, grief and jealousy; not by its own nature, but by the accidental interposure of some obstacle that hinders or endangers the fruition of its object. Were there no love of ease and pleasure, there could be no anger between competitors, no emulation or desire, no aversion or endeavour. All enmity and hostility springs from a contention, who shall enjoy what is desirable; or from some other principle of envy or revenge, in relation to what is good, as is obvious to daily experience.

[1] Delights.

Life and love are so individually united that to live without loving something is impossible. Even in hell, where their whole life seemeth to be spent in detestation and hatred, and actual love is, like fire under those embers, covered and continued; could they put off self-love, all love of felicity, and interest, their torments would be gone. Punishments and rewards are things impossible, where there is not self-love for without love to something, pains and joys are equally grateful.[1]

As love is the root of endeavour, so is it the spring of all the passions; they all depend on love alone. We are angry at that which stands in our way between our love and its object. We desire an absent good because we love it. We hope for it, when we conceive its attainment feasible. We rejoice in it when we have it; we fear to lose it; we grieve when it is gone, we despair if we cannot get or recover it; we hate all that is opposite to it. And for this cause is our love, when well regulated, the greatest virtue; because upon the right choice of its object, and true government of itself, all the powers and affections of the soul are well employed. And when we love all that we ought as we ought to do, we fulfil all laws; hope and fear and hate and grieve and desire and rejoice, and do everything in a regular manner.

There is a sensual and brutish love; there is a human and divine. Brutish love is of two sorts; the one springs from a harmony of complexions and a sympathy of bodies, the other from the consideration of pleasure abstracted. The first of these is occasioned by a secret and unexpressible agreement of tempers, by which upon the presence of each other the senses are delighted, we know not why, it being a mystery in nature; and perhaps founded in a grateful[2] transpiration of spirits from one to the other.

The consideration of beauty seemeth peculiar to the love of men; because no beast is observed to make any distinction between lineaments and features, nor upon any account of shape and colours to be delighted with each other. Wherein man exceeds the capacity of beasts, in being able to note and admire the workmanship of God, in the decent order of symmetry and proportion.

[1] Enjoyable. [2] Pleasurable.

Human affection and divine love are near allied, yet of several kinds. If you take the love of reason in its utmost height, it is always divine, for it is conformable to the love of God in its measures and degrees, in its effects and causes. For the love of God is itself the love of perfect reason. And as the reason of His love is infinite and eternal, so is its operation. But in a lower acceptation, human love differs from divine, it being founded upon temporal causes—vivacity, wit, learning, beauty, behaviour, moral honesty, fidelity, kindness, goodness, power, majesty, wealth, nobility, worth, virtue and the like. But all these may be exalted, when they are sanctified and made divine by the superadded concurrence of celestial causes. For when a man loves another because he is made in the image of God, and by the beauty of his soul is something more than human, this love is made sacred, and receives a grace from the influences of religion.

Divine love, strictly so called, is founded on eternal causes, agreeable to the life of heaven, delightful to God and pleasing to the angels.

If divine love be taken in the highest sense, there is none but in God. For it is His peculiar prerogative to love without obligation or reward, to be the sole author of all felicity, and to overflow with goodness of Himself freely, without any motive, to prevent[1] the beauty and excellence of His object, and to love from all eternity in an immutable manner; and this is the nature of divine love. Howbeit, even here are infinite ends and causes of His love, though they are all in Himself; for He loves that He may love, and begets that love which is His essence. His love is the foundation of all His treasures, the cause and end of the whole creation, and that alone by which He proceeds from Himself to all His creatures, and by those to Himself again for ever. All His kingdom and greatness and pleasure, all His wisdom and goodness, all His life and perfection is seated in love, which is His beauty and holiness, His bounty and His Godhead. He loves therefore that He may be all beauty and goodness and bounty and holiness, and that He may enjoy Himself and the eternal pleasure of His essence in glory and blessness for ever.

It is God alone that loves by His essence; angels and men may

[1] Anticipate.

love by inclination, but their affection is accidental to their nature, begins in time, may alter and cease. It is subject to chance, obligation and reward, and ought to be guided according to the pleasure of an higher agent. In this it differs from the love of God; but in many things there is a great agreement and proportion between them. For God has made the love of angels and men so like His own, by extending their knowledge to all objects, that infinite perfections are contained in their love. It is as Godlike as anything created is capable of being; for almighty power and infinite wisdom are employed in the production of it.

For the better understanding of this love, we will consider it in the power of loving, in the inclination to love, in its act and perfection. It may seem a surprising verity, but the power of loving is as necessary to blessedness and glory as life itself; an inclination to love is as necessary as the power; and the act of love is as necessary as the inclination. The world is useless without life, and life without love, the body without the soul, the soul without the power of loving, the power of loving without the inclination, the inclination without the act.

In the power of loving, I shall note nothing at present but its extent and capacity. In beasts it is confined, but in men it is endless. As a beast is unable to examine what spaces are above the heavens, so it is unable to extend its affections beyond the memory of things perceived; for a beast cannot represent to itself the ideas of its progenitors, nor see into ages that are before its birth, nor contemplate objects that will be after it is dead. But man can see and know and love any object, in any age or kingdom in the world. He can look into any region, though it be never so far removed; and be as familiarly conversant with any person or transaction there, when represented once in a clear light, as with any object in his own country. He can look into Eden, consider Adam's dust in its first creation, survey the procedure of God in His six days' works, pass out of Time into Eternity itself, run up to the original and fountain-head of all existence, ponder the nature of God, search in his bosom for His eternal counsels, pierce into the centre of the earth and survey the circumference of all immensity. His love can follow his knowledge in all its flights, while in spirit he can be present with all the angels. He is able to love not only his family and relations, but all the city and country where he liveth, all the kingdom, all the cities and kingdoms in the world, all the generations in all kingdoms, all the spirits of just men made perfect, all the cherubims and seraphims, and God blessed for ever. This is the extent. The capacity of love is so all-sufficient that his affection is not diminished; but the more he loves one, the more he is able, and the more inclined, to love all that are united to him. As in ordinary friendship, the more we love the father, the more we love his wife and all his children. For the more we love any person, the more we love all that love him or are beloved by him. As the reasons of our love increase, so may our love itself; the capacity of love being so indeficient [1] that it never can be exceeded or surmounted by its object.

The capacity of love, being so exceeding vast, multiplies and heightens in the soul of man, that is apt to overflow of its own accord. For nothing is so prone to communicate itself as that active principle of love; that soul which is generous and divine being disposed to the exercise of love, because therein it findeth its proper element. The very sun is not more inclined to communicate its beams than the soul to love. For the soul being made in the image of God, who is Love by His essence, must needs be like Him in power and inclination, and is made for nothing else but the attainment of its perfection; so that it can never rest till it actually love after His similitude. Some operation it must of necessity have. For as all life, so all pleasure, is founded in action.

If love in its perfection be considered, all that is lovely is beloved by the soul; all the capacity of love is filled with its objects, and all the goodness of the Creator and His creatures at once enjoyed. It is the life and pleasure and enlargement of the soul; it is the wisdom and goodness and glory of the soul. I confess there be many errors and diseases in love; and that love is always miserable in its effects, that is vicious; yet it so bewitches the senses that the soul, being captivated by the force of present delight, is violently carried in an irresistible appetite to those

[1] All sufficient.

things which reason condemns and advises to shun as evil. Medea's faction most prevails in the world:

Video meliora proboque,
Deteriora sequor.

Love is then a vice when it is irrational and illegal, rebellious and sensual, blind, defective, unjust, absurd; when evil things are beloved, when good things are preferred above the better, and the best neglected.

Virtuous love is that which proceedeth from a well-governed understanding, and is seated in a will that is guided by reason. It renders to all things their just due, and is the powerful parent of all kind of virtues. This love may be considered either in its properties or effects, the last of which relate to the soul itself, to the conversation of the whole man, to all its objects. When it is well understood, it will be found the proper and immediate means by which we attain our perfection and felicity.

CHAPTER VII

What benefit God Himself does receive by His eternal love. That when our love is made complete and perfect, it will be like His, and the benefit of it will be eternal

BEFORE we can fully discern the benefit of love, or see the glory of it in all its high and admirable effects, we must consider what love is and doth in God. For as we have said, the life of God is Love; nay, the Apostle saith, God is Love. By loving He begot His love. And if His Love be His Godhead, His essence is an infinite and eternal act of love, by extending which through all infinity, and by loving eternally, He begot His infinite and eternal essence; which is the Love that filleth all worlds with beauty and glory.

When you consider it well, an act of love is begotten by loving;

and if His wisdom and goodness and blessedness and glory be seated in love, His love is His wisdom, which is the Son of God, and His goodness, and His glory, and His blessedness. For all these, though we conceive them diversely, are the same thing; and of the Son of God it is said that He is the wisdom of the Father, and the brightness of His Father's Glory. He is the Life of the Father, by whom also He made the worlds; and the Love of the Father, for whom all things were created, that are in heaven, and that are in earth, visible and invisible, whether they be Thrones, or Dominions, or Principalities or Powers; all things were created by Him and for Him. For God enjoyeth all things by His Love, which is His eternal Son; and made them as perfect and delightful as it was possible for things created to be, that He might take pleasure in them. As He Himself is made glorious and delightful in the eyes of all angels and men by love, so doth His whole kingdom arise and spring from love. The beauty and felicity of all His creatures, their joys and praises, their uses and perfections, are founded in His love. By His love He begetteth all pleasures in Himself, by His love He made His treasures infinite, and by that alone doth He take infinite pleasure and delight in Himself and His kingdom. Thus useful is the Love of God.

Had not God from all eternity loved, had He never desired nor delighted in anything, He had never exerted His almighty power, never communicated His goodness or begot His wisdom, never enjoyed Himself, never applied Himself to the production of His works, never appeared in His glory to any eye whatsoever. Removing His love, we remove all the properties and effects of His essence, and are utterly unable to conceive any idea of His Godhead. For His power, though it be almighty, yet if it be dead and idle, is fruitless and deformed. Idle power is not the essence of the Deity, but a mere privation and vacuity; or at least a positive being as ignoble as it is unactive. The reason of His works is founded in Love; so are all the obligations that are laid upon His creatures to adore Him. All their rewards are founded in love, and by love prepared. All His laws are the laws of love, all his attributes and counsels are love, in several forms acting upon several occasions.

When His love communicates itself in joys to innocent creatures, it is goodness; when it attains the most perfect end by the most perfect means, it is wisdom; when it rescues guilty creatures from hell, it is mercy; when it punishes the rebellious, it is justice; when it inspires obedience into any obstinate person, it is grace; when it delights in the beauty of all its works, it is blessedness; when it appears in the perfection of its works, it is glory. For glory is the perfection of beauty, that ariseth from and is seated in the lustre of excellent actions, discovering the internal properties of an excellent agent, which is by those His properties and actions made delightful to all judicious spectators.

Nor is it only in God, but in us also, that the fruits and benefits of love are ineffable. For by loving as it ought to do, the soul acquires its own perfection, and is united to all its objects. By loving as it ought to do, it is made holy and wise and good and amiable. Only by loving does it embrace the delights of which it is capable. Love is the root and soul of those actions for which a creature is desired and praised by others.

It is an infinite advantage that we are able to live in God's image, if we please; for if God alone be infinitely glorious and blessed, there is no way for us to become glorious and blessed but by being made, either by ourselves or some other, like unto Him.

By nature He hath implanted the similitude of His power, which we are to improve by grace, turning it into act after His similitude. To be able to love is neither grace nor virtue, but a mere gift of God, a natural endowment, which may be blasted or completed. Actually to love is the work of virtue, for by that act we enjoy our felicity.

Had God limited and confined our understanding, our power of love had been shut up in bounds. Had He made it infinite, but not prepared objects for the same, our love had been deluded and had lost its force. Had He made some objects, but not so many as it was capable of loving, it had been superfluous and dissatisfied. Had He prepared objects innumerable and endless, but made them evil, our love had been irrational, had He commanded us to love them. Had He made more objects than we were able to love, we had been discontented. But having made all objects infinitely amiable and glorious, and filled His immensity and eternity with Himself and with the lustre of His actions, love is an infinite virtue, because nothing is wanting but an act of love to enjoy them.

If they are all amiable in all respects, they are all according to our hearts' desire, in their natures, places, durations, ends, occasions, causes, uses, service, relations, properties, operations, etc. All things, as they immediately proceed from Him, are in all respects most perfectly pleasing. And if we have an eye to see and discern this, and a soul able to resent [1] the benefit; if our nature be so vast and perfect as to see and take pleasure in all their circumstances; it is the most unreasonable and brutish thing in the world to withdraw our affection from them; nay, it is worse than diabolical. For we kill ourselves, we blast our felicity, we offend God, we slight the beauty of His creatures, we break His laws, we act against nature, we darken the light and splendour of our souls, we deface His image, we grieve His love, we do the most vicious and abominable thing that is imaginable. But if we excite and awaken our power, we take in the glory of all objects; we live unto them, we are sensible of them, we delight in them, we transform our souls into acts of love and knowledge; we proceed out of ourselves into all immensities and eternities, we render all things their due, we reap the benefit of all. We are just and wise and holy, we are grateful to God and amiable in being so. We are not divided from but united to Him in all His appearances, thoughts, counsels, operations. We adorn our souls with the beauty of all objects whatsoever, are transformed into the image of God, live in communion with Him, nay, live in Him, and He in us; are made kings and priests unto God, and His sons for ever. There is an exact and pleasant harmony between us and all the creatures. We are in a divine and spiritual manner made as it were omnipresent with all objects (for the soul is present only by an act of the understanding) and the temple of all eternity does it then become, when the kingdom of God is seated within it, as the world is in the eye; while it lives and feels and sees and enjoys, in every object to which it is extended, its own and its object's perfection.

[1] Feel.

If, by our voluntary remissness or mistake or disorder, we dote upon one object, or suffer some few things to engage our souls so entirely as to forget and neglect all the rest, we rob all those we desert of their true esteem, and abridge ourselves of that liberty and extent wherein the greatness of our soul consisteth. As if the sun, that is made to shine upon all the world, should withdraw its beams from the stars and the heavens, and choose to shine upon nothing else but a spire of grass, a grain of dust, or a little sand.

We lose innumerable objects and confine ourselves to the love of one; and, by sacrificing all our affection to that, become guilty of idolatry in one respect, of atheism in another. For we elevate that creature which we love alone into the place of God, and we rob the Creator of that supreme affection which is due unto Him; and in so doing bereave ourselves of the sovereign object in the fruition of which all the rest are happily enjoyed. Thus, when a man so loveth his wife or children as to despise all mankind, he forfeits his interest in all kingdoms, and the beauty of all ages is taken from his eyes; his treasures are contracted, and his felicity is maimed and made defective. When a covetous man doteth on his bags of gold, the ambitious on titles of honour, the drunkard in his wine, the lustful goat on his women, the foolish hector [1] on his dice and duels, they banish all other objects, and live as absurdly as if a king should relinquish his crown and confine all his thoughts and care to a country manor.

I will not deny but that there are many disorders and evils in the world, many deformities, sins and miseries; but I say two things. First, that in the estate of innocency, wherein all things proceeded purely from God, there was no sin nor sickness nor death, nor occasion of complaint or calamity. Secondly, that all the evils that are now in the world, men brought on themselves by the Fall; and that there is great need of distinguishing between the works of God and the works of men. For all that God did is lovely and divine; nothing is bitter and distasteful, but what we have done; Himself surveyed the whole creation, and pronounced concerning everything, that it was exceeding good. So that He

[1] Braggart.

was [1] in all His works an object of complacency.[2] To these we add two considerations more; that of all the evils and mischiefs which men have introduced, there is not one left uncorrected in His kingdom. Secondly, that God bringeth order out of confusion, light out of darkness, good out of evil, and, by a providence irresistible and a power infinite, so limiteth and divideth all that even evils themselves become the matter of His victory, the ground of His triumph; they are all improved, and He makes the greatest evils objects of joy and glory.

Now if all things before God are fit to be enjoyed, all good things perfect, all evil overcome; if without any change of place or situation, all things are naked and open before His eyes, and there be no walls to exclude or screens to hide, no gulfs to pass nor distance to overcome, but all things equally near and fair; there is some hope that the same felicity is prepared for the soul which is made in His image, and that every thing, being fit for God, is full of infinite depth and beauty. For which cause St. John, being in the Spirit, saw all the kingdoms of the world become the kingdoms of the Lord and His Christ, and heard every creature which is in heaven, and on the earth, and under the earth, and such as are in the sea, and all that is in them, saying 'Blessing and honour and glory and power be unto Him that sitteth upon the throne, and to the Lamb for evermore.' This we are the rather induced to believe, because the faithful servant is commanded to enter into the joy of his Lord, and our Master's joys are the reward of believers. Our Saviour telleth us His Lord will make His wise servant ruler 'over all his goods,' in one place, and 'over all that he hath,' in another.

To see beyond all seas, and through all interposing screens and darknesses, is the gift of the understanding; and to be able to love any object beyond the skies, anything that is good from the centre of the earth to the highest heavens, is the property of the soul; which it exerciseth here by parts and degrees, but shall at once exert at the day of consummation. The infinity of the Father in the Son, and the Godhead of the Son in the Holy Ghost, will entirely be enjoyed.

[1] ? Saw.
[2] Delight.

It is the glory of man that his avarice is insatiable, and his ambition infinite; that his appetite carries him to innumerable pleasures, and that his curiosity is so infinite that, were he monarch of the world, it could not satisfy his soul, but he would be curiously inquisitive into the original and end of things, and be concerned in the nature of those that are beyond the heavens. For having met with an infinite benefactor, he would not be fit for his bounty, could any finite object satisfy his desire; and for this cause is his reason so inquisitive, to see whether everything be delightful to his essence; which, when he findeth agreeable to his wish and to exceed his imagination, it is impossible to declare how his avarice and ambition will both rejoice, how much his appetite will be satisfied and his curiosity delighted. To sit in the throne of God and to enjoy communion with Him, in those things which neither the eye hath seen nor ear heard, nor hath it entered into the heart of man to conceive, is no mean thing; the advancement is infinitely greater than we are able to understand. No young man can gaze upon a beauteous face with greater pleasure, no epicure's sense be ravished with more delight, than that which he apprehends in so glorious a fruition.

The very sight of other men's souls, shining in the acts of their understanding throughout all eternity, and extending themselves in the beams of love through all immensity, and thereby transformed, every one of them, into a sphere of light comprehending the heavens, every angel and every spirit being a temple of God's omnipresence and perfection; this alone will be a ravishing spectacle to that goodness which delights to see innumerable possessors of the same kingdom. Much more will the perfection of the kingdom itself, which by infinite wisdom is so constituted that every one is the sovereign object, the first born, the sole heir and end of the kingdom; every one the bride of God, every one there a king, yet without confusion or diminution; every one distinctly enjoying all, and adding to each other's fruition.

To understand all this, and not to delight in it, is more miserable than not to understand it. To see it without being able to enjoy it is to pine away in a prison, from whence we see the glory of a palace and repine in our misery at the pleasures of those that are about it. To delight in these things without being affected by them is impossible. Nor is there any affection but that of love whereby we can enjoy them.

The angels see the glory of God's kingdom and delight in it. The damned see the joys of the blessed, and are tortured by them. The wicked upon earth neither see nor are affected with them. The saints upon earth apprehend them in part and believe them, desire and endeavour after them; they wait with expectation for the whole, and by certain degrees, as it were in a glass, enjoy the image and reflection of them. As many as they comprehend, they actually delight in; for their love is awakened and extended to the goodness of all they understand; which it feeds upon by meditation, and turns into nourishment for the benefit of their souls, which are made more great and strong and vigorous by their fruitions. But without love it is easy to see that no goodness can be enjoyed at all.

God does desire love from us, because His wisdom very well knows that without love the world would be in vain, and the end of the creation frustrated. His goodness is diffusive, and infinitely desires to communicate itself, which it cannot do unless it is beloved. To receive it is the highest service we can do unto it, nothing being more agreeable to the nature of His goodness than that it should be enjoyed. His blessedness consisteth in the pleasure He taketh in the felicity of others, and brancheth itself out into two parts: the pleasure of communicating all to others, and the pleasure of receiving all from others; in the satisfaction which He taketh to see others blessed, in the returns of those joys and praises which are offered up to His goodness and glory. His glory desires to be seen and delighted in. To be esteemed and beloved, to be honoured and admired, is natural to glory, the brightness of whose splendour is more sensibly pleasant in the reflection of its face and in the joy that it makes in another's soul. His holiness takes pleasure in pure and upright actions, of all which love is the fountain.

There is an objective fitness and excellency in love, for which it is infinitely valued by Him. It is one of the first and immediate properties of love to desire to be beloved, to make its object most amiable and beautiful, as well as blessed; to be united to it, to have its own goodness acknowledged, its essence approved, its excellency desired, admired and delighted in; to see all its actions, appearances, gifts and tokens esteemed; and to feel its own efficacy, in the grateful acceptance it finds, in the raptures it occasions, in the flames it enkindles in another's soul. Now love is the fountain of all honour, gratitude, praise and esteem. By love the soul is transformed into the similitude of God, by love made bright and beautiful; all its blessedness and glory are founded in love; it is by love itself made communicative and diffusive and great and rich and, as the scripture speaketh, fit for delights. All obedience and service are founded in love. And if a creature that is beloved must freely give up itself to another's pleasure, before it can show its love or entirely be enjoyed, love is of all other things in the world most fit to answer love, because the very heart and soul is given thereby to the person that desires it.

Love is the fountain of all benefits and pleasures. House, estate and lands, authority, wealth and power, life itself is consecrated and devoted by a lover to his object. So that on our side, all is given to God by love, as well as by love it is received from Him. The heavens and the earth and all the creatures are gifts and tokens of His love; men and angels are a present of His love, which He hath endlessly adorned and made endlessly serviceable to every soul that is beloved. All these His love would have us to receive with a due esteem, and therefore is it that He will have us to exercise our reason aright, and love them as much as their goodness deserveth. When we see and understand their excellence, and esteem them according to the transcendent value that appeareth in them, we adorn ourselves with their fair ideas; we enlarge and beautify our souls with bright and clear apprehensions, and, which is much more, with regular and well-ordered affections. We enrich ourselves, and increase our greatness in the fruition of His gifts; we are lively and pleasant and vigorous creatures, full of knowledge and wisdom and goodness, and fit to offer up all these things to Him again, while we empty [1] them as helps and advantages in that service which we pay unto Him. For our love to Himself is enkindled by these incentives; and while we sacrifice ourselves and them unto Him we delight in

[1] ? Employ.

nothing so much as to see Him, that is so great in love and bounty, the author and possessor of all His glories.

CHAPTER VIII

Of the excellency of Truth, as it is the object and cause of virtue. The matter and form of virtuous actions. That their form is infinitely more excellent than their matter, and the heathen morality infinitely defective and short of the Christian

I DO not see that Aristotle made the end of virtue any other than a finite and temporal felicity, which is infinitely short of that felicity which is here begun, and enjoyed for ever. He did not make God the object and end of the soul; and if all acts are distinguished into their kinds by their objects and their ends, those virtues must be infinitely base that have no other objects or ends but creatures; and those only divine and noble that flow from an infinite and eternal original, respect an infinite and eternal object, rest in an infinite and eternal end. His definition of felicity importeth all this, but his behaviour makes me to fear he did not understand it. As Seneca luckily hit upon that saying, *Deus me solum dedit toti mundo, totum mundum mihi soli*—God gave me alone to all the world, and all the world to me alone—yet could not understand it. For had he known what it was he said, he would have made a better use of it, and been more copious and explicit in the illustration.

An actual respect had to infinite obligations and rewards, a desire in every action to please an infinite and eternal Lover, to glorify a divine and endless Benefactor, to bring forth the fruits of infinite benefits, and to be truly grateful for all the advantages of a man's creation, that is made to have dominion over all the world—these are higher and better qualifications of those virtuous actions which Christians perform than heathens understood. And yet, if nature were divested of its corruption, the natural man that is no Christian might, by the light of nature, be fitted to understand them. And the truth is I wonder much, the world being so beautiful and glorious in every eye, so really deep and valuable in worth, so peculiarly applied to the use and service of every person, that the heathens did miss the fruition of it, and fail to measure themselves and their felicity by the greatness of its beauty and the joy which all the creatures ought to produce in the mind of man by their real services.

For the earth is really better than if all its globe were of beaten gold; the seas are better than if all their abysses were full of diamonds; the air is better than if all the space between us and the skies were full of sceptres; and the sun alone a greater treasure than all the wealthy mines in the Indies. Every man is surrounded with all the light of their advantages, and so much served by them as if no man but himself were alive in all the world. So it is a natural and easy investigation, even for heathens themselves, to discern the mystery of bliss, and to discover the misery of human nature to be founded in some disease of the will or understanding; and to return from inadvertency [1] and sloth to truth and right reason, which was the ready way to true felicity. For they knew not the *arcanum,* or hidden mystery of divine laws, nor the excellency and perfection of immortal souls, which make every one a sovereign and transcendent creature; yet they might easily observe the miserable effects of eternal solitude and, in external services, how useful and comfortable men were ordained by nature to be to one another.

Every man loves to have many eyes fixed on his beauty, and to have many delightful objects and transactions for his own. Be the theatre never so magnificent, the actions and actors are more delightful to the spectators than the gildings and dead engravings. Were all other men removed out of the world to make room for one, the empty theatre would remain, but the spectacle be lost. All the cities and kingdoms and ages would be removed, with all that was lively and rare and miraculous in all their occurrences. Palaces and temples had been prevented, houses and villages, fields and vineyards. The world had been a wilderness

[1] Carelessness.

overgrown with thorns and wild beasts and serpents; which now, by the labour of many hands, is reduced to the beauty and order of Eden. It is by trades and occupations that a man gets him corn and wine and oil, all which he would have been without had he never seen any company but himself, condemned to idleness and melancholy. Virtues and praises had been things unknown; admiration and honour, love and knowledge, the mysteries of religion and piety, all the speculations of wisdom, for want of education had been lost; at least, the sense and exercise of these bright and glorious things, for want [1] of conversation; corrupted nature being prone to afford no other fruits but barbarism and ignorance in that solitary condition. For the powers of the soul are improved by tradition; and it is by the information of others that our minds are awakened to perceive the dignity of our own nature, the value of all the creatures, and our interest unto them.

But religion teaches us far more: the beginning and end of the world: how highly we are honoured and beloved of God: the manner wherein we are to converse with Him: the transcendent excellency of souls, and the divine perfections of the Deity: what His omnipresence and eternity is; how we are to be enlarged in our apprehensions and desires, and prepared for infinite and eternal fruitions: in what quality and capacity we are to live in the world and exercise virtue: how we are to spend our time and employ our powers on all objects, every one as Lord of the Creation and the Friend of God! How all angels and men are commanded to love us as themselves, and by that love to serve and delight us more than by all other actions and offices whatsoever: that every soul is a more excellent being than the visible world, more nearly allied to God and more precious in itself than any treasure whatsoever: that it is endued with powers, inclinations and principles so fitly subservient and conducive to blessedness that any one of these is more delightful than all inanimate things; in the contemplation of which we may justly be lost in wonder and ecstasy. All this by the light of nature is asserted, but covered with so gross a veil that we discern it not, till it is newly revealed by the ministry of men. And upon all these accounts are men themselves, which are generally mistaken

[1] 1675, wont.

to be impediments, means and assistances of our happy living.

But however familiar and near and easy these great and evident truths appear, it so happened that the heathen philosophers were blind unto them and in the midst of their searches after felicity failed of the discovery. They became vain in their imaginations, placing felicity in a mere apathy or conceited self-sufficiency; or in a brave contempt of all misfortunes, in a forced contentment dark and empty; or in sensual pleasures, or in the goods of fortune, either alone or conjoined with those of the soul and body, which they lamely enumerated and knew not how to employ; as if the discovery of the highest and best truths in nature had been reserved for Him that redeemed nature, and the plainest truths had been appointed to honour and attend that religion which brought supernatural mysteries to light by the preaching of the Gospel.

By this last, the qualifications of a humble and pious soul, a penitent and grateful person, sensible at once of his infinite guilt and grandeur, were introduced. Another foundation laid upon the meritorious death and passion of God, the Son of God; a second love continued in the Deity to the miserable, after an infinite forfeiture: all the oracles and visions and miracles by which the nature of man is magnified and ages enlightened: the ministry of angels, and the dispensations of providence, by which the care and tenderness of God is shown: the infinite measures and violences of His love: the infinite variety and number of obligations, the present advantages and benefits, the eternal rewards: the relation of God to man as a Father and a Friend, a Bridegroom and a King, a Light and Example: the sweetness of our union and communion with Him, and the gift of the Holy Ghost sent down from heaven; all these things, which the angels desire to look into, were by the Christian religion (with the rest before mentioned) plainly revealed; with our victory over death, the resurrection of our bodies, and life eternal.

In the light of these circumstances the interior form of virtuous acts more evidently appears. For to exercise virtue in the quality and capacity of a son of God is another sort of business than to exercise virtue as an ordinary mechanic. And to do all things being clothed with a sense of our celestial grandeur, as we are heirs of the world—infinitely beloved of God, ordained for His throne, delightful in the eyes of all, angels and men; beloved and honoured by all the creatures; made partakers of the divine nature, intending and designing to please all spectators in heaven and earth by the excellency of our actions—this makes every little deed as it were infinite within. While the matter of the action seemeth nothing, it renders the form divine and blessed.

The best actions of the profaner heathens fell under the notion of dead works; by which name the Apostle calleth all wicked deeds, to intimate the privation of all that excellency which ought to be in human actions. Every deed and thought of ours ought to be inspired with life from heaven. The light of the understanding and the vigour of the will is the soul that informs it. When it is void of knowledge, and springs not from that series of God's infinite love that ought to animate it, nor regardeth those eternal joys that are set before us, nor at all considers those obligations that are laid upon us, it is bereaved of its vital and essential form. It is like a fair carcase without a soul, insensible of those interests and concerns that ought chiefly to be valued and promoted. And by this you may see clearly that the matter of a good act falls infinitely short of that perfection wherewith it ought to be inspired, if this soul or form be wanting; which, though less visible to the eye of flesh, is of as much greater excellence and importance as the soul in nature is above the body.

Thus, when a heathen giveth to the poor, the matter of the act is the very selfsame which a Christian man does. So is an act of courage or patience in encountering death; the subduing of the appetite and the denial of a lust; a piece of justice against interest and friendship; an act of prudence, temperance or fidelity. In all these, if we respect the matter of them, heathens have acted in a manner as high as any Christian, and frequently appear to vulgar apprehensions as heroic and stupendous. But consider the inside. The heathen did it that he might satisfy his conscience and please the gods; that he might acquire honour and immortal fame, or please the generous inclination of his own soul, which delighted in honour and worth; or assert his principles, or save his friends, or preserve his country. And doubtless these are great and brave considerations; but they are limited and finite, and sick of two defects, for the most part, that are incurable. They were sacrifices of obedience to false gods, plain idolatry, and attended with an ignorant loftiness and height of mind that confided in them; and besides this, they aspired to little more than a glorious name in following ages.

Whereas the Christian makes all kind of graces to meet and concentre in every action: wisdom, goodness, justice, courage, temperance, prudence, humility, penitence, patience, meekness, liberality, cheerfulness, gratitude, joy in the Holy Ghost, devotion, piety, faith, hope, charity, all kind of holiness; and his action extends to all the objects of these graces, and includes their causes. He remembers the infinite obligations that are laid upon him by that Deity which infinitely loves him; the benefit of the Creation and the glory of the Divine Image; the guilt of Fall, and that blot and misery that lies upon him; the wonder of his Redemption and the love of Christ; His death and passion; the miraculous pains and endeavours of God in all ages to reclaim him; the giving of the Holy Ghost, and his holy baptism; the new covenant which he is in with God; the height and glory of his place and station; the beauty of the world and His dominion over all the living creatures; the joy and amity of all the angels; the benefit and welfare of all his neighbours; the joy and prosperity of future ages; the glory of God, the honour of His Church and the propagation of religion; the salvation of others' souls and the external state and condition of his own; the acquisition of a celestial and eternal kingdom, and the delight he taketh in an infinite sphere of eternal joys; the fervent desire he has to be grateful to the Almighty; all these, by the light of his divine and celestial knowledge, enter into the act; for want of which the other work, that is wrought by an ignorant heathen, is in a manner rightly called a work of darkness.

I do not speak this as if I would discourage a heathen from doing the best that he is able, or condemn those reasons upon which he proceedeth in his virtuous deeds. No; nor as if all this were necessary to the acceptance of an action. But to show how highly Christianity does ennoble the soul of man, how far more sublime its principles are, and how far more perfect it makes his actions, when they are what they may be: and withal to provoke

Christians to a more intelligent and lofty practice of Christian virtues, lest they differ not in their morals from the better sort of heathens. All these things are necessary to the perfection of an action, though not to its acceptance. And God's omnipresence and power and wisdom and love ought to be considered in all places, among all persons, upon all occasions; and the blood of Christ, and the infinite glory of eternal bliss. But that which above all I chiefly intend is to show what influence the great perfection of felicity hath upon all our virtues; not only to stir us up to do them, but by entering their constitution to inspire them with their beauty and form, for their fuller lustre, glory and perfection; that we may see also how great and transcendent that life must be, wherein every act is capable of so much majesty and magnificence, if I may so speak, by reason of the variety of its ends and causes. And how abominable and absurd they are all that exclude God out of their thoughts and considerations, who is alone the fountain of all beauty in every virtuous deed, and the proper fullness, cause and end of all its perfection.

How ambitious we ought to be of knowledge, which is the light wherein we are to adorn and complete ourselves, we may learn and collect from all that is said. It is rightly called the key of knowledge. It admits us into the spacious recesses of every virtue, openeth the gate by which we enter into the paths of righteousness, that lead to the temple and palace of bliss, where all the treasuries of wisdom are exposed to the eye of the soul, though hidden from the world. How great and amiable every virtue is, how great and perfect it may be made, is only discerned by the eye of knowledge. It is by this alone that men come to discern how full of reason religion is, and with what joy and security and sweetness it may be practised.

CHAPTER IX

Wisdom is seated in the Will. It attaineth the best of all possible ends by the best of all possible means

KNOWLEDGE, how excellent soever it may be conceived, is, without wisdom, like skill without practice; which, whether it be in music or painting or any other art, as government, navigation, preaching, judicature, is altogether vain and fruitless, if it be not reduced into act and exercise. For wisdom is that excellent habit of the soul by which we choose the most excellent end of all those which may be known, and actually prosecute it, by the best means that are conducive thereunto.

To know the best of all possible ends and not to embrace it is the greatest folly in the world. To choose and embrace it without endeavouring after it is a folly contending with the other for eminence. To choose any means less than the best in order thereunto is a new piece of folly, even then when we pursue what wisdom requires. For no less than the best of all possible means is requisite to the acquisition of the best of all possible ends. And by all this we discern that wisdom is not a mere speculation of excellent things but a practical habit, by virtue of which we actually achieve and complete our happiness. For it is impossible for the best of means, when they are well used, to fail. We may grow remiss and suspend our endeavour, which is another kind of folly, and so be diverted from the best of all possible means by some strong temptation, or cease from using them through our own inconstancy, or yield to some light and easy allurement, or be discouraged by some terrible danger, and thus may abandon the best of all possible ends; but without some such folly it can never be lost.

Possibilities are innumerable, so that nothing less than infinite wisdom can find out that which is absolutely the best. But when the best of all possible ends is by infinite wisdom found out, it is an easy thing for wisdom to discover that end to the knowledge of others, to whom it is able to communicate itself by way of gift and participation.

What the best of all possible ends is, only God fully comprehendeth. But in general it is such that it includeth all kind of goods in the highest perfection, infinite varieties and degrees of possibility turned into act. All sweetness and beauty, empire, dominion and power, all riches, pleasures and honours, victories triumphs and possessions will be in it, and nothing possible or desirable be wanting to it.

God alone is the best of all possible ends, who includeth all things in Himself, as their cause and end. The perfection of His will is His blessedness and glory, and His essence the only means by which He can attain unto it. By Himself it is that we come unto Him, in a manner afterwards more fully to be explained. His essence is the best of all possible means, by which He attains Himself and by which He is enjoyed. Our conformity to His essence is our way, by a wise application of our souls to that eternal act which is His end.

That sweetness and beauty are attributes of the best of all possible ends is evident and clear; as it is also that these must be infinite in their degree and measure, because nothing but what is infinitely convenient is absolutely eligible. Now what is infinitely convenient is infinitely sweet and beautiful. What is infinitely desirable is infinitely good, because it is agreeable to that Love wherewith every existence intends itself and pursues its own sublime happiness.

It is easy to conceive how God should be the end of His creatures, but how He should really be His own end is difficult to understand; because His creatures are defective, and have something beside themselves to aspire after, but God from all eternity is infinitely perfect and, being all that He can be, needeth nothing that He can endeavour to attain. But if we consider the nature of wisdom, which is a voluntary act, we may be freed from the despair of understanding the mystery.

For wisdom must of necessity intend itself in its operation, because it becometh wisdom by doing the best of all excellent things, and doth them all that it may be wisdom, or wise in doing them. It implies deliberation and freedom, being a virtue seated in the will and understanding. It implies a power of knowing and choosing and doing all things. It consisteth not in the power of knowing only, nor in power of choosing, nor in the power of doing. Nothing else is wisdom but to choose and do what we know is absolutely most excellent. Wisdom then is founded in the act of doing; nay, it is the act of doing all that is excellent. And if it be a free and voluntary act, as it needs must be—because nothing is wisdom but that which guideth itself by counsel freely to a known end, which it discerneth to be most excellent—it implies an ability to forbear, in him that is wise, by choosing to do what he might forbear. Had it forborne to do what is most excellent, it had turned into folly, because it had by that means lost the most excellent end; but by choosing to do all that was best, it became an act of wisdom; which being most lovely it chiefly desired to be. And so by choosing and doing the most excellent of things, begot itself; and by itself proceeded to all its operations; which must needs be infinite, if wisdom be so, because anything less would, if rested in, be infinitely defective. That riches and pleasures may be infinite is evident from the nature and extent of space, which is illimited and endless, from the omnipresence and eternity of God, in which there is infinite room for innumerable varieties, especially from His wisdom and goodness, which are infinite treasures. It appears also from His almighty power, which is able in all parts of His omnipresence and eternity to work without any bound or period; without cessation at once to work in all places of His dominion, and throughout all His immensity to act and do what He will. So that in one instant He can fill both Eternity and Time with enjoyments, every part and particle of which shall be infinitely delightful, because of the vigour of His eternal power in every operation. Thus is He entirely acting in heaven and earth and hell at the same time, and at all conceivable distances beyond all heavens ever acting, because He is willing, decreeing, seeing and ruling there, and everywhere accomplishing His counsel and pleasure. His essence and His will are both the same; His essence is His act, and His act His pleasure.

By exerting His almighty power He begot that act which is the means and end of all His endeavours. An act of wisdom infinite and eternal is His blessedness and glory. We must take heed of conceiving God to be one thing and His act another, for all His wisdom and goodness, all His blessedness and life and glory are in the act by which He became the fountain and the end of all things. He became so freely, and yet was so by His essence from everlasting; for eternity is an infinite length of duration, altogether present in all its parts in a stable manner. To fill one part of space with treasures and leave another empty was not wise. Common reason will instruct us that it is better to have all spaces full of delights than some few or none. And by His infinite wisdom it is that He knows how to enjoy what He never needed, and to improve His enjoyments by giving them away.

Infinite and eternal wisdom does not only imply the possibility but the certain reality and existence of eternal treasures; where, lest you should wonder how such should be infinite, you must needs be informed that God is His own best and most perfect treasure. For if treasures are by nature those precious things which are means by which we acquire our ends, or those things which we most esteem, as the sovereign objects of our joy, God is in both those respects His own wealth; because His essence is the means by which He achieveth all His ends, and the sovereign end of all those means which He by His wisdom useth for His ends. *For of Him, and by Him, and to Him are all things,* as the Scripture witnesseth.

Matter is the dreg of nature, and dead without power. Power is the abyss of nature, but void without act. Act is the top and perfection of nature, it is the fullness of power, the fountain and means of all that is; for power by transforming itself into act becometh an act, and by that act produceth and perfecteth all its works both outward and inward. So it is the means of all its productions; being so infinitely simple and various together that nothing but power exerting itself is in the nature of the act by which it is exerted. And the essence of that act is the complete exertion of eternal power, and yet to it alone we ascribe the original and means of all. It is the cause and means and end of itself, as well as of other things, which for its own sake are produced by it. For idle power can do nothing. Mere power is neither the cause nor the means nor the end of anything. Power not idle, but exerted and thoroughly employed, is all act. And this is the cause of all its productions; because of this power exerting itself they spring; and the means of all, because by this power exerting itself they are; and the end of all, because it did all that it might not be idle, but power exerting itself, or a glorious act in its full perfection.

It was an effect of infinite wisdom, wherein God by one act acquired Himself and all his dominion, prepared His own and all His creatures' blessedness, made Himself and all His kingdom glorious. But this is scarcely intelligible, because the manner of His life is incomprehensible. We cannot tell how to conceive what the learned constantly affirm, that all eternity is at one time. All I shall observe, in order to the explaining of this mystery, is only this: that though the world begins and ends with time, yet eternity does immutably include time, and the operations of Divine Wisdom are various and exactly fitted to their several seasons; yet all the parts of eternity are filled with operations which, though they are one in God, like that of shining in the sun, are manifold in effects, as the beams of the sun in their different works among all the creatures.

It is a natural effect of infinite wisdom to make every of its treasures suitable to its own excellence. And that the wisdom of God has done, by making every the smallest thing in His kingdom infinitely serviceable in its place and station, for the manifesting of His wisdom, goodness and glory to the eye of a clear beholder. And this He hath done by making all His kingdom one entire object, and everything in it a part of the whole; relating to all the innumerable parts, receiving a beauty from all, and communicating a beauty to all, even to all objects throughout all eternity, while every one among millions of spectators is endued with an endless understanding to see all and enjoy all in its relations, beauties and services.

I cannot stand [1] to enlarge on this, otherwise I might illustrate it by a familiar example. No single part of a stately monument is so beautiful out of its place as it is in its place; because it is seen alone, it is not understood; for the beauty that results from all consists in order and symmetry, which by any division is broken

[1] Delay.

to pieces. He knoweth nothing as he ought to know, who thinks he knoweth anything without seeing its place and the manner how it relateth to God, angels and men, and to all the creatures in earth, heaven and hell, time and eternity.

It is an act of wisdom to prize and enjoy what is by wisdom prepared; and because infinite wisdom includeth all wisdom, infinite wisdom at once knoweth, chooseth, doth, esteemeth and enjoyeth all that is excellent. It is an act of wisdom to make one's self good and delightful to others, and for that cause to be infinite in bounty. For what is infinitely good is infinitely glorious. And therefore it is that God, needing nothing in Himself, gives all things to others; gives them in enjoying them, enjoys in giving them; while His goodness delights in the felicity of others, and in being the felicity of others. For by making them great and blessed He magnifieth Himself; and by replenishing them increaseth His treasures.

How little soever of this you are able to conceive, you may understand that to be like God is the way to be happy; and that if God hath put it in your power to be like Him, it is the extremest madness in the world to abuse your power and to neglect His treasures. But it is infinite wisdom by the best of all possible means to embrace and enjoy them, because an infinite end is thereby attained, even God Himself, who is thereby made the portion of the soul and its reward for ever.

The best of all possible means whereby we can acquire His eternal treasures is to imitate God in our thoughts and actions; to exert our powers after His similitude, and to attain His image, which is after God in knowledge, righteousness and true holiness. For by knowing all things as God knoweth them, we transform our souls into an act of knowledge, most bright and glorious. By loving all things, as God loveth them, we transform our wills into an act of love, which is most sweet and blessed. We enrich and beautify ourselves with the image of His goodness, while we communicate our souls, in our powers, to all objects in His whole eternity. We magnify ourselves by magnifying Him in all His works. We do right to ourselves by doing right to God and all other things. Which forasmuch as we must here on earth learn by degrees, and can never perfectly accomplish the work till it is given us in heaven, it is wisdom to walk in the paths of righteousness as far as we are able, and to do those things here, though small and defective, which He will recompense with a reward so perfect hereafter.

If ever we be so happy as to come to heaven, His wisdom shall be our wisdom, His greatness our greatness, His blessedness our blessedness, His glory our glory. All His joys and treasures shall be ours, His life and love ours, and Himself ours for evermore.

His wisdom is made ours because it is the light in which we shall see light, and learn thereby to inherit all things; the exemplar and original of our wisdom, the fountain and pattern of all our joys, the author and inventor of all our delights, the end and sum of all our desires, the means of all our felicity, our very blessedness and glory.

CHAPTER X

Of righteousness. How wisdom, justice and right reason are shut up in its nature. What God doth, and what we acquire, by the exercise of this virtue

RIGHTEOUSNESS and wisdom are near allied. For to be just towards all objects is to render them their spiritual due, their due esteem. It is wisdom, because thereby we attain our end, and enjoy their excellency. It is right reason, because to value all things just as they are, rendering to them neither more nor less than they deserve, is to do right to ourselves and to them. It is a virtue, because by force thereof we attain our happiness.

For the better understanding of this virtue, we must know that there is a righteousness of apprehension, a righteousness of esteem, a righteousness of choice and a righteousness of action.

Righteousness of thought is that habit by virtue of which we think aright; forming and framing within ourselves aright apprehensions of all objects whatsoever. This, though it be the first

F

and smallest part of righteousness, is of great importance; because no man can use that aright, the nature of which he does not apprehend. He that mistakes his hand for his meat will rise hungry from the table. He that mistakes a fiddle for an axe will neither cut wood well, nor make good music. The misapprehension of great and transcendent objects, whether visible or spiritual, is not perhaps so gross, but more pernicious and destructive. He that apprehends God to be a tyrant can neither honour God, nor love Him, nor enjoy Him. He that takes virtues to be vices, and apprehends all the actions of religion unpleasant will loathe and avoid them. He that conceits [1] nothing in the world to be his own but his low cottage and coarse diet will think it needless to praise his Maker, and will deny himself to be happy in those narrow and mean enjoyments. He that thinks all the wealth is shut up in a trunk of gold will little regard the magnificence of the heavens, the light of the sun or the beauty of the universe.

Righteousness in esteem is that habit by virtue of which we value all things according as their worth and merit requires. It presupposes a right apprehension of their goodness, a clear knowledge of all their excellencies. It is a virtue by which we give to everything that place in our soul which they hold in nature. It is wonderful both for its extent and value. For there is room enough for all objects in the esteem of the soul, and it is by esteem that they are honoured, perfected and enjoyed.

A wise man will actually extend his thoughts to all objects in heaven and earth, for fear of losing the pleasure they afford him, which must necessarily spring from his esteem of their excellency.

Honour and esteem are near akin. How the creatures are honoured by esteem needeth not to be unfolded; but how they are perfected by it is a little mysterious. A thing is then perfected when it attains its end. Now, the end for which all things were made is that they may be seen and enjoyed. They are seen that they may be esteemed, and by an intelligent and right esteem are all enjoyed. In our esteem therefore they find and attain their end, and by attaining that are consequently perfected. The application of actives to passives is a mystery in nature of very great and general importance in all pleasures, cures and productions.

[1] Conceives.

All satisfactions, joys and praises are the happy offspring of powers and objects well united. Both the one and the other would lie void and barren if they never met together; and when they meet, their union must be regular, wise and holy.

God is an object of man's esteem; which, unless it were able to render Him His due and quadrate [1] with His excellencies, a man could never be righteous towards God. For that esteem is void of righteousness, that either exceeds or falls short of its object. If it becometh us to fulfil all righteousness, it becometh God to endue us with the power of esteeming all that is good and excellent according to the worth and value thereof. For which cause He enables us to esteem all that we can see in heaven and earth, and in the heaven of heavens. For this esteem is the foundation of that choice which is the original spring of all excellent actions.

Even God Himself meeteth His honour in the esteem of our souls. He is injured by the sacrilegious impiety that robs Him of His esteem. Being infinitely quick and tender in apprehending, He is more jealous of His honour, and more grieved when He loseth it, than any other. His wisdom and love are infinitely offended when they are slighted and profaned, but pleased extremely when they are sanctified and honoured; and that they are by a just esteem. And for this cause He hath made us able to attend Him in all His works and in all His ways, and to have communion with Him in all His counsels and perfections; that, as our Saviour saith, The Father loveth the Son, and hath given all things into His hand; and again, The Father loveth the Son, and showeth Him all things that Himself doth. So we might become the Sons of God, and see His love and delight in all that He hath done. For which cause He afterwards saith: Henceforth I call you not servants, for the servant knoweth not what His Lord doth; but I have called you friends, for all things that I have heard of my Father I have made known unto you.

The omnipresence and eternity of God are so far from filling the soul that they fit it only to be filled with infinite objects. For by the indwelling of God all objects are infused and contained

[1] Correspond.

within. The spiritual room of the mind is transcendent to time and place, because all time and place are contained therein. There is a room in the knowledge for all intelligible objects, a room in our esteem for all that is worthy of our care and desire. I confess this room is strange and mysterious. It is the greatest miracle perhaps in nature; for it is an infinite sphere in a point, an immensity in a centre, an eternity in a moment. We feel it, though we cannot understand it.

Whatever we close our eyes against, we exclude out of our knowledge. Whatsoever we hate, we reject, though we know it. We give a place in our heart only to that which we receive and embrace with a kind affection.

Eternity itself is an object of esteem, and so is the infinity of Almighty God; there are infinite causes for which they ought to be esteemed. Our esteem of these cannot be abridged, for upon the least subtraction of the smallest part, infinity is lost, and so is eternity. We must be able to esteem the utmost extent of every perfection of God, or our righteousness in relation to that will be infinitely defective. The proportion between our esteem and its object is that wherein righteousness is seated; if our esteem be finite, it is utterly destroyed; for where the object is infinite, instead of proportion, there is infinite disproportion.

From righteousness in esteem we proceed to righteousness in choice. We weigh and consider what is fittest to be valued, and what we find of greatest esteem we most desire. To prefer the better above the worse is a righteous choice; but to prefer the worse is abominable impiety. The election of God may be more strictly or generally conceived. His election of particular persons from the rebellious mass of mankind, to be employed as ministers in restoring the residue, is a matter of grace; which, as arbitrary and free, is occasioned by an accident of their general rebellion, and His mercy thereupon. Howbeit, it is righteous; for He does right to Himself and to all His creatures and perfections therein. For thereby, notwithstanding the universal apostasy of the world, He upholdeth and continueth His righteous kingdom. But the primitive election, by which, when He had considered the nature of all possible things, He chose the fittest and the best, was wholly natural. For according to the merit of all objects He chose them, which merit nevertheless was to be infused by Himself in their first creation. Whether a star were a thing fit to be made, whether the sun should be limited, whether His image should be infinite, whether naked spirits or bodies should be created, or bodies and spirits personally united; whether men should at first instant be placed in glory or in an estate of trial, whether when they fell into sin they should be redeemed or no, what laws were most fitting under the covenant of works, what conditions were most proper for the covenant of grace; what helps and assistances men should have, what impediments and obstacles; all these and many millions of objects more passed His examination, in order to the perfection of His kingdom; as it did also whether He should create a kingdom or no. And look, what surpassed in esteem, as best and most eligible, that He chose to create and perform.

To fail in a tittle had been an infinite fault; because had He in any one particular preferred the worse above the better, He had contracted a blot upon His own wisdom and goodness, and made the whole creation deformed. For there is such a love to righteousness implanted in our natures that, should God be unjust to a poor Indian beyond the seas, we should be grieved at the blemish; and any blemish in Him would blast our felicity. For the justice of the soul is an impartial thing, and its severity greatest where its expectation is the highest.

It is more easy with God to be infinitely wise than with man to be anything. He may be exact and perfect in every action with greater ease than any other of His creatures can, because He is almighty, omniscient and omnipresent. All the advantages of His wisdom and knowledge and goodness and power would be aggravations of His fault, should He sin against Himself. The least offence would be an infinite blot in Him, because committed against all wisdom, goodness and power; and a misery to us, because it would tend to the ruin of His creatures. The accurate perfection which He acquires in all His ways, having to do with so many millions of objects, becomes our infinite joy, our amazement and wonder, a transcendent cause of complacency[1] and

[1] Delight.

adoration; it fills eternity with delights and praises. The possibility of doing otherwise, in Him that is subject to no laws, awakens our concernment; but the prevention of our fear, by the establishment of our security, supplies our contentment. He is an absolute and free agent, and therefore we may fear a miscarriage in His choice; but as from all eternity He hath determined Himself, and is by His essence an eternal act of wisdom and righteousness, He secures our felicity; and makes it more great, because He is not imposed on by another, but freely of Himself delights in the most excellent things.

This relateth to the righteousness of action, whereby God did execute all His decrees, and does eternally. For nothing is past, but all things in Him are infinitely near and present for ever. If you desire further information concerning the nature of righteous actions, those actions are properly called righteous that are adequately fitted to their ends and causes. And in this respect there is in every being under several [1] circumstances a several righteousness.

The effect of righteousness with men is peace and assurance for ever, because righteous men are agreeable to God and all His creatures, rightly answer all their natures and assist in the harmony of the whole creation. It is fruition and blessedness, because all the perfection and goodness of God is with His kingdom, received into the soul by the righteous esteem of all objects. It is the beauty and glory of the inward man, because a voluntary agent that does incline himself to such excellent actions is highly amiable and delightful to be seen. Not only because his soul is transformed into an intelligible world, transcendent to all that is created, by the ideas of God and His works erected in the mind; but his affections are framed in a living and incomparable order, according as every cause and object requires. There is something in the soul of a righteous man that fitly answers all obligations and rewards. It is transformed into the image of God in such a sort that, in the righteous act which it becomes, God for ever dwelleth and appeareth.

The effect of righteousness in God is so great that, whereas all impossibles are stark naught, all things which it is possible

[1] Distinct.

for God to do are fair and excellent; all the best are made actual, by the execution of His righteous decree. By this the Son of God is in the bosom of the Father, and the Spirit of God proceedeth throughout all eternities to His own perfection. For the righteousness of God is not like the righteousness of men, that may be permitted to sleep and intermit their operations; an accidental habit, distinct from their essence, which may sometimes exist when it doth not work. But it is quick and powerful and ever in action; and is indeed the act itself which is His eternal essence and His Son begotten of itself for ever. *'For Wisdom is more moving than any motion; she passeth and goeth through all things by reason of her pureness. It is the breath of the power of God, and a pure influence flowing from the glory of the Almighty; the brightness of the Everlasting Light, the unspotted mirror of the power of God and the image of His goodness. Being one, it can do all things; and remaining in itself maketh all things new; and in all ages entering into holy souls, she maketh them friends of God and prophets.'*

God's righteousness is the end and effect of itself. His essence is an infinite and eternal act of righteousness and wisdom, which filleth His kingdom with the majesty of its glory, and by coming into being in a voluntary manner giveth to all things their essence and perfection. Because it cometh into being in a voluntary manner, it is mysterious and incomprehensible.

The glory of this act is derived from Himself, and springeth purely from the perfection of its pleasure. Of its pleasure it is what it is; and as the Son of God is Light of Light, so He is Wisdom of Wisdom, Righteousness of Righteousness, Life of Life and Goodness of Goodness. For it is infinite wisdom that found out the perfection of this act, and eternal righteousness that first achieved it. The righteousness achieved would not spring from any but eternal righteousness in itself achieving it; which is unbegotten in the Person of the Father, begotten in the Person of the Son, and proceeding in the Person of the Holy Ghost to all creatures and operations; in its actions existing and abiding perfect for ever.

In God, to act and to be are the same thing. Upon the suspension of His act, His essence would be gone; whereas our essence may without its act or operation remain. And if His act existeth, by acting His righteousness is and existeth of itself, and by itself completeth its essence for ever. It is not the power of being righteous, but the exertion of that power, which is the parent of eternal righteousness.

God having such an infinite delight in the righteous act, which Himself is, designed to make us such righteous acts as Himself is. And when we perfectly do what we ought, we shall in operation and extent be like unto Him; being 'perfect, as our Father which is in heaven is perfect; for we shall see as we are seen, and know as we are known.'

In the meantime, God hath taken care to endue us with power to make our particular actions completely righteous. Every little act we perform is a fruit and offspring of the whole creation. Infinite Love is delighted by it, infinite glory and blessedness acquired. A creature of infinite value is preserved, the crown is put upon all God's works, and all the spectators—angels and men—are eternally pleased. For, being done, it is admitted into eternity, and shall remain in its place and be visible for ever. 'For the Lord will come, who both will bring to light the hidden things of darkness, and will make manifest the counsels of the hearts; and then shall every man have praise of God.' All that was done shall be remembered for ever, and be praised and admired by the holy angels, esteemed by all saints, and crowned with acceptance by God Almighty; which will turn to the joy of the righteous, because of the innate goodness of their souls; which moveth them to delight in nothing more than in becoming, in all their righteous actions, objects of complacency [1] to God and His creatures.

[1] Delight.

CHAPTER XI

Of Goodness, natural, moral and divine; its nature described; the benefits and works of goodness

GOODNESS is a virtue of the first estate, a divine perfection in God, by which He is and enjoys His blessedness. In men it is a habit or act of the soul, by force of which they love and delight in all that is blessed. 'Tis that by which all creatures communicate themselves to others' benefit. All living creatures affect others, and delight in doing good unto them. In God it is that infinite and eternal act from which all other goodnesses spring, and on which they depend. The nature of goodness is founded in a convenience [1] between that which is good and that to which it is profitable. If we consult its several kinds, there is a natural goodness, a moral and a divine.

Natural goodness is the aptitude of corporeal beings to produce such profitable and healing effects as the enjoyer desires. The nutritive power in aliments, the medicinal quality in herbs, the pleasing quality in perfumes, the grateful lustre in precious stones, the comfortable heat in fire, the beautiful splendour in the sun, the refreshing moisture in the sea, the reviving nature of the air, the solid convenience [2] and fertility of the ground, all these are physically good. But this is goodness in the meanest degree, being no more than the natural fitness of dead agents that are made to act by a fatal necessity, without sense or desire, though their action be answerable to the several exigencies of other creatures.

Moral goodness includeth all the perfections of the former, and something more. For life and liberty enter its existence, and it is wisely exercised in love and virtue. A clear understanding and a free will are the principles of those actions that are morally good. They must flow from ingenuity [3] and desire, though the person doing them be subject to another's empire, and made

[1] Agreement.
[2] Fitness.
[3] Sincerity.

to give an account of his actions. The nature of its excellence is very deep and retired, because it consists more in the principle and manner of its operation than in the thing that is done, and is measured more by the intention than the benefit. A madman or a fool may by accident save a man's life or preserve an empire, yet be far from that goodness which is seated in the will and understanding; which plainly shows that the goodness chiefly regarded is in the soul of him that does anything convenient; not in the benefit received, but in the mind of the benefactor. And the truth is that the external benefit, though it saves the lives and souls and estates and liberties and riches and pleasures and honours of all mankind, acts but physically, by a dead or passive application. The root of its influence and value is seated in another place—in the soul of him whose goodness was so great as to sacrifice his honour and felicity for the preservation and welfare of those whom he intended to save. It is seated in the counsel and design of the actor.

It is a hard matter to define it, but it is something like a willing conformity to the interests and affections of his fellow-creatures, attended with a voluntary convenience in a person obliged and subject to laws to all those obligations that are laid upon him, and to all the rewards that are set before him; but especially to the desires and commands of his superior, to whom he naturally owes himself and desires to be pleasing. To act upon great and mighty principles, in a vigorous, free and generous manner, for the sake of those that obliged him and for the sake of those to whom his kindness is shown, increases the measure of moral goodness; but its perfection is seated in a loyal respect and perfect gratitude to God Almighty, who, by being infinitely good to us, has infused and created such a goodness in the soul that its principal joy and delight is to please Him. For though all creatures consult themselves and their own preservation, yet the force of gratitude upon an ingenious soul is very powerful. Moral goodness is an alacrity and readiness of the will to sacrifice itself, upon consideration of the benefits a man hath received, to another's benefit, enjoyment, comfort, satisfaction.

Divine goodness is an active and eternal principle, stirring up itself without obligation or reward, to do the best and most excellent things in an eternal manner. It is proper only to God. Its excellency is supreme, its beauty infinite, its measure endless, its nature ineffable, its perfection unconceivable. It hath no cause, but is the cause of all other things whatsoever. It is a living and eternal act of free and underserved love; an indeficient [1] ocean of bounty, which can never be fathomed or by finite degrees be wholly received. It is invisible in its essence, but apparent in its effects; incomprehensible, but manifest enough to be believed and adored. It is an infinite and eternal essence, which is good to itself by being good to all; infinitely good to itself by being without measure good to all its objects. It is an infinite and eternal act, which continually ponders and entirely desires the welfare of others, and establishes its own, in a voluntary manner, by that intention; an act whose essence is seated in the preparation of all delights and the communication of all its glories. Its felicity is eternal and infinite, yet seated entirely in the felicity of others. It doth infinite good to all its recipients, merely for the sake of the excellency of the act of doing good. It delighteth in the excellency of that act, and useth all its power in doing good, that the act in which it delighteth might be infinitely perfect. And the perfect act in which it finally resteth is the goodness which all adore and desire. Its sovereign joy and pleasure is to be delightful to others. All its creatures are delightful to itself only as they imitate and receive its goodness. Should we run into its properties, they are innumerable and endless, but as infinite in beauty as variety and greatness. It is the utmost height of all goodness, as well as the original and end of all. It exceedeth moral goodness as much as that exceedeth natural, and infinitely more. In physical goodness there is a mechanical fitness and dead convenience; but all it can pretend to is the benefit and pleasure of moral agents. For the sun and moon and stars, the trees and seas and minerals are made for men. Whereas moral goodness is made to enjoy all physical goodness, that in a higher sphere it might be pleasing to God, and is immediately subservient to His divine and essential goodness.

This divine goodness is the first perfection of the efficient cause of the world's creation, which of necessity derives an immediate

[1] All-sufficient.

excellency into all the creatures, because it is the most communicative and active principle that is. But the necessity is attended with a liberty no less than infinite. For it freely pleaseth itself in its operations, and its pleasure is to delight itself in the acquisition of felicity for others. Its freedom is a necessary circumstance of its operation. For the glory of its inclination and kindness could not be, much less be seen, did it act by necessity of nature, imposition, chance or accident. When the act is in being, it worketh physically; and it is no wonder that such an act should produce such effects and be so beneficial. For when it is done, it cannot be otherwise but that such and such effects must follow its existence; they are as natural as if they were essential to it. All the wonder is, what should determine the liberty of the agent at first to do such great and mighty things for others' sake. And all that can be said is, His own goodness and the excellency of the action. For it is not with God as it is with men. Few men will be at the expense of doing what all admire. All that receive the benefit applaud and delight in the action, and so much the more by how much the more hazardous and great and painful it was; but scarcely one will endure the difficulty of a heroic deed for the sake of others. God, on the contrary, takes infinite delight in the action which all admire; and because it is infinitely great and heroic and perfectly divine, finds His liberty and ease in that act, and is so taken with the beauty of the work that His infinite pleasure exceeds all the necessity and fate in nature.

That pleasure which He taketh in promoting the happiness of all existences created and increased is His goodness. It is the infinite use of perfect liberty freely delighted in; as pleasant to Himself as to all intelligent spectators and enjoyers. It is easy to discern that this goodness is the foundation and essence of His happiness and glory.

By it He becomes delightful to Himself, by it He becomes delightful to others. By it He communicates all His powers and perfections with pleasure, and receives the services of all the creatures with satisfaction. By it He is concerned in the joys of others and enjoys their blessedness. By it He is capable of all their affections and of the services which His laws require. By it all angels and cherubims are moved to admire and adore

His glory. By it all creatures visible and invisible are made His treasures. By it He is multiplied and magnified in every soul, as the same object is in several mirrors, being entirely represented in every living temple of His eternal essence. By it He becometh His own end, and the glorious author and the king of heaven. By it He liveth a divine and a blessed life, and by it He is what He is for ever. By it all the graces, exaltations and virtues of His creatures are made His joys, and their persons and praises are delightful to Him.

Of all His laws and decrees and counsels His goodness is the fountain. It is the original and final cause of all our thanksgivings. Our ease and repose and satisfaction, our bliss and enjoyment, are founded in it and caused by it. For its own pleasure, all our delights are made exquisite in their place, and most of them eternal. For its own glory it maketh all its creatures glorious, and prizeth its own glory because it is the sovereign delight of all its creatures. It is every way complete and perfect, as infinitely convenient as it is great in bounty, as good to itself as to all others. There is no end of all its perfection, and for that cause it is incomprehensible.

To be made partaker of the divine nature without having the goodness of Almighty God is impossible. Nor can we enjoy His goodness or bear the similitude of His glory, unless we are good in like manner. We enjoy the goodness of God, and may be said to have it, either when we have its similitude in ourselves or the pleasure of it in others. Since the goodness of God is the great object of our joy, its enlargement is our interest; and the more there are to whom He is good, and the more He communicates His felicity to every one, the greater pleasures He prepares for us and the more is our goodness therein delighted. To see innumerable millions in communion with Him, and all of them made glorious and blessed, and every one seated in His throne, is the greatest elevation of our souls, and the highest satisfaction in the world. When our goodness meeteth His in all places, and congratulates [1] the felicity of every person, we may then use the words of our Saviour, because we are endued with the same mind and affection. And as He accepts all the good that is done to His members as

[1] Rejoices in.

done to Himself, saying 'Inasmuch as ye have done it to the least of these my brethren, ye have done it to me,' our souls will reply, 'Inasmuch as Thou hast done all this to the least of these my brethren, Thou hast done it to me.' For loving our neighbours as ourselves, all angels and men will be our fellow members, our brethren, our other selves. As we delight in all acts of goodness for their own sake, that are done to us, so shall we delight in all the bounties of God for theirs, who are the partakers of them; and in God for this very reason, because He is good to all. We shall be as happy in others as in ourselves; and esteem the goodness of God our felicity, because it hath prevented [1] our goodness, and done all for them which, were it undone, we should desire to do ourselves; because our goodness is a principle that carries us to delight in their perfect felicity. Which that we may do the more sweetly, and with more full satisfaction and perfect reason, His goodness to all others is but the perfection of goodness to us; for they are all made blessed for our fuller and greater felicity.

Had God withheld or withdrawn His goodness from all others, it had not been greater to us, but less. The stars are no hindrance to our enjoyment of the sky, but the light and beauty of the place which we contemplate. Were they all annihilated, the heavens would be obscure. They do us many services, of which we should be bereaved by their absence or destruction. God, by giving beams and influences to them made our treasures more rich and fair, which are increased and multiplied by their beauty and number. Did the sun shine upon us and upon nothing else, it would be less beneficial to us than now it is. Its beams that are scattered seem to be lost; yet were they contracted upon one, his body would be consumed, and all the rest of the world would be dark about him. Those rays which fly from the sun to the utmost parts of the world illuminate all objects, and from them more conveniently return to the eye with their beauty and glory which, by those rays that are dispersed, become visible and profitable. They fall not all upon every single man, but work for him in other places; begetting herbs and fruits and flowers and minerals and springs and trees and jewels, with all that is rich

[1] Anticipated.

and delectable in the world for his fruition. It serves beasts and fowls and fishes, for my sake; and for my sake does it serve even men and angels, that they, being more divine and glorious creatures, might adorn heaven and earth with their persons, which without them would be void and empty. For we all desire to be seen and known and beloved, and for that cause, without living agents, should be very desolate and discontented.

Thus you see, if God had given all eternity and immensity to a man, if He had made no other creatures but him alone, His bounty had been defective; whereas by the creation of these He hath filled eternity and immensity with treasures. All which He hath made ours, by commanding them to love us as themselves; fit to be enjoyed and beloved by us, by filling them with His goodness and making them in His image. For every one of them is to love all His creatures as He does, and to delight in the beauty and felicity of all, and be the joy and delight of all, as He is. And the greater, and the richer, and the fairer they are, the more great and happy are we, because they are made our lovers and friends, our brides and brethren, our sons and daughters, our fathers and our servants; which the more honourable and excellent they are, the more delightful; the more glorious and blessed these are, their love is the more precious and acceptable. True goodness removes all envy and contention out of the world, and introduces nothing but peace and bounty and joy, unspeakable and full of glory.

We love nothing more than to be delightful to others, and to have our glory seen is a natural desire, which our Saviour has countenanced by His own petition. It is our interest that the eyes should be innumerable that see and admire the glory which we had with the Father, in some sense, before the world was; that they should see, I mean, how much we are beloved of God from all eternity; that there should be millions of blessed persons to whom we may communicate ourselves concerns our glory, as it doth also that they should be great and perfect, that are made to admire and delight in us. If we enter into His eternal glory, as the Scripture saith, and our bliss be individually one with His, or so perfectly like His as is promised, it is no fault to desire glory; for it is goodness itself that desires glory and esteemeth all those its best and sovereign treasures that are capable of loving and delighting in it.

There is in the goodness of God and men and angels a living power, that is exquisitely tender in sense and feeling; which, as it feels and apprehends itself, doth also feel its object, and apprehend both its own and its object's excellences, by virtue of which living power it is able to delight in its own goodness and its object's glory. The apple of its eye is not more tenderly regarded than the person which it loveth. It is afflicted in all our afflictions, and crowned and delighted in all our prosperities. It tendeth by its nature to the benefit of others, and cannot endure the least damage or detriment to any. It infinitely hates the least defect in itself or in its creatures. Nothing can be evil to it but what is evil to another. Its interests and its objects are so united that it entirely lives and sees and feels and enjoys in others; as its inclination is to be doing good, and it has no other element than the felicity of its creatures. In friendship it appeareth and from love it proceedeth; it endeth in felicity. It hath many great and glorious designs, all contending with each other for supremacy. It clothes itself with glory and adorns its essence with all kind of beauties. It endures all afflictions and hazards; it undertakes all labours; it builds a palace and provides a kingdom for its beloved. And yet, when all is done, nothing can exceed the delight which it taketh in the person of its beloved. All the honour and esteem and glory it desires, it findeth there. The use and value of all its treasures consists in the benefit they do to its beloved. Infinite goodness can be seated nowhere but in Love alone, for that only is capable of infinite benevolence and complacency.

The liberal soul deviseth liberal things, and by liberal things shall he stand. The more good it doth, the more good it is; and the more good, the more great and honourable, the more perfect and happy. There can be no excess in goodness; because the more delightful it is to its object, and the more divine and glorious its object is, the more abundant pleasure it taketh in communicating all felicities to its object. And the more great and manifold its treasures are, the more sweet and precious the things are which it giveth away, and the more its beloved delighteth in them. By so much the more admirable and divine it is, its goodness and its blessedness are both the greater.

There is no inconvenience which it can possibly meet, but a stop or impediment. It cannot be hurt by itself, because its essence is always overflowing, and the only evil it can fear from others is the unkindness of its object or the wrong that it may receive from free agents. For angels and men being made free, that they may love and honour and praise in a voluntary manner, and be and become good of their own accord (because they cannot be made morally or divinely good without the liberty of their concurrence and their own consent), there is some fear that they may abuse their power, because for the most illustrious use of it they are left in the hand of their own counsel. Howbeit, He has endeavoured as much as is possible, without prejudicing their excellence, to secure their duty. He hath infused into them the greatest inclinations to goodness imaginable, and the greatest principles of honour. He hath shown them the glory and felicity of goodness by His one [1] example. He hath commanded them by the severest laws that are possible to be good. He hath founded their peace and pleasure in goodness. He hath made the suspension of goodness uncouth and unnatural, all evil actions dark and disagreeable. He hath laid infinite obligations upon them to exercise goodness, and set eternal rewards before them. He hath made the object unto which they must show it extremely amiable. He hath given them all advantages, helps and assistances. He hath prepared the severest torments to punish the omission of it; and for a complement of all, will be extremely grieved if they fail to show it. This in the estate of innocency. Since the Fall indeed we must be kind and good to injurious persons; but this is founded in His own goodness toward us sinners; and though it be a difficult work in the first appearance, carries us to higher and more perfect glory.

That such goodness as this should be cannot be incredible to them that are acquainted with the nature of the universe; though it seemeth hard at least, if not impossible, to them that converse with peevish men. Being corrupt in their understandings, they are narrow and base and servile in their affections. They start at a

[1] ? Own.

shadow and boggle at a feather. Sin hath transformed them into slaves and cowards. They misapprehend the nature of their duty like fools, that were made to be great and mighty as kings. They think they shall be undone, if they become too great and good. They fear they shall become weak and contemptible by goodness; whereas nothing makes them so amiable and glorious as excess of goodness.

To show that there is such a goodness as that, which infinitely delights in pouring out its glory upon all creatures, the sun was made; which continues night and day pouring out its streams of light and heat upon all ages, yet is as glorious this day as it was the first moment of its creation. To show this, the stars were made, that shine in their watches and glitter in their motions only to serve us. The moon was made to show this goodness, which runs her race for ever to serve us. The earth was made to support us; springs and rivers expend their streams to revive us. Fruits and flowers and herbs and trees delight us. All corruptible things waste and consume away, that they may sacrifice their essence to our benefit. For if they were made stiff and unalterable, they could not feed us nor communicate their essence and perfection to us. The emanations and effusions of minerals are unknown, but that of spices and odours is well understood. And if these by disbursing their proper sweetness become more sweet and enlarge themselves, if they are made bright and fair for our sake, if they enjoy any light and pleasure in their service—as the sun and stars do, as herbs and flowers do, as beasts and birds and fishes do—the goodness of the Creator is abundantly more clear and apparent herein. For in all those creatures that perfect themselves by the service which they do, the service itself is a sufficient recompense; while those upon which we feed, being more corruptible, are exalted in their beings by being turned into ours. And the trade of bees, in the honey they make for us, and the warmth of sheep, in the fleeces they bear for us; the comfort of birds in the feathers they wear and the nests they build for us; and the pleasures of beasts in the offspring they beget and bring up for us, these things show that God is good to all, and His mercy is over all His works. And if any perish in our service, the bloody characters of His love and goodness are the more stupendous. All nature is sacrificed to our welfare, and all that we have by pure nature to do (till sin mars all) is to admire and enjoy that goodness, to the delight of which we sacrifice ourselves in our own complacency.[1] And in real truth, if it be a great wonder that any goodness should be thus infinite, the goodness of all other things without that goodness is a far greater. If it be wonderful, admire and adore it.

(AUTHOR'S MARGINAL NOTE—All this is spoken for encouragement and imitation.)

CHAPTER XII

Of Holiness: its nature, violence and pleasure. Its beauty consisteth in the infinite love of righteousness and perfection

THE infinite love of His own goodness is the holiness of God. There are infinite pleasures and perfections in its nature that merit an infinite esteem and desire. His goodness is all beauty, and His holiness all fire and flame in pursuing it. His holiness is all beauty, and His goodness all fire and flame to enkindle it. The infinite excess of His eternal goodness is its own holiness, and the beauty of holiness is excess of goodness. For if righteousness and holiness be well distinguished, righteousness is that virtue by which God doth apprehend, affect and esteem all excellent things according to their value, and choose and do always the best and most excellent. Holiness is the love which He beareth to His own righteousness, which, being infinite, makes Him infinitely enflamed with the love of the most perfect actions, and carries Him with an infinite ardour to the performance of them. For though it be a righteous thing to esteem the righteousness of God in an infinite manner, yet there is as much difference between righteousness and the love of righteousness as between

[1] Delight.

an object and the affection embracing it. Though here also the affection and the object are the same thing; for this holy esteem and love of righteousness is righteousness itself; for it does but render righteousness its due, though the affection be infinite which it bears unto it.

Holiness, if it be strictly defined, is that virtue in God by which He loveth the most perfect things, and infinitely delighteth in them. For by virtue of this affection He shunneth and hateth all that is profane, pursuing and delighting in all that is holy; for the object of holiness may be holy, as well as the affection. Whereupon it followeth that holiness is of two kinds; either the holiness of the affection, or the holiness of the object. They bear a relation to each other, yet are absolute perfections in themselves. For the hatred of all defects, imperfections, blemishes and errors is a glorious thing in itself, yet relates to the perfections of those objects from which it would remove those odious imperfections. The perfection of all objects when they are free from all blemishes is a glorious thing in itself too, yet is acceptable to that affection that desires to see a completeness and perfection in every object. And all is resolved into the same goodness of which we have been speaking.

For infinite goodness must needs desire with an infinite violence that all goodness should be complete and perfect; and that desire, which makes to the perfection of all goodness, must infinitely avoid every slur and miscarriage as unclean, and infinitely aim at every grace and beauty that tends to make the object infinitely perfect which it would enjoy. It cannot desire less than infinite perfection, nor less than hate all imperfection in an infinite manner. All objects are made and sanctified by the holiness of God. It is the measure and strength and perfection of goodness.

The holiness of God is sometimes called in His oracle, *the Beauty of Holiness,* as if all the beauty of God were in this. It extends to all objects in heaven and earth, from the highest to the lowest, from the greatest to the meanest, from the most pure to the most profane, with a goodness and wisdom so infinitely perfect disposing all, that some way or other everything might answer its infinite affection. It infinitely hates all that is bad, and as infinitely desires to correct the same. The influence of that affection, by which God abhorreth the least spot in His kingdom, reaches to the perfection of every object, and is the real and proper fountain of all the perfection of life and glory. And for this cause, in all probability, do the angels so continually cry, *Holy, Holy, Holy, Lord God of Hosts;* because the brightness of His infinite glory and perfection appeareth in His holiness, the violence of His eternal love and the excess of goodness. It may be also because all the heights of created perfection owe themselves to this holiness, all the raptures and ecstasies of heaven depending on the zeal wherewith God is carried to perfect blessedness; all which are occasioned by those pure and quintessential joys, those most sublime and perfect beauties, which they see and feel everywhere effected by the irresistible strength of that eternal ardour.

Sins of omission have an unknown guilt and demerit in them. They insensibly bereave us of infinite beauty. To let alone that perfection which might have been infinite, to pass by or neglect it, to exert almighty power in a remiss and lazy manner, is infinitely base and dishonourable, and therefore unclean because so odious and distasteful. Lukewarmness is profane, as well as malice. And it hath pleased God to brand it with a worse and more fatal censure. No folly or iniquity can dwell with Him; omission is both. To be hated is to be rejected; but to be beloved lukewarmly is to be embraced with polluted and filthy arms. And for this cause, the fire of His jealousy burns most devouringly about the altar. He will be sanctified in all them that draw nigh unto Him, and but to touch His ark irregularly is to be consumed. Nor is this any other than a concomitant of His holiness, and an evident testimony of His love to perfection. For it first shows that on His own part He maketh our powers perfect, that we may be able to see and adore Him worthily; and next, that He delights in no adoration but the most worthy. It moreover shows that He infinitely delights in the perfection of His own actions, for otherwise He would not be so severe against the imperfections of ours.

Nor is the reason of His love to the utmost perfection less than infinite. You know that all impure things upon earth are dull and obscure; as vile in esteem as base and faint in their operations. Neither will a lump of dirt shine like the sun, nor a mud wall be resplendent like polished marble. All glorious things have a height of intenseness in them, and owe most of their beauty to the motion of their strength and activity. But God is a more high and necessary thing than these. Perfection is His essence, and He could not be Himself upon any abatement. It is a great wonder! But the smallest thing in the world may spare somewhat of itself rather than that which is infinite. Upon the least subtraction, that which is infinite is made finite, and the loss is infinite. We cannot be at all beloved by Almighty God unless we are infinitely beloved. For to love and neglect us at the same time is impossible, and to be able to do infinite things for us and yet to do but some of them is to love and neglect at the same time. 'Tis love in what it does, and neglect in what it leaveth undone. The reason why it is our duty to love Him infinitely is because He infinitely loved us. Did He not exert all His power Himself, He would never command us to exert ours. The love of all perfection is His essence, and must be infinite for its own perfection. The least flaw in a diamond abates its price; one tooth awry or wanting in a clock doth make it useless. *Dead flies corrupt the apothecary's ointment; so doth a little folly him that is in reputation for wisdom and honour.* The greater his reputation and wisdom is, the more grievous a disparagement is any stain. Nor is God above these rules, for His essence itself is the ruler of ours; and the higher His divinity is, the more exquisite is its care of its own perfection. There is no danger of being severe in our expectations, for God does infinitely hate any defect in Himself more than we, though we infinitely hate it; and enjoys Himself only as He is an object worthy of His own infinite love and honour.

From God's love of righteous action it proceedeth that He made ours so completely capable of becoming righteous, and that He adventured a power into our hands of offending. It is a strange thing that the excess of the hatred of all sin should make sin possible, and that the most perfect righteousness should be the accidental cause of unrighteousness. But yet it is so. An infinite love to the best of all possible things made the worst of all things that could be possible; excepting those that are impossible, which yet we need not except.

To read these riddles aright, you must understand that even impossibles themselves are conceivable things, and actual; that the highest and best of all that are possible are the most easy with God and most near to His nature; that inferior possibles are more remote, and only thought on in the second place; that things impossible are the worst of evils, and things actual the best of goods. For nothing is impossible but that God should lie, or dishonour or displease or deny Himself; or abuse His power, or suspend His goodness, or injure His creatures, or do some such thing, which is contrary to His nature; yet very conceivable, because He is a free agent and has a kind of power, were it not prevented by His eternal act, whereby He is able to do these impossible things. Nothing is eternally actual but the goodness and wisdom and holiness of God, or some such thing as His righteousness and blessedness and perfection; all which spring from His will, and are eternally His pleasure as well as His essence. In the idle power of being and doing all excellent things, there is much hazard and danger; but He freely and voluntarily became all these from all eternity. He wrought all righteousness and wisdom and goodness from everlasting, and by so doing became the fountain of all that is glorious from all eternity. The worst of all possible evils are the sins of men, which have an infinite demerit and vileness in them, yet are truly possible; and the reason of their possibility is thus accounted. Impossible, which are worst of all, are sins in God.

To make creatures infinitely free and leave them to their liberty is one of the best of all possible things, and so necessary that no kingdom of righteousness could be without it. For in every kingdom there are subjects capable of laws and rewards and punishments, and there must be free agents. There is no kingdom of stones nor of trees nor of stars; only a kingdom of men and angels; who, were they divested of their liberty, would be reduced to the estate of stones and trees; neither capable of righteous actions, nor able to honour or to love or praise; without which operations all inferior creatures and mere natural agents would be totally useless. So that all the glory of the world depends on the liberty of men and angels, and therefore God gave it to them, because He delighted in the perfections of His creatures; though He very well knew there would be the hazard of their abusing it, and of sin in that abuse, when they had received it. The abuse of it He infinitely hated, yet could not prevent it without being guilty of a greater evil. He infinitely hated it, because those actions of love and honour, which should spring from the right use of it, were the only fair offspring for the sake of which the whole world was made; and without the right use of their liberty all creatures, angels and souls would be in vain. He could not prevent it without being Himself guilty of what in them He abhorred.

For Himself to be guilty was the worst of evils, and absolutely impossible. 'Twas better to let them make their power vain themselves, than do so Himself. For the author of that vanity, be it who it will, is the author of the sin. If they would make it vain, He could not help it. For Him to divest them of the use of liberty after He had given it was as inconsistent with Himself as it was with their beauty to abuse it; the act of giving it, by taking it away, being made vain. He infinitely hated that the liberty should be frustrated which He gave unto men for their more perfect glory. He laid all obligations upon them to use it well, and deterred them, as much as was possible, from abusing it; but would not transfer their fault upon Himself, because He foresaw they were about to do it; which He certainly had done, had He made their power vain Himself, after He had given it. Either to refuse to give the power, or, having given it, to interpose and determine it without their consent, was alike detrimental to the whole creation. For indeed it is impossible that He, by determining their wills, should make them the authors of righteous actions, which of all things in the world He most desired. There is as much difference between a willing act of the soul itself and an action forced on the will, determined by another, as there is between a man that is dragged to the altar, whether he will or no, and the man that comes with all his heart, with music and dancing, to offer sacrifice. There is joy and honour and love in the one; fear and constraint and shame in the other. That God should not be able to deserve our love, unless He Himself made us to love Him by violence, is the greatest dishonour to Him in the world; nor is it any glory or reputation for us, who are such sorry stewards that we cannot be entrusted with a little liberty but we must needs abuse it.

God adventured the possibility of sinning into our hands, which He infinitely hated, that He might have the possibility of righteous actions, which He infinitely loved. Being a voluntary and free agent, He did without any constraint love and desire all that was most high and supremely excellent of all objects that are possible to be thought on. His own essence, which is a righteous act, is the best; and the righteous acts of saints and angels are the highest and best next that, which creatures could perform. The very utmost excellence of the most noble created beings consisted in actions of piety freely wrought; which God so loved, that for their sake alone He made angels and souls and all worlds. These righteous actions He so loved that for their sake He prepared infinite rewards and punishments. All the business of His laws and obligations are these righteous actions. That we might do these in a righteous manner, He placed us in a mean [1] estate of liberty and trial; not like that of liberty in heaven, where the object will determine our wills by its amiableness, but in the liberty of Eden, where we had absolute power to do as we pleased, and might determine our wills ourselves; infinitely desiring and delighting in the righteous use of it, hating and avoiding by infinite cautions and provisions all the unjust actions that could spring from it.

If we love righteous actions as He does, and are holy as He is holy, in all manner of wisdom and righteousness, then shall we delight in all righteous actions as He doth, shall love virtue and wisdom as He doth, and prefer the works of piety and holiness above all the miracles, crowns and sceptres in the world. Every righteous and holy deed will be as pleasing to us as it is to Him. All angels and men will be as so many trees of righteousness, bearing the fruit of good works, on which we shall feast in communion with God. Or, if our righteous souls be vexed, as Lot's soul in Sodom was, in seeing and hearing the unlawful deeds of the wicked, they shall be recreated and revived with the sight of God's most righteous judgments, and with the beauty of His holy

[1] Midway.

ways, by which He rectifies the malignity of the wicked, overcomes the evil of their deeds, and turns all the vices of men into His own glory, and ours, in the kingdom of heaven.

The delights of wisdom and righteousness and holiness are suitable to their nature as those of goodness are to the nature of goodness; which no man can enjoy but he that is qualified for them by the principles of goodness and holiness implanted in his nature. For as he that has no eyes wanteth all the pleasures of sight, so he that has no knowledge wanteth all the pleasures of knowledge, he that is void of holiness is void of the sense which holiness inspires, and he that is without goodness must needs be without the pleasures of goodness; for he cannot delight in the goodness of God towards other creatures.

To be good, to be holy, to be righteous, is freely to delight in excellent actions; which unless we do of our own accord, no external power whatsoever can make us good or holy or righteous, because no force of external power can make us free. Whatever it is that invades our liberty, destroys it. God therefore may be infinitely holy, and infinitely desire our righteous actions, though He doth not intermeddle with our liberty, but leaves us to ourselves, having no reserve but His justice to punish our offences.

CHAPTER XIII

Of Justice, in general and particular. The great good it doth in empires and kingdoms, a token of the more retired good it doth in the soul. Its several kinds. That God's punitive justice springs from His goodness

THOUGH, following the common course of moralists in our distributions of virtues, we have seated Justice among the cardinal moral, yet upon second thoughts we find reason to reduce it to the number of divine, virtues; because upon a more near and particular inspection, we find it to be one of the perfections of God, and under that notion shall discover its excellence far more completely than if we did contemplate its nature as it is limited and bounded among the actions of men.

The universal justice of angels and men regards all moral actions and virtues whatever. It is that virtue by which we yield obedience to all righteous and holy laws, upon the account of the obligations that lie upon us, for the public welfare of the whole world; because we love to do that which is right, and desire the fruition of eternal rewards. There is much wisdom and goodness, as well as courage and prudence, necessary to the exercise of this virtue, and as much need of temperance in it as any. For he that will be thus just must of necessity be heroical, in despising all pleasure and allurements that may soften his spirit, all fears and dangers that may discourage and divert him, all inferior obligations and concerns that may entangle and ensnare him. He must trample under foot all his relations and friends and particular affections so far as they incline him to partiality and sloth. He must be endued with great wisdom to discern his end, great constancy to pursue it, great prudence to see into temptations and impediments; and, to lay hold on all advantages and means that may be improved, he must have a great activity and vigour in using them, a lively sense of his obligations, a transcendent love to God and felicity, a mighty patience and long-suffering; because his enemies are many, his condition low, his mark afar off, his business manifold, his life though short in itself yet long to him, his undertaking weighty and his nature corrupted.

They otherwise define justice to be that virtue by which we render unto all their due; which is of large extent, if the apostle's commentary comes in for explication: *For this cause pay you tribute also, for they are God's ministers, attending continually on this very thing. Render therefore to all their dues; tribute to whom tribute is due, custom to whom custom, fear to whom fear, honour to whom honour. Owe no man anything, but to love one another; for he that loveth another hath fulfilled the law.* Kings and magistrates and ministers and parents and children must have all their due; and so must God, blessed for ever, adoration to whom adoration is due, and obedience to whom obedience. In strict justice we must render hatred to whom hatred is due, and love to whom love. Hope is due to certain grounds of encouragement, and sorrow to certain sorrowful objects. But all our passions must still be guided by the rule of the law, and all our actions as honour and equity require.

Particular justice is conversant in the distribution of rewards and punishments; or else it observes the rules of equity and reason in buying and selling. It is called particular, because the exercise of it is not allotted to all; the power of rendering rewards and punishments being committed to a few, namely to the magistrates; and among private persons many not at all accustomed to buying and selling. This virtue, being to be exercised by some particular men, is particular justice. However, it has occasioned a distinction in the thing, whereby justice is divided into distributive and commutative; the one being used in courts of judicature, the other in the market.

It was a notable observation of Plato, that by reason of our dim eyes we are not able to see immediately what virtue does in secret in the soul. And therefore he says that as an old man that is blear-eyed, if he hath something given him to read in little characters, finds it necessary first to see the same in capital letters; so to observe first what virtue doth in a commonwealth is expedient to him that would understand what it doth in his own soul. The throne is upholden by justice; the majesty of kings and the glory of kingdoms is preserved by justice. When virtue is rewarded and vice suppressed, the city flourisheth. As the laws are the ramparts of men's estates, justice is the rampart of the law, the guardian angel of every family, state and kingdom. Kings and counsellors and priests and soldiers and tradesmen have all their several offices and proper duty in a kingdom; and that nation is blessed with order and beauty where every one contains himself in his proper duty. But where tradesmen invade the priests' office and defile the altar, the soldiers turn counsellors, and every counsellor deposes the king, nothing but confusion can follow in such a state. The senses and members of the body are like tradesmen; they traffic with sensible objects. The irascible passions of the soul are soldiers, and very apt to rebel and mutiny.

The conscience is the priest in the temple of the mind; right reason is the king, and the concupiscible affections, or smoother passions, especially avarice and ambition, may pass for counsellors. They may do well to put a man in mind of his interest, but when they despose right reason and usurp the throne, ruin must follow in the soul. The passions will turn counsellors, the tradesmen invade the temple, and all rights, sacred and profane, be blended together. To sell offices of trust and places of judicature is for a king to do that himself which rebels attempt in violence —to put unworthy men in places of trust promiscuously, that will sell justice by retail, as they bought it by wholesale. Justice is a severe virtue, and will keep up all the faculties of the soul upon hard duty, for otherwise it would not pay to felicity its due; but where its care is remiss in taking an account, and solid goods are bartered away to counterfeit false commodities, the soul will grow loose and poor in a moment. All its powers, subordinate and superior, will forget their duty, and the healthy estates of the mind fall into anarchy and confusion. All its hopes and felicities will be lost, for want of that justice which distributes to every power its proper office.

There are two passages that I mightily desire to be imprinted in the memory of all the world, and they are both of our Saviour. The one is, *He that is faithful in a little shall be ruler over much.* The other is this: *Who then is that faithful and wise servant, whom his Lord hath made ruler over his household, to give them meat in due season? Blessed is that servant whom his Lord, when he cometh, shall find so doing. He that is faithful in a little is faithful also in much.*

To be just in a little silver and gold, and accurate in deciding causes between a man and his neighbour, are actions that in their own nature seem to have little tendency to bliss and glory. But when we consider that we are servants for a time, entrusted by a Lord that will come and examine what we have done, we are not to measure our hopes by those little acts as they determine in a moment, but in relation to the recompenses which our Lord will give when he cometh. For our Saviour hath added, *But and if that evil servant shall say in his heart, 'My Lord delayeth his coming,' and shall begin to smite his fellow servants and to eat and drink with the drunken, the Lord of that servant shall come in a day when he looketh not for him, and in an hour that he is not ware of, and shall cut him asunder and appoint him his portion with hypocrites; there shall be weeping and gnashing of teeth.*

If God should be loose and careless in His kingdom, as it is infinitely greater than all other dominions, so would it quickly be more full of confusions; especially since the King would then himself be so loose and careless. For licence and profaneness are of a spreading nature, and such as the king is, such is the people. The vices of kings do always punish themselves in the imitation of their subjects, especially where the distinction between profane and holy is lost, and there is no hope or fear of punishments or rewards. If God should declare it by any act of His, to be a thing indifferent whether men did well or ill, it would mightily abate the rectitude of His nature and eclipse His majesty. His sovereignty would be slighted and His will despised, which ought infinitely to be dreaded. While justice is infinite and there is an infinite difference put between good and evil, His creatures, we see, are apt to abuse their liberty, and rebel and become apostates; though they have an infinite pleasure to aspire after, and an infinite destruction or wrath to fear. What would they do if the divine will were feeble and remiss, and exacted no reverence to its law and pleasure? It is the height and glory of God that He sets an infinite rate upon excellent deeds, and infinitely detests and abhors the wicked. Their last ends are not more distant than their first beginnings, in His esteem and displeasure. Because He is infinitely offended and displeased at evil deeds, He guards and fortifies His law, deters men from displeasing Him by the fear of infinite punishments, encourages men to please Him by proposing infinite rewards. And the truth is, the infinite approbation and esteem which He hath for wise and holy deeds produceth a delight and complacency [1] in them which is a principal part of the reward. Nothing is more honourable than to be praised and honoured by the King of kings. The infinite hatred of evil deeds is the very torment itself that afflicts the wicked. 'Tis but to see how much we are hated of God, and

[1] Satisfaction.

how base the action is; no other fire is needful to hell. The devil's chiefest hell is in the conscience. They are obdurate and seared that cannot discern and feel the wound which they inflict on themselves, when they grieve and offend their Creator. It is easy to see the necessity of that justice which springs from holiness; and that God could not be infinitely holy, were He not infinitely just in like manner.

That His punitive justice springs from His goodness is next to be observed. He punishes them that are harmful to others. He is most severe in pleading the cause of the fatherless and the widow. Himself is persecuted when His saints are molested; and the faults for which the untoward servant was punished are particularly those of *beating his fellow servants.* A good man, by how much the more tender and compassionate he is, by so much the more is he provoked at any gross affront or abuse of the innocent. Every soul is the bride of God; and His own infinite goodness, which deserves infinite love, is infinitely beloved by Him. He infinitely tenders [1] it and avoids its least displeasure; but its displeasure is infinite at every step, and consequently His anger, when such a sovereign beauty as His infinite goodness is offended by it.

The foundation of His righteous kingdom, and of the room prepared for His eternal justice to act in, is infinitely deeper, and must in other discourses more full and copious on that theme be shown; and to those we refer you. All we shall observe here is that this punitive justice being God's infinite zeal, whereby He vindicates His abused goodness, His goodness must of necessity precede it and be abused before He can be angry, and before His anger can be accounted justice. His dominion is infinite, but cannot be arbitrary, in a loose construction, because it is infinitely divine and glorious.

[1] Cherishes.

CHAPTER XIV

Of Mercy. The indelible stain and guilt of sin. Of the kingdom which God recovered by mercy. The transcendent nature of that duty, with its effects and benefits

SUCH is the infinite justice of God and the severity of His displeasure at sin, His holiness so pure and His nature so irreconcilable, His hatred so real and infinite against it, that when a sin is committed, His soul is alienated from the author of the crime, and His infinite displeasure will ever see the obliquity and ever loathe the deformity therein.

The person of a man is concerned in, and always represented in the glass of, his action. Union between him and his deeds is marvellous. 'Tis so close that his soul itself is hated or loved in his actions. As long as it appeareth in that deed which is odious and deformed, he can never be beloved.

How slight soever our thoughts of sin are, the least sin is of infinite demerit, because it breaketh the union between God and the soul, bereaveth Him of His desires, blasteth His image, corrupteth the nature of the soul; is committed against infinite goodness and majesty, being (as the scripture speaketh) *exceeding sinful,* because it is committed against infinite obligations and rewards; displeasing to all the glorious angels, abominable to all the wise and holy, utterly against all the rules of reason, and infinitely opposite to the holiness of God, who is of purer eyes than to behold the least iniquity. So that unless there be some way found out to deliver the soul from the guilt of sin, to blot out the act and to purify it from the stain, there can be no reconciliation between God and a sinner. That an offence so infinite should be eternally punished is the most reasonable thing in the world.

Nothing but infinite power and wisdom is able to wash away leprosy of guilt, and to restore the soul to its former beauty and perfection; without which all pardon is vain, and the soul dishonourable and sick unto death, as long as the shame and confusion of its guilt does lie upon it; which cannot be removed by feeble tears, nor by acts of indignation against ourselves, nor by any penitence or sorrow of ours; for if these could prevail, devils might repent, and be cleared of their trespasses long ago.

That no law of works can justify sinners is evident enough from that of the apostle, *For if there had been a law given which could have given life, verily righteousness should have been by the law.* God was not so prodigal as without an infinite cause to expend the blood of His Son. And the principal cause for which He came was that He might be *made a curse and sin* for us, that we might be delivered from the curse of the law, and be made *the righteousness of God in Him.*

The reason why the devils cannot be saved is because the Son of God *took not upon him the nature of angels, but the seed of Abraham.* And there is no other name given under heaven among men whereby we may be saved, but only the name of Jesus, who offered up Himself a sacrifice for us, that He might purify to Himself a peculiar people zealous of good work. He pacified the wrath of God by His death, and satisfied His justice in our nature, and washed us in His blood, and made us kings and priests unto God. To Him be glory and dominion for ever, Amen.

It was the design of Christ, and it became the mercy of God in our redemption, to take away all the filth and deformity of guilt; in which the perfection of His love and power appeareth. *Even as Christ also loved his Church, and gave himself for it, that he might sanctify and cleanse it with the washing of water, by the Word; that he might present it to himself a glorious Church, not having spot or wrinkle or any such thing, but that it might be holy and without blemish.* For the Church of God being His Bride, and we *members of his body, and of his flesh and of his bones,* it was meet that we should be restored to the perfection of beauty, and if not recover the same, enjoy a better righteousness than we had before.

The light of nature could discover nothing of all this, and therefore it was taught by revelations and miracles and oracles from heaven.

As all things before his fall were subservient to man's glory and blessedness, so all things after his fall became opposite to him. All creatures upbraided him with his guilt, everything aggravated his sin and increased his damnation. The glory and blessedness which he lost was his torment; the honour which he had before was turned into shame. The love of God, which he had offended, increased his guilt; eternity was a horror to him, his conscience a tormentor, and his life a burden. Nothing but shame and despair could follow his sin; the light of nature itself condemned him, and all he could see was that he was deformed and hated of God. For that of the psalmist is an eternal verity: *Thou art not a God that hath pleasure in wickedness, neither shall evil dwell with thee. The foolish shall not stand in thy sight; thou hatest all workers of iniquity. Thou shalt destroy them that speak leasing; the Lord will abhor the bloody and deceitful man.*

The express declaration of God assured Adam that his recovery was impossible: *In the day that thou eatest thereof thou shalt die the death.* For not being able to dive into the secret reservation, which depended absolutely upon God's holy will and pleasure, as an act of sovereignty above the tenor of the law, all that he could see was that he must die the death, because the veracity of God (as well as His nature) obliged Him to fulfil the denunciation of the sentence; at least as Adam conceived.

In the midst of this black and horrid condition, the mercy of God appeared like a morning star, and the redeeming love of God was that alone which was able by its discovery to dispel the mists of darkness that were round about him.

As all things were before turned into evil by the force of sin, and conspired to sink him lower into the bottomless pit; so all the evils of his present condition were, by this infinite mercy, turned to his advantage, and his condition in many respects far better than before.

It is fit to see how sin enfeebled his soul, and made him unable to serve God, that we might the better understand the manner of his recovery, and how his spiritual life and power is restored in the new strength which he received in his Saviour.

The account of it is this: by his self-love he was prone to desire all that was profitable and delightful to him. While therefore God infinitely loved him, being apparently the fountain of all his happiness, he could not choose, as long as he considered it, but love God and delight in Him. It was natural and easy to celebrate His praises. But when he was hated of God, though he could not choose but acknowledge that hatred just, yet his self-love made him to look upon God in a malevolent manner, as his greatest enemy and his eternal tormentor. All that was in God was a terror to him. His power, His eternity, His justice, His holiness, His goodness, His wisdom, His unalterable blessedness, all was a grief and terror to his soul, as long as the hatred of God continued against him, it made him desperate to think it would continue for ever, and reduced him to the miserable slavery of hating God even to all eternity.

But when the love of God towards man appeared, the joy wherewith he was surprised was, in all likelihood, so far beyond his expectation, and his redemption so far above the powers of nature, that his very guilt and despair enflamed him with love. God appeared now so welcome to him, and so lovely above all that was before, that it was impossible for him to look upon God and not to love Him with greater amazement and ardour than ever. Self-love, that before compelled him to hate God, carried him now most violently to the love of God. And the truth is, the love of God in the eye of the understanding is the influence of the Holy Ghost proceeding from the Father by the Son into the soul of the spectator. For God is Love, and we therefore love Him because He first loved us. A fallen man is still a reasonable creature and, having more reason to love God than he had before, is by the pure nature of his essence infinitely more prone to love God and delight in Him and praise Him for ever, because he is so mercifully and strangely restored. Thus are we in Christ restored to the exercise of that power which we lost by sin; but without Him we can do nothing.

When all the kingdom of God was at an end by the fall of man, and all the labour of creation lost by the perverseness of him for whom the whole world was made, God by His mercy recovered it, and raised it out of the rubbish of its ruins, more glorious than before; which is the chief reason for the sake of which we introduce the mercy of God as our best pattern. For when a man has injured us, by nature there is an end of all the lovely exercise of peace and amity, if natural justice should be strictly observed; but then the season of grace arrives, and the excellency of mercy shows itself in the lustre of its wisdom; and so our empire is continued, our loss retrieved. For by showing mercy we often recover the love of an enemy, and restore a criminal to the joy of our friendship. We lengthen out our goodness and heighten its measure; we make it victorious, and clothe it with a glory above the course of nature. And all this we are enabled to do by coming to Jesus Christ, who hath restored us to hope of salvation, and taught us a way to increase our own goodness by other men's evils, to turn the vices of others into our own virtues, and to live a miraculous life of worth and excellency in the midst of enemies; dealing with men better than they deserve, adorning ourselves with trophies by the advantages of their vileness, making ourselves more honourable by the ignominy they cast upon us, more lovely and desirable by the hatred which they bear towards us.

The foundations upon which we exercise this virtue are wholly supernatural. To be kind to the innocent is but justice and goodness, but to be kind to the malevolent is grace and mercy. And this we must do, because *our Father which is in heaven causeth his sun to rise on the just and the unjust, and his rain to descend on the righteous and the wicked.* Because Mercy is the headspring of all our felicities, therefore should we show mercy, as we have obtained mercy. As the blood was sprinkled on the tabernacle and all its utensils, so is the blood of Christ upon the heathens, and the earth, and all our enjoyments. They are daily monitors of mercy to us, because they were purchased by the blood of Christ. For of Him it is that the heavens declare the glory of God, and the firmament showeth His handiwork to us sinners at this day; the salvation of sinners being the only end for the sake of which we can be permitted now to enjoy them.

The Incarnation of our Lord Jesus Christ is an incredible mystery to them that do not consider the love of God towards men in the creation of the world. But they that measure it by His laws and works, and see it in the value of their own souls, would think it very strange if that love which appeareth so infinite in all other things should be defective only in its ways of providence. They easily believe it may express itself in the

Incarnation. Especially since all ages are beautified with the effects and demonstrations of this verity, that *God so loved the world that he gave his only-begotten Son, that whosoever believeth in him should not perish but have everlasting life.* For love is apt to transform itself into all shapes that the necessity of its object requires; and as prone to suffer as rejoice with it, as apt to suffer for it as with it. Many fathers have died for their children, many for their country; but the love of God exceedeth them all. To be beloved in our guilt is exceeding wonderful; but this also is in the nature of love. It may be provoked with the guilt or moved with compassion at the misery of a sinner.

Where the love is extremely violent and the weak estate of the object fit for compassion, it is more inclined to pity than revenge; though where the object is strong and endued with all advantages, it is more offended at the outrage of its rebellion.

Whether we consider the nature of man or his estate before the fall, we have some reason to believe that he was more beloved than the holy angels; for there was more exquisite care and art manifested in the creation of his person, and his condition was fitted for a more curious tenderness and compassion, if he offended.

If you look into the nature of angels and men, you will find this mighty difference between them. Angels are more simple spirits; men are images of God, carefully put into a beautiful case. Their souls would seem equal to the angels, were they not to live in human bodies; and those bodies are superadded, certainly for unspeakable and most glorious ends. The visible world was made for the sake of these bodies, and without such persons as men are, it would be utterly useless. The hypostatical union of two natures so unspeakably different as the soul and body are is of all things in the world the most mysterious and miraculous. Man seems to be the head of all things visible and invisible, and the golden clasp whereby things material and spiritual are united. He alone is able to beget the divine image, and to multiply himself into millions. His body may be the temple of God, and when it pleased God to become a creature, He assumed the nature of man. Angels are made ministering spirits for the sake of man, and by him alone God and His works are united.

If you respect his condition, he was made a little lower than the angels, that he might be crowned with glory and honour; lower for a time, that he might be higher for ever. The angels were placed in such an estate that, if they fell, it would be with more shame; yet if they stood, it would be with less glory. For having the advantages of greater light and strength, to sin against them was more odious, and to stand in them less wonderful; while man, being more remote from God, was more obnoxious [1] to dangers and more weak to resist them. His want of clear light, if he fell, would lessen his offence; and the difficulties wherewith he was surrounded, if he stood, would increase his virtue; which by consequence would make his obedience more pleasing, and much augment his eternal glory. All which put together, when angels and men both fell, fitted man rather to be chosen and redeemed, he being the greater object of compassion and mercy.

The degrees and measure of that mercy which was shown to man in his redemption are very considerable. When he was weak and unable to help himself, when he was an enemy, when he was leprous and deformed, when he was miserable and dead, before he desired or thought of such a thing, God freely gave His Son to die for his salvation, and condescended to propose a reconciliation; which should teach us, though higher than the cherubims and more pure than light, though our enemies are never so base and injurious and ingrateful, nay, obstinate and rebellious, to seek a reconciliation by the most laborious and expensive endeavours, to manifest all our care and kindness toward them, pursuing their amendment and recovery. For the same mind ought to be in us that was in Christ Jesus; *who, being in the form of God, thought it no robbery to be equal with God, yet took upon him the form of a servant, and being found in fashion as a man, humbled himself to the death of the cross; wherefore God also hath highly exalted him, and given him a name above every name, that at the name of Jesus every knee might bow.* The very reason why we so infinitely adore Him being the incomparable height and perfection of His mercy, expressed in His humiliation and abasement for us. If we would enter into His glory, we must

[1] Liable.

walk in the way which He hath trod before us, for that only will lead us into it.

Though God hath in His infinite mercy redeemed us from the unavoidable necessity of being damned, yet hath He with infinite prudence ordered the way and manner of our redemption in such sort that we are not immediately translated into heaven, but restored to a new estate of trial, and endued with power to do new duties, as pleasing to Him as those which He required from us in Eden. For He loved a righteous kingdom from the beginning, wherein His laws were to be obeyed, rewards and punishments expected and administered in a righteous manner.

The great and necessary duties in this second kingdom are faith and repentance; introduced by His wisdom and occasioned by sin; necessary for our justification and sanctification, and superadded to the former.

This kingdom of evangelical righteousness, being founded on the blood of Christ, is, by death and sin and by the supernatural secrets of love and mercy, made infinitely more deep and mysterious than the former.

CHAPTER XV

Of Faith. The faculty of believing implanted in the soul. Of what nature its objects are. The necessity of faith; its end, its use and excellency. It is the mother and fountain of all the virtues

FAITH and repentance are the principal virtues which we ought to exercise in the kingdom of evangelical righteousness; because by them alone a sinner is restored to the capacity and power of living in the similitude of God, in the practice of His divine and eternal virtues. For *without faith it is impossible to please God;* because we can never believe that He is the rewarder of all those that diligently seek Him, without that credit which is necessary to be given to the discovery of His love to them that are defiled by the guilt of sin. For as long as we think God to be an infinite and eternal enemy to all offenders, we cannot use any endeavour to please Him, because we know there is no hope of reconciliation; and the vanity of the attempt appears like a ghost that always haunts us, and stands in our way to oppose and discourage us in the achievement we would undertake. For to fight with impossibility is so foolish a thing that nature itself keeps us back from doing it. Till, therefore, we believe our reconciliation possible, we have no strength at all to endeavour our salvation. Our despair oppresseth and frustrates our desires, with the inevitable necessity of our eternal shame and guilt and misery.

To believe that God will be so gracious as to pardon our horrible apostasy and rebellion is a work so great that God accepteth it instead of all other works of innocence and piety. To believe that He hath given His eternal Son to die for us, and that He so loved us as to come down from heaven, to suffer the wrath of God in our stead, is so much against the dictates of nature and reason that God *imputeth this faith alone for righteousness.* Not as if there were no good works necessary beside, but by this alone we are justified in His sight, and our justification cannot be ascribed to any other work of ours whatsoever. Howbeit, that which maketh faith itself so great a virtue is that we thereby receive a power and an inclination withal to do those works of love and mercy, the performance and the reward of which was the very end of our Saviour's coming.

That there is implanted in man a faculty of believing is as certain as that his eyes are endued with the faculty of seeing, or his soul with knowledge or any other faculty; and that this power is of some use in nature is as sure as anything in the world. For nature never gave to anything a power in vain. This, therefore, being one of the powers of the soul, must have a certain end ordained for it; and its use is the exercise of faith, in order to that end.

Objects of faith are those things which cannot be discovered but by the testimony of others. For some things are known by sense, some by reason and some by testimony. Things that are known by sense are present, some time or other, to the senses themselves. Those things which reason discovers are known as effects are by causes, or causes by effects; a good and rational demonstration being made by the concatenation of causes and effects depending upon each other, whereby things remote from sense are evident to reason, because the one is necessarily implied by the existence of the other. But some things there are which have no such necessary dependence at all. Such are the fortuitous occurrences that have been in the world, with all those actions of free agents that flow merely from their will and pleasure; for of these there can be no certain knowledge when they are past, but by history and tradition. That the world was made so many years ago, that man was created in an estate of innocency, that he fell into sin, that God appeared and promised the seed of the woman to break the serpent's head, that there was a flood, that Sodom and Gomorrah was burnt by fire, that all the world spake one language till the confusion at Babel, that there were such men as Julius Caesar or Alexander the Great, or such as Abraham and Moses and David; that the children of Israel were in Egypt and were delivered from thence by miracles; that they received the law in the wilderness, and were afterwards settled in the land of Canaan; that they had such and such prophets and priests and kings; that Jesus Christ was born of the Virgin Mary, that He was God and man, that He died and rose again, that He ascended into heaven, and sent the Holy Ghost down upon His apostles; nay, that there is such a city as Jerusalem; all these things can no other way be understood but only by faith. For no light of nature nor principle of reason can declare such verities as these; among which we may reckon these—that all the nations in the world, except that of the Jews, were pagans and idolatrous, till the gospel began to come forth from Jewry; that by the miracles and persuasions and faith and patience and persecutions and deaths of the martyrs they were converted, and forsook their dumb idols, and erected temples to the God of heaven; that His eternal Son was crucified in Judea; that such emperors made such laws, that such councils were held in such ages, that such and such fathers sprung up in the church; that there is such a place as Rome, and Constantinople; these and many millions of the like objects, to them that live in this age and never stirred any further than the

English coast, are revealed only by the light of history, and received upon trust from the testimony of others. Nevertheless there is as great a certainty of these things, as if they had been made out by mathematical demonstration, or had been seen with our eyes.

For though there are some false and some doubtful testimonies, yet there are also some that are true and certain. And lest all faith should be utterly blind and vain and uncertain, there are external circumstances and inward properties by which those testimonies which are true and infallible are distinguished from others.

All those things that are absolutely necessary to the welfare of mankind, the knowledge of which is of general importance, that are unanimously attested by all that mention them, and universally believed throughout all the world, being as firm and certain as the earth or the sun or the sky itself. We are not more sure that we have eyes in our heads than that there are stars in the heavens, though the distance of those stars are many millions of leagues from our bodily organs.

The objects and transactions which in former ages occur to our eyes (I mean the spiritual eyes of the intelligible soul, that are seated within) are by faith received and brought to the understanding. When they are transmitted to our knowledge, their nature is apprehended immediately by the soul, and their existence examined by reason; there being certain clear and infallible rules, by which their truth or falsehood may be discerned. And for this cause is it that we are commanded to *Try all things, and hold fast that which is good.* It is our duty to be *ready always to give a reason of the hope that is in us.* For reason is a transcendent faculty, which extendeth to all objects and penetrates into all mysteries, so far as to inquire what probability may be in them; what agreement or repugnance there is in the nature of the things revealed; what harmony or contradiction there is in the things themselves; what correspondence in all the circumstances; what consistence between those things which we certainly know and those which we are persuaded to believe; what authority the relation is of, what is the design and integrity of the relaters; what is the use and end of the things revealed; whether they are important or frivolous, absolutely necessary, merely convenient or wholly superfluous; things to be abhorred or things to be desired, absurd or amiable; what preparations went before, what causes preceded their existence, what effects followed, what concomitants they had; what monuments of them are now left in the world; how the wise and learned judge of them; what consent and unity there is in all the relations and histories and traditions of the things reported.

Where there is no repugnance between the object offered to our faith and the things we already know, no inconsistence in the things themselves, no difference, no contention between the relators, no fraud in promoting nor folly discernible in the first embracing of the things that are published; no want of care in sifting and examining their reality, nor any want in the hearers of industry, skill and power to detect the imposture; there is a fair way laid open to the credibility of such objects attested and revealed with such circumstances. But if the things attested were openly transacted in the face of the world, and had millions of spectators at the first; if they were so public as to be taken notice of in all kind of histories of those times and places; if they were founded on great and weighty causes; if they were pursued by a constant series and succession of affairs for many ages; if they produced great and public alterations in the world; if they overcame all suspicious oppositions, obstacles and impediments; if they changed the state of kingdoms and empires; if old records and monuments and magnificent buildings are left behind, which those occurrences occasioned; our reason itself assists our belief, and our faith is founded upon grounds that cannot be removed.

Much more if the things be agreeable to the nature of God, and tend to the perfection of created nature; if many prophecies and long expectations have preceded their accomplishment; if the mysteries revealed are attested by miracles, and painted out many ages before by types and ceremonies, that can bear no other explication in nature, nor have any rational use besides; if all the beauty of former ages is founded in and compounded by their harmony; if they fitly answer the exigencies of human nature, and unfold the true originals of all the disorder and corruption in the world; if the greatest and best part of learning itself consists in the knowledge of such affairs; if the doctrines on which they attend be the most pure and holy and divine and heavenly; if the most of them are rooted in nature itself, when they are examined and considered, but were not discerned nor known before; if they supply the defects of our understanding and lead us direct to felicity; if they take off our guilt, and are proper remedies to heal the distempers and maladies of our corruption; if they direct and quiet the passions of men and purify their hearts, and make men blessings to one another; if they exterminate their vices, and naturally tend to the perfection of their manners; if they lead them to communion with God and raise up their souls to the fruition of eternity, enlarge their minds with a delightful contemplation of His omnipresence, enriching them with infinite varieties of glorious objects fit to be enjoyed; if they perfect all the powers of the soul, and crown it with the end for which it was prepared: where all these things meet together, they make a foundation like that of the great mountains which can never be moved. But if there be any flaw or defect in these things, if any of them be wanting, our faith will be so far forth lame and uncertain as our reason shall discern its cause to be failing.

Now of all the things that the world doth afford, the Christian religion is that alone wherein all these causes of faith perfectly concur; insomuch that no object of faith in all the world is for certainty comparable to that of religion. Never had any truth so many witnesses, never any faith so many evidences. They that first taught and published it despised all the grandeurs and pleasures in the world, designed nothing but their eternal felicity and the benefit of men, trampled all honours and riches under feet, attested the truths they taught and revealed by miracles wrought, not in obscure corners but, in the eye of the sun. Many nations far distant from each other were in a moment reduced and changed at a time. Millions of martyrs were so certain of the truth of these things that they laughed at persecutions and flames and torments. The Jews, that are the great enemies of Christianity, confess those histories and prophecies and miracles and types and figures upon which it is founded. They reverence the Book wherein they are recorded, above all the writings in the world, confess that they had it before our Saviour was born, and glory that it was theirs before it was ours. Their whole faith and religion is made up of such materials, which being granted, it is impossible the Christian religion should be false; Turks acknowledge the historical part. The artifices of corruptors have been all detected, and must of necessity so be as long as there are inquisitive men in the world. All schismatics and heretics have cavilled and disputed about the true interpretation of certain texts, but never so much as doubted, much less shaken, the foundation. Nay, when you look into matters well, the very certainty of the one was the occasion of the other. The great moment of what they took for granted made the strife the more eager.

This advantage our faith has above all; it is suspected only by lazy and profane, half-witted men, that are as empty as self-conceited, as rash as wanton, and as much enemies to felicity and virtue as to truth and godliness. But the more you search into it, the more light and beauty you shall discern in the Christian religion. The evidences of it will appear still more deep and abundant; as endless in number, force and value as they are unexpected.

Among other objects of felicity to be enjoyed, the ways of God in all ages are not the least considerable and illustrious. Eternity is as much beautified with them as His omnipotence is with the works of the creation. For time is in eternity, as the world is in immensity. Reason expects that the one should be beautiful as well as the other. For since all time may be objected [1] to the eye of knowledge altogether, and faith is prepared in the soul on purpose that all the things in time may be admitted to the eye of the soul, it is very displeasing to human reason that time should be horrid and dark and empty; or that He that has expressed so much love in the creation of the world should be unmindful of our concerns in the dispensations of His providence. Especially since the world, how glorious soever it is, is but the theatre of more glorious actions, and the capacity of time as great and large as that of the universe; ages are as long and wide as kingdoms. Now if God have altogether neglected the government of the world, all time will be dark and vain, and in-

[1] Presented.

numerable bright and delightful objects, which were possible to be desired, denied to the soul, and the better half of God's love be removed. But if God's will and pleasure be uniform in His operations, and time itself be beautified by this wisdom, goodness and power, as well as the world, our faith will have a peculiar excellency; because it is that by which all the beauties in time and providence are enjoyed; especially if it be able to see and feel them in clear light, and in as lively a manner as the reason of the soul can do, when most fully informed. It is evident that without this faith the greater half of our felicity can never be enjoyed.

To know that we are men, encompassed with the skies, and that the sun and moon and stars are about us, with all the elements and terrestrial creatures, is matter of sense and reason; as it is also that we have the dominion and use of them, and that such excellencies and degrees of goodness are connatural to them. But their utmost perfection is discovered only by the truth of religion. That alone discloses their first cause and their last end, without which all their intermediate uses are extremely defective. It is far more pleasant to see the infinite and eternal Godhead, from the incomprehensible height of His glory, stooping down to the abyss of nothing and actually making all these transcendent things out of nothing for our sakes, than to see ourselves at present surrounded with them. This is the first act of all the ornaments of time and nature; which, though it be founded on clear reason, yet is it an object of our highest faith, as it is revealed by the world of God; and therefore is it said, *Through faith we understand that the worlds were made.* For faith and reason are not so divided but that, though formally distinct, they may enter into each other's nature and materially be the same. The very same object, I mean, that is known to reason may by faith be believed; reason not destroying but confirming faith, while it is known upon one account and believed on another. For there is a mutual convenience [1] between these two; faith is by reason confirmed, and reason is by faith perfected.

To see God stooping down to create the world, and nothing follow, is not so beautiful as to see Him afterward in the act of making man and giving him dominion over all the creatures.

[1] Agreement.

It is more pleasant to see man made in God's image than to see the world made for the use of man. For the end of the creation is that upon which all the perfection of its glory does depend; and the more noble man is, for whose use the world was made, the more sublime and glorious its end is. To see him placed in the estate of innocency, light and glory, wherein he was secure from death and sin and sickness and infelicity, if himself pleased, is very delightful. So it is to see that nature never intended any of those abortive errors that now so confound us. But to see the end why man was placed in such an estate to be his trial, and the end of that his friendship with God, whose exercise consisteth in voluntary acts of gratitude and amity; and the end of those the beauty of his life, and his fuller exaltation of bliss and glory —this is far more pleasant than the other. To see him fall is infinitely displeasing; but the fault is entirely charged on himself. And had God eternally destroyed him, though we perhaps had never lived to see it, yet we confess it would have been just in itself, and the justice adorable. But to see God exalting His mercy in pardoning the offence, and for all our sakes redeeming man by the death of His Son is sweeter still; as it is also to see His infinite justice and holiness in the manner of our redemption. To see Him lay the foundation of our hope on a certain promise, seconded with His long-suffering, yet defer the accomplishment of it for our greater benefit, wisely forbearing to send His Son till the fullness of time, is very transporting; but the reason of it is very difficult to understand. His foresight of our obstinate blindness and incredulity was the cause of His delay, that He might gain time, before our Saviour came, to speak of Him, to paint Him forth, to make Him the expectation of the world and the hope of all nations.

To see Him for that end reveal Himself to Abraham, Isaac and Jacob, and bringing down their posterity into the land of Egypt, that He might make that nation, out of which the Saviour was to spring, famous by miracles, and by His conduct and government of them more glorious than all nations; to appear Himself among them, and give His oracles unto them, and to make them conspicuous to the eye of all the world by mighty signs and wonders and judgments; punishing them for their offences, yet graciously continuing a seed among them, that Christ might be raised up according to the prophesies that went before concerning Him: to see all the mysteries of the gospel painted out in so lively a manner, in all the types and figures of the ceremonial law, and that service with so much splendour and glory continued before He came, by the space of two thousand years, wherein all the mysteries of His kingdom are exhibited: to see *the volumes of the Book in which it was written of Him* so highly magnified and exalted, by them that crucified Him after it was written and that now continue so much to oppose Him as the Jews do: to see the prophets at various times and in divers manners so clearly to describe all the particulars of His life and doctrine, His eternity, His Godhead, the hypostatical union, His incarnation in the Virgin's womb, His poverty, His meekness, His miraculous life, His death and passion, His resurrection and ascension into heaven, the sudden and miraculous conversion of the Gentiles (compared to *a nation's being born at once*), the very town where He should be born, and the city from whence the law should go forth into all the world, and the temple in which the gospel should begin to be preached: to see the accomplishment of all these things attended with so many glorious and transcendent wonders, and the utter subversion of that nation for their incredulity when they had slain Him: to see kings and queens become the nursing fathers and mothers of the Church, and so many glorious empires receive His law, that was hanged on a tree: to see temples erected all over the world to a crucified God, and nations upon earth adoring His glory in the highest heavens: especially to see the manner of His satisfaction, by way of a sacrifice in our stead; the laying of our sins upon His head, and the sprinkling of His blood upon all nations so lively represented; the necessity of such a Saviour exhibited by the rigour and severity of the law, His person and His office being pointed out in so particular a manner: all this, as it is sweet and heavenly, so does it enrich the contemplation of the soul, and make it meet to walk in communion with God in all ages, adoring His wisdom and power, admiring and delighting in the fullness of His love. And all these most great and transporting things we receive into our souls by faith alone.

But that which above all other things is most satisfactory is to see Jesus Christ *the end of the law* and the centre of time, the main business of all the dispensations of God's providence, and the only hinge upon which all mysteries both of the law and gospel principally turn.

Had He come in the beginning of the world, there had been no room nor place for all these prophesies and figures and expectations and miracles preceding His birth. We had had nothing but a bare and naked tradition that He had been in the world, which by the carelessness of men had passed away like a dream and died unprofitably; as we may plainly see by their backwardness to believe these things, notwithstanding their strength and beauty and the reiterated appearances of God to excite and awaken mankind, notwithstanding His care to erect a ministry among us for this very end, *that Jesus Christ might be known.*

Had He not been God and Man in one person, had no satisfaction been necessary for our sins, had He not made satisfaction for us, there had been no necessity of believing on His name. The light of nature had been sufficient to guide us to sorrow and obedience. All this trouble and care might have been spared, all this economy might have been changed into a government of less expense, and the most of these proceedings had been impertinent [1] and superfluous; for they all receive their attainment and perfection in Jesus Christ, who is the fullness and substance and glory of them.

Nor is it the excellency of faith alone, that it looks back upon ages past; it takes in the influences of all these that it may bring forth fruit in our lives for the time to come. For what is it but the faith of these things, attended with the glory which is intimated by them, that made so many divine and heavenly persons, so many wise and holy heroes, so many saints and martyrs? What can enflame us with the love of God, inspire us with courage or fill us with joy, but a sense of them? A true and lively faith is among sinners the only root of grace and virtue, the only foundation of hope, the only fountain of excellent actions. And therefore it is observed by the apostle Paul that by faith Abel offered a more excellent sacrifice than Cain; by faith Enoch walked with God;

[1] Irrelevant.

by faith Noah prepared an ark in which, being warned of God, he saved himself from the general deluge; by faith Abraham did such things as made his seed to multiply above the stars of heaven; by faith Moses despised the honours and treasures of Egypt, and endured, as seeing Him that was invisible. *What should I say more,* said the Apostle, *for the time would fail me to tell of Gideon and of Barak and of Samson and of Jephtha, of David also, and of Samson, and of the prophets; who through faith subdued kingdoms, wrought righteousness, obtained promises, stopped the mouths of lions, quenched the violence of fire, escaped the edge of the sword, and of weakness were made strong, waxed valiant in fight, turned to flight the armies of the aliens. Women received their dead raised to life again; and others were tortured, not accepting deliverance, that they might obtain a better resurrection. And others had trial of cruel mocking and scourges, yea moreover of bonds and imprisonments. They were stoned, they were sawn asunder, were tempted, were slain with the sword; they wandered about in sheepskins and goatskins, being destitute, afflicted, tormented; of whom the world was not worthy; they wandered in deserts and mountains and in dens and caves of the earth.*

All these things were done through faith, while yet there were but a few things seen to encourage them. But the whole accomplishment of mysteries and miracles is far more fair and vigorous and enflaming; the beauty of the whole body of God's dispensations fitly united in all its parts being an eternal monument of His wisdom and power; declaring the glory of His love and kingdom in a more eminent manner, and making us *more than conquerors, in and through Jesus Christ, who loved us and gave Himself for us.*

CHAPTER XVI

Of Hope. Its foundation, its distinction from faith, its extents and dimensions, its life and vigour, its several kinds, its sweetness and excellency

JANUS with his two faces, looking backward and forward, seems to be a fit emblem of the soul, which is able to look on all objects in the eternity past, and on all objects before, in eternity to come. Faith and hope are the two faces of this soul. By its faith it beholdeth things that are past, and by its hope regardeth things that are to come. Or if you please to take faith in a more large and comprehensive sense, faith hath both these faces, being that virtue by which we give credit to all testimonies which we believe to be true, concerning things past, present and to come. Hope is a virtue mixed of belief and desire, by which we conceive the possibility of attaining the ends we would enjoy, and are stirred up to endeavour after them. Faith respects the credibility of things believed to be true; hope, the possibility and goodness of their enjoyment. The simple reality of things believed is the object of the one; the facility of their attainment and our interest united are the object of the other.

Hope presupposes a belief of the certainty of what we desire. It is an affection of the soul of very general importance, which forasmuch as it is founded on faith and derives its strength from the sure belief of what we hope to attain (and there can be no fruition of that which is not really existent), to lay the foundation of our hope more firmly we will again consider the objects of faith, in the best light wherein their apparent certainty may be discerned.

The objects of divine faith revealed in the holy scriptures may fitly be ranked into three orders; for the matter of the Bible being partly historical and partly prophetical and partly doctrinal, the objects of divine faith fall under the three heads of doctrine, history and prophecy.

The doctrine of the scripture is of two sorts; for some doctrines are natural, some are supernatural. The natural are again divided into two; for some of them are laws that teach us our duty, some of them propositions only, or bare and simple affirmations, which we call articles, guiding our apprehensions in the truth of those things which are meet to be known. Speculation is intended in the one, and practice in the other.

Natural doctrines are objects of divine faith only as they are revealed by the word of God; for the authority of the witness is that which maketh our faith divine. They are called natural because, however blind any man is in his present condition, upon a diligent search those things may be clearly discerned by the light of nature. Those doctrines which are objects of divine faith, and yet may be found out by the investigation of reason, are such as these: that there is a God, that the world was made, that man was created in God's image, that he hath dominion over the works of His hands, that he is (or ought to be) tenderly beloved of all mankind, that he is to be good and full of love to others, that he is to render all objects their due esteem and to be grateful for the benefits he hath received of his great Creator; that the first estate of the world's creation was pure and perfect, that sin came in by the accidental abuse of the creature's liberty, that nature is corrupted, that death was introduced as the punishment of sin; that the soul is immortal, that God is infinitely just and wise and holy, that He will distribute rewards and punishments according to right; that there is such a thing as eternity and immensity; that the body is frail and subject to diseases, that we receive all things from God and depend in the fruition of all upon His power and providence, that it is wise to please Him and foolish to displease Him; that punishment is due to sin and that God hateth it, that reward is due to virtue and that God delighteth in it; that there is a conscience in the soul, by which it feels and discovers the difference between guilt and innocence; that man is a sinner, that he is prone to evil, that nevertheless he is spared by the long-suffering of God, and that God loveth him and desireth his salvation; that there is a felicity—and a supreme felicity—appointed for man; that he is a free agent, and may lose it, if he pleases; that misery is the consequent of the loss of felicity; that God delighteth in all those that love and practise virtue, that He hateth all those that drown their excellences in any vice; that sorrow and repentance are necessary for all those that have offended God; that there is a hope to escape the punishment of sin, if we endeavour to live as piously as we ought. All these things are evident in themselves by the light of nature, because they may either be clearly deduced from the principles of reason or certainly discerned by plain experience; and are therefore taught by the word of God, either because they had need to be revived and raised up to light from under the rubbish of our fall; or because God would sanctify nature by His express consent, or make its dictates more remarkable and valid by His approbation, and confirm all by the seal of His authority; or because a fair way is laid open by these to more retired and celestial mysteries.

For when we know these things, we are prone to inquire what God hath done, what way there is to recover our ancient happiness, what remedies are prepared for the corruption of nature, how the guilt of sin may be removed, how we may be aided and assisted in the works of virtue, by what means our reconciliation with God is wrought, and in what manner we ought to demean [1] ourselves that we may be accepted of Him. For the knowledge of our former health is necessary to the clear apprehension of our present sickness, and the sense of our infirmity fits us for the physician. When we know all that nature can teach, and see something needful that nature cannot unfold; when we are condemned by our conscience, yet feel ourselves beloved; find that we have forfeited all, yet see the glory of the creation continued for our use and service; stand in need of an atonement, yet know not where to get it—our exigency meeting with the grace of God, the sense of our misery and hope united, our own guilt and God's mercy (of both which we have the feeling and experience) adapts us for the reception of the holy gospel, wherein those things are revealed that come in most fitly to answer our expectations.

Satisfaction for sin by the death of Christ, and the incarnation of His Godhead, above the course of nature, for that end; His active and passive obedience in our stead, our justification thereby;

[1] Behave.

the application of His merits to our souls by faith; the glory which we owe Him for so great an undertaking; the coming down of the Holy Ghost to sanctify our nature, and the dignity of both these Persons by reason of their unity in the eternal essence, for the manifestation of which the mystery of the Trinity is largely revealed—these supernatural points come in so suitably and are so agreeable to nature, so perfectly fit in their places, so marvellously conducive to the perfection of the residue, that the very harmony and sweetness of all together is enough to persuade us of their credibility. And then the matter of fact comes in, with the testimony and authority of God's word, assuring us that these things are so, by history and prophecy. The miracles at our Saviour's birth alone one would think enough to clear the business; much more, if we take in all the miracles of His life, where in His glory appeared, as of the only-begotten of the Father; more fully yet, if we take in the miracles of His death, and abundantly more, if the glory of His resurrection and ascension be added. But especially the coming of the Holy Ghost and the power the apostles received from heaven, all the prophecies that went before and all the successes that followed after; all the faith and learning of the fathers, all the canons and decrees of councils, all the transactions of the world drawn down to our own age in a continued series, illustrate and confirm all that is revealed.

But you will say, how shall we know such histories to be true, and that such prophecies and prophets were in their several ages, since we never saw the same with our eyes, and there are many sleights and fables in the world. How dost thou know there are any antipodes? Thou didst never see them! Or that there is any sea, which thou didst never behold? Or that the next river has a fountain head? Is not the universal tradition of all the world (wherein the Church of Rome, nay, the Catholic Church, is but a little part) a clear light for a matter of antiquities, attended with a stream of effects and clear monuments, concurring together without any dissonancy in the things themselves, or contentions of parties? How dost thou know that there was such a man as King James or William the Conqueror? Is he not a madman that will doubt or dispute it? All that thou hast to confirm thee in the certainty of these, and infinitely more, conspires together to confirm thee in the certainty of the other. The history of the Bible is confessed by Turks and Jews and Infidels, and (which is far more) by the testimony of the Church, which deserves to be believed above them all. And if the history be true, there were such persons as Adam, Enoch, Noah, Abraham, Joseph, Moses, Samuel, David, Solomon, Elias, Elisha, Josiah, Isaiah, Jeremiah, Ezekiel, Daniel and the rest of the prophets; such persons as Jesus Christ and His apostles in such ages; such prophecies and such accomplishments at vast distances; such acts and such miracles, and such doctrines upon such occasions. And if all this matter of fact be true, 'tis impossible but these doctrines must be divine, which the devil and wicked men so much oppose and blaspheme in the world. And if these doctrines are true, then all the promises of God are true, and there is a large foundation of eternal hope prepared for the soul; because, if all these preparations be not eternally disgraced by the feebleness of their end, the glory and felicity which is designed by them is infinite and eternal.

That all these things are intended for thy benefit thou mayst clearly see, by thy very power to see them and by the natural influence which they have upon thy estate and condition. For though it may happen, by some succeeding accident, that thy power to see and enjoy all may be bereaved of its objects, when thine interest is eclipsed and forfeited by thy rebellion; and the influence of all may at last, through thine own default, be ineffectual and malevolent to thee; yet thou art assured by the nature of God and of thy own soul that it could not be intended evil from the beginning. Nay, the very order and disposition of the things themselves importeth the design to be felicity and glory. For all these things were written for our admonition, upon whom the ends of the world are come; and the Apostle expressly saith that *whatsoever things were written aforetime were written for our learning, that we through patience and comfort of the scriptures might have hope.*

This hope maketh not ashamed, because the love of God is shed abroad in our hearts. We delight in beauty, and by that very inclination that we have unto it are very apt to delight in anything that is amiable. We delight to see the order and perfection of God's ways, and God Himself taketh pleasure in manifesting His wisdom and goodness for the behoof of our souls, because He is great in bounty and infinite in love by His very essence. Nay further, we are every one capable of all the benefit that accrueth thereby, and by nature fitted to celebrate His praises for all the advantages that by any of His dispensations are imparted to us, and have liberty to improve them all for the acquisition of that glorious end to which we are ordained. The nature, of God, which is hereby manifested to be love to His creatures, is that which enableth thee by this very means to honour and adore Him, and by so doing to enter into His kingdom; where He, that did all these things for a farther end, will appear in glory, and show thee a perfection of life and bliss that is worthy of all this care and providence, being as great as thy heart can wish or desire.

Hope is for its dimensions vast and wonderful. All the honour, advancement, exaltation, glory, treasure and delight that is conceivable in time or eternity may be hoped for; all that the breadth and depth and height of the love of God, which passeth knowledge, is able to perform; all that ambition or avarice can desire, all that appetite and self-love can pursue, all that fancy can imagine possible and delightful. Nay, *more than we are able to ask or think* we are able to desire, and aspire after (if it be promised to us) the very throne of God and the joys of His eternal kingdom. And the more sublime its objects are, the more eagerly and violently does our hope pursue them, because there is more goodness in them to ravish our desire.

To fall from the height of one's hopes, where the kingdom and glory was infinite to which we aspire, is to fall from the height of heaven into the depths of hell. It produceth a misery and anxiety in the soul, an indignation and sorrow, answerable to all the greatness of our objects and the expectancies of our hopes; especially where the hope is lively and tender and strong, and sensible of what it conceiveth.

For it is the property of a true and lively hope to elevate the soul to the height of its object. The dull and drowsy hope makes no impression or alteration in the mind. The soul extends itself with a kind of pleasure in its wishes, and in touching the possibility of such goodnesses as it proposes to itself in its own imagination. Love and beauty, even in romances, are delightful; the very dreams and ideas of the perfections of bliss have a pleasure, as well as their reality. The desires of it are something more rich and sacred than the fancy or imagination; but to hope for such a thing with a clear and joyful expectation is to grasp at its fruition, with a faint kind of promise that it shall at last be ours. Had our hopes in spiritual things as much sense as they have in temporal, those beams of allegiance that enlighten our hope and fill it with glory would infuse a solid strength into our desire, and our pleasures would be so great that we should not exchange them for all the empires in the world. Especially if it ascended so high as to be founded on infinite and eternal causes, and the only fears that did chequer our hopes sprung from nothing but the danger of being wanting to ourselves. For who would think that, when our lives and liberties are at stake, we should be false to ourselves; that infinite love and power should be tendered to us, infinite beauty and goodness be before us, infinite honour and pleasure be offered us, eternal delights, inestimable riches, ever-flourishing joys, an infinite empire be without fraud attainable, and we be so treacherous and false to ourselves as to slight it all! It is an absurdity so incredible, that we should lose all these enjoyments by our own default and bare remissness, that we shall hate ourselves eternally if we lose so fair an advantage. Yet this is our case; we daily do that which, in point of reason, is impossible to be done, and for doing which we judge ourselves guilty of eternal tortures. All the misery that is lodged in infinite despair has comfort and refreshment answerable to it in infinite hope. 'Tis the present food and support of our lives; 'tis the anchor of our souls in the midst of all the storms and tempests in the world; 'tis the foretaste of bliss and celestial glory, a glimpse and appearance of the beatific vision, without which to live is to die, and to die is to perish for evermore.

The great reason for which a right hope is accounted so great a virtue is because its objects do really surpass all imagination. The fullness of the Godhead in the soul of man, the perfection of the divine image, a transformation for glory to glory, even as by the spirit of the Lord; communion with the Father, Son and Holy Ghost; infinite love and bounty; the estate of a bride in communion with God, the possession of His throne with another kind of sweetness than the bridegroom himself enjoys; the resurrection of the body and life eternal, in a kingdom where all occasions of tears and fears shall ever be removed; where all regions and ages and spaces and times and eternities shall be before our eyes, and all objects in all worlds at once visible, and infinitely rich and beautiful, and ours! Our very appetites also being ravished with sensible pleasures in all our members, not inconsistent with, but springing from, these high and superior delights; not distracting or confounding our spiritual joys, but purely superadded and increasing the same, while our bodies are *made like to his most glorious body, by that almighty power whereby he is able to subdue all things to himself;* all these infuse their value. And the hope that is exercised about these things is a virtue so great that all inferior hopes, which this doth sanctify, are made virtues by it; but without this, all other hopes are debasements and abuses of the soul, mere distractions and delusions, and therefore vices.

I know very well that presumption and despair are generally accounted the extremes of hope, and the only vices that are opposite thereto. But I know as well that there may be many kinds and degrees of hope, of which some may be vicious and some virtuous; and that some sorts of hopes themselves are vices. Whenever we make an inferior desire the sovereign object of our hope, our hope is abominable, idolatrous and atheistical. We forget God, and magnify an inferior object above all that is divine. To sacrifice all our hopes to things unworthy of them, or to be remiss and sluggish in hoping for things of infinite importance, is apparently vicious. But to be just to all our encouragements, and to lift up our eyes to the eternal God with a humble expectation; to wait upon Him, and to hope for all that from His bounty which His goodness has promised; to desire the most high and perfect proofs of His love, is the property of a most great and noble soul, by which it is carried above all the world, and fitted for the life of the most high and perfect virtue.

CHAPTER XVII

Of Repentance. Its original, its nature; it is a purgative virtue. Its necessity, its excellencies. The measure of that sorrow which is due to sin is intolerable to sense, confessed by reason and dispensed with by mercy

REPENTANCE is a sour and austere kind of virtue, that was not created nor intended by God, but introduced by sin; made fair by mercy, in remitting the offence and pardoning the sin. It is a strange kind of offspring which flows from parents so infinitely different, and has a mixture in its nature, answerable to either; an evil which it derives from sin, and a goodness which flows from mercy. Its evil is that of sorrow, indignation and shame; its goodness is the usefulness and necessity of the thing, considering the condition we are now in. It is highly ingrateful [1] to sense, but transcendently convenient [2] and amiable to reason; for it is impossible for him that has once been defiled with sin ever to be cleansed, or to live after in a virtuous manner, unless he be so ingenious [3] as to lament his crime and to loathe, acknowledge and detest his error.

The union of the soul and body is mysterious; but that sin and mercy should be united, as causes so infinitely different, for the production of a child so black and so beautiful, is the greatest wonder which the soul can contemplate on this side heaven; and will continue to be remembered for ever, and appear more wonderful than before, when the perfect disparity and opposition between them is clearly seen in the light of glory.

The efficient cause of repentance is either remote or immediate. Its immediate efficient cause is the gracious inclination or the will of the penitent: its remote efficient is God, the Father of Lights, from which every good and perfect gift descended. Its material cause is sorrow. Its formal cause, which makes it a virtue, is the

[1] Displeasing.
[2] Agreeable.
[3] Honest, sincere.

reason and manner of that sorrow, the equity and piety wherewith it is attended, containing many ingredients in its nature, too long a particular to be described here. Its final cause is either immediate or ultimate; the first is amendment, the last salvation.

Being thus bounded by its causes, its definition is easy. Repentance is a grace, or Christian virtue, wherein a man confesses, hates and forsakes his sin, with grief that he hath been guilty of it; and purposes of amendment of life in order to his peace and reconciliation with God; that he may answer the obligations that lie upon him, discharge his duty, lay hold on the advantages of God's mercy, escape everlasting damnation, and be made a partaker of eternal glory.

Among the virtues, some are purgative and some are perfective. The purgative virtues are all preparatory to bliss, and are occasioned only by the disorder of the soul. The perfective are essential to our formal happiness and eternally necessary by the laws of nature. Repentance is not in its own nature, if simply and absolutely considered, necessary to bliss. But in relation to sinners, it is as necessary as physic to the recovery of health, or as the change itself is, by which we pass from the distemper we are sick of to the right and sound estate which we had lost by the disease. As the malady is accidental, so is the cure; for the nature of man may be well and perfect, without either this or the other. He that is originally pure has no need of a purgative virtue; but he that is fallen defiled must needs rise and wash away the filth, before he can be clean.

For this cause, even among the heathens themselves, the more knowing and learned have a conscience of sin. Their priests and philosophers devised several rites and manners of purgation, which they taught and imposed on their disciples with much circumstance and ceremony in order to their reception. Nor was there any temple or religion in the world that pretended not something to diviner mysteries; which were not graced and beautified with preparatory washings, humiliations, fashions, attires, watchings, retirements, shavings, sprinklings, anointings, consecrations, sacrifices or some other disciplines like unto these, to be endured and passed through before their votaries could be admitted to their mysteries. All which rites, as they made a great show, because they were sensible,[1] so were they apt to put a magnificent face on their religion, to dispose the persons exercised by them to a more complying obedience, and to beget a reverence mixed with awful admiration in their ignorant spectators. All which nevertheless were but emblematical ordinances, signifying something invisible that was necessary to be done, of which the priests themselves knew not the meaning. They had the name of *penitentia* in their common conversation, but applied it to profane and trivial occasions. But repentance in religion, which is the soul and substance of those mystical observances, a broken and contrite heart, an internal sorrow for their sin, was a thing unknown; so that all their appearances, how magnificent soever, were but empty shells.

Repentance alone, though never so simple and short in its name, being of such value, that God accepts one contrite groan above all the ceremonies even of His own law; and therefore He saith, *Thou desirest not sacrifice, else would I give it; thou delightest not in burnt offering. The sacrifices of God are a broken spirit; a broken and a contrite heart, O God, thou wilt not despise.*

For though repentance be not in itself a desirable virtue, nor so much as a virtue till there be a sphere and occasion for it wherein to be exercised; though repentance in itself be far worse than obedience; yet upon the account of our Saviour's merits, and God's love to sinners, it is preferred above the greatest innocency and purity whatsoever. For *there is more joy in heaven over one sinner that repenteth than over ninety and nine just persons that need no repentance.* If the soul be of greater value than the whole world; if the loss of anything that we esteem increaseth the sense of its excellency; if our Saviour justly and rationally compared Himself to a shepherd, that leaveth ninety and nine sheep in the wilderness, to seek one that is gone astray; if He rejoiceth when He hath found it, more for that one that was lost than for the ninety and nine which He had in safety; if His delight in the success of His labours be answerable to their greatness; if the frustration of all His desires and painful endeavours in seeking it be infinitely grievous, and the virtues more amiable

[1] Apparent to the senses.

and wonderful which sinners exercise after their redemption; if their love and their joy and their praise be increased by the extremity of their distress and the multitude of sins that are forgiven them; if their communion with God be more sweet and their happiness more exalted, and the kingdom of God itself made more sublime and glorious thereby—repentance hath something more in it than perfection had before the Fall. And as sinners have made themselves more infinitely indebted, so are they infinitely more subject to the arbitrary disposal of almighty power, infinitely more capable of obligations and rewards, infinitely more obliged for pardon and deliverance, as well as infinitely more obnoxious [1] to divine justice. Their fear and danger is infinitely greater, they stand in need of infinite grace and mercy; which when they receive and enjoy, their love and gratitude are proportionately greater, their delights are more quick and vigorous and full, and so are their praises.

But before a sinner can achieve all this, or God enjoy the fruit of his salvation, he must needs repent; for repentance is the true and substantial preparation of the soul, the only purgative virtue, by which it is fitted for these divine attainments. It is, we confess, in outward appearance a slight invisible act; but as great within, as wide and comprehensive, as the heavens. It receiveth the virtue of the divine essence of the whole creation, of infinite mercy, of the blood of Christ, of His humiliation, merit, exaltation, intercession and glory, of all the work of redemption into itself. And having fed itself, digested them, it receiveth strength by the influence of these to dispense all their virtue again, in the production of those fruits for the sake of which God hath filled all the world with miracles; the verdure and maturity and perfection of which shall, with their beauty and sweetness, continue in life and flourish for ever.

If we respect man alone, and the things that are done in him by repentance, it seemeth a virtue of infinite value. It divests him of all his rebellion, pride and vainglory, strips him of all his lust and impiety, purges him of all his corruption, anger and malice, pares off all his superfluities and excesses, cleanseth his soul of

[1] Exposed.

all its filthiness and pollution, removeth all that is so infinitely odious to God, and makes him amiable and beautiful to the holy angels. It fits and prepares him for all the exercises of grace and piety, introduces humility and obedience into his soul, makes him capable of a divine knowledge and makes way for the beauty of his love and gratitude; inspires fortitude and prudence and temperance and justice into his soul; renews his nature and makes him a meek and patient person; restores him to that wisdom and goodness he had lost, clothes him with righteousness and true holiness, and seats him again in the favour of God. By repentance he recovers the divine image, and by consequence it extends to all that blessedness and glory which is for ever to be enjoyed.

Repentance is the beginning of that life, wherein all the sweat and labour of the martyrs, all the persecutions and endeavours of the apostles, all the revelations of the prophets, all the examples of the patriarchs, all the miracles of old time, all the mysteries of the law, all the means of grace, all the verities of the gospel, begin to take full force and effect, in obtaining that for which they were intended; which sufficiently intimates the value of the grace, and how highly well pleasing it must be to God.

It is the conception of felicity and the new birth of the inward man, the dereliction of the old and the assumption of a new and more celestial nature. It is the gate of the heavenly kingdom, which they that refuse to enter thereat can never enjoy. It is one of the keys of death and hell, by which the gate of the prison is unlocked—nay, the very knocking off the chains and manacles of Satan, the very act wherein we regain our liberty and become the sons of God and citizens of heaven.

It was fitly typified in the old law by the laver that was set at the door of the tabernacle for the priests to wash in, before they entered into the sanctuary, to walk in the light of the golden candlesticks, to offer their devotions at the incense altar and to partake of the shewbread on the golden table. In the outward court they enjoyed the society of the visible church, the sight of the bloody altar (which answers our Saviour's cross erected in the world) and the benefit of their outward profession, which consisted in their admission to the visible ordinances and exterior rites of religion. But that court was open overhead, obnoxious [1] to showers, in token that a bare profession is not enough to shelter us from the dangers and incommodities that may be rained down in judgments upon us from the wrath of God; whence the face of heaven is overcast with clouds, and covered with black and heavy displeasure, till we wash and be clean, and enter by penitence into the invisible church, of which the second court is a figure; wherein we are illuminated by the Holy Ghost, and offer up the sweet perfumes of our thanksgivings and praises, being admitted to feed upon the heavenly feast, represented by the shewbread table.

Without repentance, we are never received into the society of the saints and angels, painted out in the cherubims and palm trees round about on the inside of its walls, nor covered overhead with a veil to protect us; a veil of blue to represent the inferior heaven, wherein cherubims were interwoven to represent the angels looking down upon us; a veil of goat's hair concealed and unseen above that of blue, to signify the fruits of our Saviour's life; and another of ram's skin dyed red, to signify the blood of Christ, by which we are secured from all the displeasure which otherwise, for sin, was due to us. The goat's hair fitly resembles the active obedience or the righteousness of Christ, forasmuch as hair may be clipped off and a covering made of it, while the beast is alive; for so might Christ have been perfectly righteous, though His life had never been taken away. But red is the colour of blood, the skin importeth death, forasmuch as it cannot be flayed off without the destruction of the creature. These veils, therefore, as they were above the other, were of higher and more mysterious importance, and spread over the enclosed and invisible court, into which none but priests and levites entered, that washed at the laver; to intimate the security only of those that are washed in the laver of regeneration, and made kings and priests unto God, being purged from their old sins, and sanctified and illuminated in a secret spiritual manner. For as they only, that tarried in their houses, were under the protection of the paschal lamb whose blood was sprinkled on the lintels of their gates and doors, when the destroying angel passed through the land of Egypt to kill the first-born of man and beast; so only they that

[1] Exposed.

keep within the pale of the invisible church are under the shadow of the Almighty. Because they only dwell in the secret place of the Most High, and they alone are under the coverture of that powerful Blood, which speaketh better things than the blood of Abel, but pleads for the preservation of them only that repent and believe, and is therefore effectually spread over the invisible church alone. Which in another type is exhibited by the mixture of blood and oil which was sprinkled upon the priests and lepers that were cleansed; sanctification and justification moving always hand in hand; the unction of the Holy One, or the oil of love and gladness, anointing all those that are washed; and only those are washed in clean and pure water, they alone being effectually sprinkled with the blood of Christ, *who of God is made unto us wisdom and righteousness and sanctification and redemption.*

For if God should take pleasure in us before we were pure, His complacency [1] would be false and His delight unrighteous. Till we be delightful to Him, we can never be honourable nor glorious before Him; nor ever be pleasing to that goodness which is indelible, though latent, in our own souls, till we feel ourselves clean and beautiful.

If anything in the world can commend the value of repentance, or discover the infinite use and necessity of it, this will certainly be a consideration effectual; that though God love us with an infinite and eternal love, though He magnifies His mercy infinitely over all our deservings, though Jesus Christ loved us so as to sacrifice Himself in our places, though He made infinite satisfaction to the justice of God for our sins, though the Holy Ghost came down from heaven for our sakes, nay, though we ourselves were taken up into heaven—all of this would be of little avail, and we should quickly be tumbled down again, if only sin were delightful to us, and our wills so obstinate that there was no place for repentance in our hearts, no sorrow, no contrition for the offences we had committed.

It is not the love of God to us, so much as our love to Him, that maketh heaven. It may surprise you, perhaps, but shall certainly instruct you; for the love of God may be infinite, yet, if it be unseen, breed no delight in the soul; if it be slighted and

[1] Satisfaction.

despised, it shall increase our guilt, shame and deformity, and make us the more odious, which it must needs do, when we are impenitent. For so long, it is manifest that we are neither sensible of His love nor just unto it. The taste of its sweetness, and the pleasure we take in His infinite love, is the life of blessedness and the soul of heaven. It is the concurrence of our love and His, when they meet together, that maketh heaven.

Here upon earth we ought actually to grieve and repent for our sin. But should God require a measure in our grief answerable to its causes, our repentance itself would be hell unto us, for the grief would be endless and insupportable. Right reason requires that we should be infinitely afflicted for the infinite folly and madness of sin. But the mercy of God dispenseth with our grief so far that it takes off the pain, which its infinite measure would inflict upon our sense, and accepts of an acknowledgement made by our reason, that it ought to be infinite if strict justice were exacted at our hands. Our intention is, in the course of reason, to be infinitely and eternally grieved for the baseness of the act and the vileness we have contracted; and so we should be, did its effects continue and abide for ever; for then we should be hated of God, and become His enemies world without end. But the removal of that hatred, and the infinite mercy whereby we are forgiven, hath a kindly operation on the soul of every penitent; and the joy it infuseth restrains and limits the excess of our sorrow. It leaves the intention of grief, and its inclination, in the mind, yet stops the persecution, and relieves our reason by diverting the stream of its operations and exercises. It engageth its actual resentments [1] upon other objects, which turn it all into love and adoration, praise and thanksgiving, joy and complacency. For the love of God continued after our fall; and the felicity to which we are called out of the depth of our misery, all the advantages we receive upon our redemption, the improvements of our miserable estate, the degrees and ornaments that are added to the beauty and perfection of God's kingdom upon so sad an occasion as sin is—all these things take up our thoughts in such a manner that, while we are actually and fully just to these, and loving God (for His eternal love) infinitely more than we love

[1] Feelings.

ourselves, we live in Him, and are all in raptures of blessedness.

Yet is there a virtual sorrow, which reason conceives as most due to sin; which being, expressed only in the humility of our souls, and seen, as it were, under the fruition of our joys in the lowly conceit we retain of ourselves, in the confession of our vileness and the deep sense of our own unworthiness, is far greater (now we are restored to the favour and love of God), far sweeter to be seen and deeper to be understood than the grief for sin would have been, had we been not redeemed but damned for ever.

CHAPTER XVIII

Of Charity towards God. It sanctifieth repentance, makes it a virtue, and turns it to a part of our true felicity. Our love to all other objects is to begin and end in God. Our love of God hath an excellency in it that makes it worthy to be desired by His eternal majesty. He is the only supreme and perfect friend. By loving we enjoy Him

REPENTANCE without love is so far from seating us in the felicity of heaven that it is one of the ingredients of the torments of hell, a natural effect of sin and a great part of the misery of devils. Love is a genuine affection of the soul, and so powerfully sweet, when it is satisfied and pleased, that it communicates the relish of its own delightfulness to everything near it, and transforms the most virulent affections into smooth, healing, perfective pleasures. Insomuch that in heaven our sorrow for sin shall perhaps be infinite, yet the malignity of it so perfectly corrected that, though we continue eternally just in rendering our sins that grief which is their due, it shall not discompose our peace, nor corrode our delights, but increase our repose in the beauty of our souls, and make our joys more full of ecstasy, by those melting, lively, bleeding resentments [1] which our love will occasion in the very grief wherewith it perfects our felicity.

For as the falling out of lovers is the renewing of love, so is the mercy and kindness of the one, even of him that was injured, and the calm and secure indignation wherewith the other hates himself for being guilty of so vile a miscarriage, the very grace and beauty of the reconciliation. It is a great means of their mutual endearment and tenderness ever after; the compassion of him that is innocent, and the humble grief of the guilty, making the joy of their future correspondence more deep and serious, more vigorous and enflaming, more lasting.

Love is that which sanctifies repentance, and makes it pleasant both to him that is beloved and to him that is adored; acceptable and delightful to him that repenteth, as well as to him that had been injured. For the sinner's restoration makes it as natural to grieve for his fault as to rejoice in his felicity. His sad and humble resentments are his own satisfaction, because he sees himself just and rational in them. He delights in his sorrow, because it is honourable, and finds a new kind of pleasure in his abasement, because it is relieved by the wonder of his happy condition; and what he hath lost in himself is regained in the perfection and goodness of his object.

That God is the sovereign object of love I scarcely need to mention. All I shall observe upon this occasion is, that we are more to love Him for His mercy and compassion towards us as sinners than for His goodness and bounty expressed at first, as we were innocent creatures. The bleeding spectacle of His incarnate deity, and the perseverance of His miraculous and transcendent love after all our offences, is another kind of motive to heighten our charity, and gives it another form, as much more mysterious, so much more perfect and delightful than ever. Our sorrow for sin infuses a new sense into nature, a new beauty into love, and gives as much unto it as it receiveth from it. But this being better known by experience than by description, I shall refer you to the life of heaven and grace, for more ample satisfaction.

[1] Feelings.

Love, as we have showed, may be extended to all objects in heaven and earth, all that is goodly and amiable being capable of that affection. Hereupon the word Love is generally used for that liking and esteem we have for anything, whether dead or alive. We can love life, and desire to see good days; we can love the sun, and wine, and oil, and gold; love our dogs and horses, fine clothes and jewels, pleasures, honours, recreations, houses, riches, as well as love men and women, souls and angels. And evermore our love expresseth itself in tenderness and care for the preservation of what we love, in esteem of its worth and delight in its beauty; in endeavours also to promote its welfare as far as it is capable.

But there is another sort of love towards living objects, divine and reasonable, which we call Charity. This is that virtue of which the Apostle saith (after he had spoken of all the miracles, helps, governments, prophecies, tongues and other gifts of the Holy Ghost that were then in the Church). *And yet I show unto you a more excellent way.* And in the next chapter, *Though I speak with the tongue of men and of angels, and have not charity, I am become as sounding brass or a tinkling cymbal. And though I have the gift of prophecy, and understand all mysteries and all knowledge, and though I have faith so that I could remove mountains and have not charity, I am nothing and though I bestow all my goods to feed the poor, and though I give my body to be burned and have not charity, it profiteth me nothing.* It is that concerning which our Saviour speaketh: *The first of all the commandments is, Hear, O Israel, the Lord our God is one Lord, and thou shalt love the Lord thy God with all thy heart and with all thy soul and with all thy mind and with all thy strength. This is the first commandment; and the second is like, namely this, Thou shalt love thy neighbour as thyself. There is none other commandment greater than these.* Nay, perhaps it is that of which He said to His apostles, when they had admired at His miracles, *He that believeth on me, the works that I do shall he do also, and greater works than these shall he do, because I go to the Father.* For faith worketh by love. Love is the life of faith, and without the works of the one the other is dead. The works of love are the end of all miracles, and more blessed than they. Nay, love is the end of faith, as well as it is of the law; for the Apostle saith, *The end of the commandment is charity, out of a pure heart, and of a good conscience, and of faith unfeigned.*

It is the end of the very creation of the world, of all God's labours and endeavours, of all His ways in all ages, all the faculties and powers of the soul; the very end of the redemption of mankind, the end of the Jewish economy under the law, the end of all the dispensations of grace and mercy under the gospel; the end of our Saviour's coming down into the world, the end of all His miracles, tears and blood; the end of the Holy Ghost's appearing upon earth; the end of all the means of grace, and in some sort the very last end of all rewards and punishments whatsoever. The everlasting continuance of this love is the end of eternity itself, in a manner; and if our love be not the end of God's love, His is of ours. And if the truth be deeply inquired into, the intermixture is so sweet that His is the end of ours, ours of His. For He loveth us with the love of benevolence, that we may love Him; and He desires to be beloved of us, that He may love us with another kind of love, distinct from the former, even that of complacency [1]; which love of complacency is the crown of ours, and so delightful to us that it is the very end of our desire, and begetteth in us a new love of complacency fitly answering His unto us.

Now, if love be the end of all the laws, works and ways of God, of all our Saviour's labours and sufferings, of our souls and bodies, of the whole creation, of all the endeavours and desires of the Deity, in all the dispensations of His grace and providence, there must be something in its nature equivalent to all these transcendent undertakings, to justify the wisdom that selected love for its sovereign object. For it is the office of wisdom to suit the means and their end together, so that the excellency of the one may be worthy of all the cost and difficulty of the other. For it is a foolish thing to pursue a base and feeble end by glorious and wonderful methods, because its vileness will disgrace the design, and with it their beauty; their very grandeur will be absurd, where the issue is but contemptible. The Apostle there-

[1] Satisfaction.

fore telleth us that *Love is the fulfilling of the law,* and that it is *the bond of perfectness.* And pursuing the properties a little more amply, he saith, *Charity suffereth long, and is kind; charity envieth not, charity vaunteth not itself, is not puffed up, doth not behave itself unseemly, seeketh not her own, is not easily provoked, thinketh no evil, rejoiceth not in iniquity but rejoiceth in the truth; beareth all things, believeth all things, hopeth all things, endureth all things.*

It is one noble effect of charity that it suffereth afflictions cheerfully and patiently for the sake of its beloved. Another is its kindness to its object, its sweet and courteous inclination to do all manner of good. Another, for which it is highly valuable, is that it envieth not the felicity or glory of its beloved, but taketh pleasure to see it far higher and greater than its own; is not apt to vaunt and brag of its perfections, but hath an honourable esteem of all its achievements; doth not behave itself in a distasteful manner, but studies and designs the honour, benefit and satisfaction of its object. But that which of all other is its greatest perfection is that *it seeketh not its own.* It is not mercenary or self-ended, but truly generous and heroic in its performances. It sacrificeth itself and all its interests to the advantage of its object. It prefereth the person it loveth above itself, desires its exaltation and delights in its glory more than its own. *It is not easily provoked,* because it puts the best sense upon all that is done by its object. *Thinketh no evil,* is not suspicious or malevolent or censorious, but frameth honourable and fair ideas of all that is thought or done by its beloved; hateth all impurity that may displease its object, all black and crooked apprehensions that may wrong and disguise it. *Beareth all* with hope and equanimity, because it believeth its object to be good and wise, till it must of necessity change its opinion and entertain a judgment tending to its condemnation. It is no longer charity then, but dislike and aversion, when it ceaseth to think well of its object; for it is another principle, as distinct in nature from love, as its actions are from the actions of love; the diversity of effects evidently proving a difference in their causes.

The quality by which charity *rejoiceth in the truth* is an incomparable excellence and commendation of its nature, because the truth is God's infinite goodness and love and providence, which are exercised in preparing delights and treasures for His beloved. The truth is the felicity and glory of the soul. And if it be true that all eternity is full of joys, and all the world enriched with delights, that a man is infinitely beloved of God and made in His image on purpose that he might enjoy all the best of all possible treasures in His similitude, he may well rejoice in the truth; because no truth can be greater or more delightful than that himself is exalted to the throne of God and ordained to live in communion with Him.

But that quality by which the soul believeth and hopeth all things that concern the honour and fidelity of its beloved is yet more acceptable and delightful than the former. For a good opinion of the nature and intention of the person with whom we are united is the basis and foundation of all our respect, the cement of our peace, and the life and soul of all that honour which is paid unto him. The very grace and beauty of all our conversation dependeth upon it, and if it be true that we are more to love God for the intrinsic perfections of His essence than for all His gifts, the chief business of our knowledge is to frame glorious apprehensions of His nature, and to believe Him in all things so kind and wise that He is true and faithful in all His declarations, and most to be honoured in all the dispensations of His providence; because He is ever mindful of His protestations and promises. For then we can believe that all things shall work together for our good; can safely trust ourselves and all that is ours in His hands; resign ourselves up to His disposal with joy, and say *Thy will be done,* for it is holy, good and acceptable. Thy will alone is of all other wills most perfect and desirable. There are on earth, indeed, more nice [1] emergencies, many obscurities and riddles, in the midst of all which to think so well of God as He deserveth is the most acceptable thing in the world; for it argues a great confidence of His worth, and a love that is founded on substantial causes never to be removed. It feedeth the soul with a lively hope and fair expectations of great things from Him; by which alone we do right to His Godhead, in acknowledging the perfection of His love and goodness; and

[1] Particular.

by which alone we are made able to adore Him and to live in union and communion with Him.

There is great talk of friendship. It is accounted the only pleasure in the world. Its offices are highly magnified of all: kindness of behaviour, a thorough and clear communication of souls, a secure reliance upon each other's fidelity, a perfect discovery of all our thoughts, intentions and resentments,[1] an ardent willingness to impart lives and estate for the benefit of our friend, the reposing of all our secrets in each other's bosoms, to do all services and suffer all afflictions for each other's sakes, to prefer the concerns of our friends upon all occasions above our own—these are the *magnalia amicitiae et arcana mutuae benevolentiae,* the great and mighty effects for which friendship is admired. But all these, without a good opinion of our friend, are nothing worth. They are but externals of friendship. The greatest secret of its nature is the mutual agreement of souls and spirits, the delight which either taketh in the other, the honour and esteem they give and receive, the approbation and love of each other's dispositions, the sense and admiration of each other's virtues, the continual desire of being always together, peculiar ecstasy which the beauty of either occasioneth in the other, when of all other treasures in the world their persons are the greatest to one another. Either is the proper element and *refrigerium* of the other's soul. Their bosoms are the mutual receptacles and temples of each other's accomplishments, whereinto they are received in all their desert, and have justice done to every degree and perfection in their nature. Their hearts are the thrones where they are exalted and magnified and live at ease, are honoured and worshipped and extolled, and reign as absolute in each other's souls.

There are some slight aims and adumbrations of this friendship on earth, but the best and highest degree of it here beneath is but a rude and imperfect shadow. Only God is the sovereign friend. All adoration paid to any one beside is mere idolatry. Our hearts can be absolutely sacrificed to none but Him; because He alone is immutable in His goodness. We cannot infinitely honour and delight in any but Him: it is He alone that can infinitely honour and delight in us. All our lives, estates and

[1] Sentiments.

services are due to Him; His will alone is to be wholly ours, because no other will is infallibly right, wise, holy, but His alone.

The union of our wills is a perfection of love; but that at which He aimeth by all His labours and gifts and benefits is our right and good opinion of His excellencies and perfections. That we should see and discern His interior properties, admire His graces, adore His perfections, adore and magnify His beauty and glory—this is the end for which He communicateth Himself in all His works and ways unto us. It is the end of the whole creation, and of all the excellent things in the universe. For by this He establisheth His empire in our souls, and makes us pleasing to Himself in all our operations. And for this cause it is that the Apostle plainly tells us that, though we give our body to be burned, and all our goods to feed the poor, without charity it profiteth nothing. To render to God the honour that is due to His name, to receive and admire all His bounties, to rejoice in all His operations, to adore Him in all His ways, to take pleasure in all His works, to fill heaven and earth with our joys and praises, is a work which cannot but be agreeable by its nature to His eternal essence. And if this be the work of love, it is that which is most excellent, because He is therein both pleased and enjoyed. God and all His creatures are united together by love alone, and in the eternal exercise of pure and perfect love all blessedness and glory consisteth.

If you require what it is to love God, you will find it worthy of His highest desire, because thereby all our souls, nay, all His creatures and His whole kingdom are perfected; for to love God as we ought to do is to honour Him as our Father, Benefactor, Bridegroom and King; to contemplate Him as our cause with complacency,[1] and to rest in Him as our end; to delight in Him as our Creator, Preserver, Lawgiver and Redeemer; to dedicate ourselves wholly to that service, whatever it be, wherein He is chiefly pleased and delighted. It is to love Him in Himself; in all His works, in all His ways, in all His laws, in all His attributes, in all His thoughts and counsels, in all His perfections. It implies the knowledge of all objects, the use of all means, the attainments of all ends; all wisdom and goodness, all obedience and gratitude,

[1] Delight.

all righteousness and holiness, all joy and praise, all honour and esteem, all blessedness and glory. For it is to love Him with all our heart and with all our soul, with all our strength and with all our might, with all our understanding, with all our will, with all our affection, with all the powers of our soul, with all our inclinations and faculties; in all His creatures, in all His appearances, in heaven and earth, in angels and men, in all kingdoms and ages. It is to see and desire, to esteem and delight in His omnipresence and eternity, and in everything by which He manifesteth Himself in either of these; so that all enlargement, and greatness, and light, and perfection, and beauty, and pleasure, are founded in it. And to love Him to perfection implies all learning and attainment, because we must necessarily be acquainted with all things in all worlds, before we can thoroughly and completely do it; which, here upon earth, to do by inclination and endeavour to the utmost of our power is all that is required of us. And if we do it to our utmost, it shall be rewarded in the beatific vision, with a full and blessed perfection, with an actual love exactly resembling His, and fully answerable to it in the highest heavens.

There are two common motives of love among men; the one, the goodness and excellency of the person; the other, his particular kindness and love to us. And both these are in the highest degree in God. He is of infinite goodness and excellency in Himself, for there is nothing good in the world but what hath received all its goodness from Him. His goodness is the ocean, and all the goodnesses of creatures little streams flowing from that ocean. Now, you would think him a madman that should say the sea were not greater than a trifling brook; and certainly it is no less folly to suppose that the goodness of God doth not as much, nay, infinitely more, exceed that of all the creatures. The sun is a lively mirror of that eternal act of love which is the glory of its essence; but it is infinitely less prone to communicate its beams, and doth less good to itself, and infinitely less to all other creatures. It shines for their sakes, nevertheless, and clothes itself with glory by the splendour of its beams; and is an emblem of God, who exerteth His power with infinite pleasure, and, by communicating His essence in an infinite manner, propagates His felicity and glory to the utmost height and perfection.

By proceeding from Himself to all objects throughout all worlds, He begets and dwelleth in Himself; He inhabits eternity in a blessed and more vigorous manner, by establishing the felicity of all his creatures, and becomes their infinite and eternal glory; wherein His particular kindness and love to us appeareth, because He hath fitted us with qualities and powers adapted for so great an end, and as particularly appropriated all to us as the sun to the eye of every spectator. For our bodies and souls are made to enjoy the benefit of all, and His desire is that we should attain the end for which we are created. On His side all is prepared; on ours, nothing is wanting but love, to embrace and take pleasure in His goodness, which shineth in all these things, and created them on purpose that, being manifested by them, we might delight in it for ever.

He that loveth not God with all his heart liveth a life most contrary to nature. For to love is as natural for the soul as to shine for the sun; and the more lovely anything is, the more prone we are to delight in it. If anything be infinitely amiable, we are prone to love it in an infinite measure. We prefer the better above the worse, and cannot rest but in the best of all. Reason is the essence of the soul, and tends always to the utmost perfection. The more divine and glorious anything is, the more high and noble is the love that we bear it. No beauty less than the most perfect, no pleasure, no wisdom, no empire, no learning, no greatness, wealth or honour less than the most sublime, can be our full satisfaction. No little degree of love, nothing less than the most supreme and violent can content us. So that God, being most truly perfect in all these, is the adequate object of all our desires, and the only person to be esteemed in an infinite manner. It is as natural for man to love Him, as to desire and delight in any being which supplies the ordinary and daily necessities of his life.

To love Him as we ought implies two things that are agreeable to the nature of love, yet very rarely to be found among the sons of men: a desire to please Him, and a desire to enjoy Him. The desire of pleasing is a constant fruit and effect of love. For he that loves is very desirous to approve himself, and to do whatever he thinks will be grateful to his beloved. According to the degree of love, the desire is more or less. Where we love earnestly, we are extremely earnest and careful to please; where love is remiss, there is little need or regard of anything. But infinite love! It is impossible to declare what fervour and zeal it will produce. If we love God, we shall keep His commandments with a tenderness and desire so extreme that no joy will be so great as the observation of His laws. It will be with us as it was with our Lord Jesus Christ; it will be our *meat and drink to do the will of our Father which is in heaven.* The measure of our love will not infuse some slight and faint endeavours of pleasing, but put on us the most painful and costly duties, make us willing to forsake our own ease, goods, friends, nay, life itself, when we cannot keep them without offending our Creator.

The desire of enjoying is constantly seen in our love to one another. If any man hath a friend whom he entirely loveth, he desireth his conversation, wishes to be always in his company, and thinketh the time long till he and his friend be together. And thus will it be in our love to God, if as great and hearty as it ought to be. In this life, our enjoyment of God is more imperfect; more complete and perfect in the life to come. Here upon earth we desire to converse with Him in His ordinances; in prayer, meditation, hearing His word, in receiving the Sacrament; which are intended all for this purpose, to bring us into a nearer intimacy and familiarity with God, by speaking to Him and hearing Him speak and show Himself to us. If we love Him indeed, we shall highly value these ways of conversing with Him. It is all, here upon earth, whereby we can enjoy Him. It will make us, with David, esteem one day in His courts better than a thousand. We shall delight in all the means of approaching to Him as often as possible, and use them diligently, to the end of uniting us more and more unto Him, who is the object of our desire and the life of our souls. And forasmuch as there is another enjoyment of God, which is more complete and perfect, we shall groan earnestly, *desire to be dissolved and be with Christ,* where we may see no more as in a glass, but face to face, and know as we are known. For many waters cannot quench love, neither can the floods drown it. Affliction, persecution, sickness, anything that will bring us to heaven, will be acceptable and delightful.

If you would know more fully why God desires to be beloved, you may consider that love is not only the motive and incentive to virtue, the cause of obedience, but the form and essence of every grace, and the fulfilling of the law. We shall choose Him for our God and have no other gods but Him; no delights, no sovereign enjoyment but Him alone. We shall honour Him with all our souls, and adore Him with every power of our will and understanding. We shall not regard images and shadows but worship Him immediately in spirit and in truth. We shall not take His name in vain, nor contentedly stand by when others abuse it, but shall praise His name, and desire to see it glorified throughout the world. For love desires the honour, and delights in the glory and advancement, of its beloved. We shall reverence His sanctuary and keep His sabbaths, desiring rest from other avocations, that we may contemplate His glory in all His works.

For His sake we shall observe the laws of the second table, and love our neighbour as ourself; for to love Him is no impediment, but a strong engagement and incentive to the love of all His creatures. We shall honour our parents for His sake, and preserve the life of our neighbour. We shall not rob him of his happiness in his wife, nor wrong him in her chastity and fidelity towards him. We shall not steal from him, nor diminish his possessions. We shall not defame him, nor hurt him by lies, but vindicate and preserve his reputation; it will be our joy and satisfaction to see his honour clear and unblemished. We shall not injure him so much as in a thought, nor covet aught that is his, either for necessity or pleasure, but study to add to his contentments.

Were all the world as full of this love as it ought to be, paradise would still continue, and all mankind would be the joy and glory of the whole creation. The love of God towards all would dwell and abide in every soul, and the felicity of all would be the particular joy of every person. All the earth would be full of repose and peace and prosperity; nothing but honour and kindness and contentment would replenish the world; which leads me to that other branch of charity, which is charity to our neighbour.

CHAPTER XIX

Charity to our neighbour most natural and easy in the estate of innocency. Adam's love to Eve and his children a great exemplar of our love to all the world. The sweetness of loving. The benefits of being beloved. To love all the world and be beloved by all the world is perfect security and felicity. Were the law fulfilled, all the world would be turned into heaven

CHARITY to our neighbour is love expressed towards God in the best of His creatures. We are to love God in all the works of His hands; but in those especially that are most near unto Him, chiefly those in which He manifesteth Himself most clearly; and these are they that are most like Him, most exalted by Him, most loved of Him, and most delightful to Him.

Angels and men are so distinct from the residue of the creation that all the works of God, as if they were things of another kind, are put in subjection under their feet. They were made in His image, and are often called the Sons of God. They are the sovereign objects of His eternal love; every one of them, considered apart, is so glorious as if he were the sole individual friend of God and king of the universe; so that they are to be treated in another manner, as high and sacred persons, elevated above the race of ordinary creatures, as a progeny of kings that are all of them friends to the King of kings; ambassadors representing His person, in whom He is injured or obliged.

I confess there are many disguises that overcast the face of nature with a veil, and cloud these sovereign creatures. The excellency, the absence and distance, and unknown nature, of angels; the perverseness of nature; the ignorance, and unkindness, and disorders of men, darken and eclipse this glorious duty, and make it uncouth and difficult to use. But all these disorders came in by sin, and it is expedient to remove the confusions that blind us in our miserable estate, and to look upon this virtue of charity in the naked beauty which appeareth to us in the light of Eden.

In the purity of nature, men are amiable creatures, and prone to love; two great advantages, of which sin and misery hath bereaved us, and to which we are restored but in part, even then when we are sanctified. Where the beauty of the object is entire and perfect, and the goodness of the spectator clear and undefiled, to love is as natural and easy as for fire to inflame when it is applied to convenient matter. For the beauty of the object is oil and fuel to the affection of the spectator. It is not more easy to delight in what is pleasant than it is to desire what is good and amiable. To be commanded to take pleasure in it is liberty, not constraint. To be forbidden would be hard. A prohibition would be the severest law and the most cruel bondage. There was no positive law in Eden, that required a man to love his neighbour; it was a law of nature. The nature of the object required it, and our nature prompted itself thereunto. The service that law required was perfect freedom.

Adam was commanded to love Eve by a silent law, surprised by her beauty and captivated by the chains of nature. He was amazed at so fair a creature; her presence was so delightful that there was no need of a law; an injunction had [1] imported some sluggishness in the zeal of his affection. His appetite and reason were united together, and both invited him to lose himself in her embraces. She was as acceptable a present of the love of God as wisdom and goodness could invent for him. He was too apt to admire her, had not her soul been as worthy as her symmetry was transcendent. He admired the bounty of the donor in so great a gift, and great part of his life was to be spent in the contemplation of his treasure. He had a noble creature made in the image of God, for him alone. Her soul was far more excellent in beauty than her face, a diviner and more glorious object than the whole world. Her intelligence and vivacity, her lofty and clear apprehensions, her honour and majesty, her freedom of action, her kindness of behaviour, her angelical affections, her fitness for conversation, her sweet and tender principles, a million of graces

[1] Would have.

and endowments conspiring to enrich her person and perfection, made all the world to serve Adam with one degree of pleasure more in serving and pleasing her. The universe seemed to be nothing but the theatre of their mutual love; as if all the world were made for nothing else but to minister to her for his sake, and to make him happy in the enjoyment of her, while the fruition was sanctified by a just acknowledgment and thanksgiving to the Author.

We produce Eve only for a precedent.[1] This first sweetness is but a pattern and copy of what follows, fair prologue to a more magnificent scene, and used by us as a mere introduction. Adam was able to love millions more, and as she was taken out of his side, so were they to spring from his bowels; all to be as great and fair and glorious as she, as full of soul and as full of love. As the woman was the glory of man, so were their offsprings the glory of both; I mean, they had been so, by the law of nature, had not the due course of it been disturbed; which accident is wholly to be fathered on Adam's fondness to please his wife, and to be mothered upon her lightness and credulity. But we being here to disclose the felicity which is hid in the fulfilling of God's laws, and to justify His love in commanding this charity to our neighbours, must not regard the malevolence of men, but look upon the pure intention of the law, and the success that would have followed, had it been (as it might have been) perfectly observed.

All Adam's children had been himself divided and multiplied into millions, and every one a greater treasure to him than the whole world. The stars had not been by a thousand degrees so great an ornament to the skies as they to the earth; an offspring of incarnate angels, an assembly of corporeal seraphims, a race of celestial kings; every one loving and honouring Adam, as the fountain of their being and the author of their well-being; of the one in begetting them, of the other by standing and abiding in his integrity. They had all been so many pledges of his wife's affection; monuments of love, new and powerful endearments, enlargements of their parents; being mirrors and memorials of

[1] President, 1675.

L

both their perfections. For all had been made for every one, and every one had been the joy, nay, and the beauty of all. All had been every one's objects, and every one the spectator of all; every one would have delighted in the beauty of all, and all had conspired and strived together in the love of every one. Their concurrence would have banished all sin and oppression, discontentment and sorrow, wrong and injury, theft and murder and adultery and lying out of the world. There had been no noise of war or contention, no anger or envy, or malice or revenge; this accursed *the blackguard* had never appeared. But all would have been delightful to one another; affections, honours, benefits and service, pleasures, praises and prosperities, these alone had filled the world with beauty, security, peace and glory. Wisdom, goodness, love and felicity had been all that had been known, had love been entirely and inviolably observed.

But where God's laws are broken, there is confusion and every evil work; which nevertheless does more highly commend the excellency of His nature, and reflect a praise upon that authority which must first be despised before any misery can come into the world. If the duty which the law requires be all sweetness and felicity and glory, completely good, and on every side advantageous and profitable, we that fail in the discharge of our duty may be condemned; but God is to be admired, and still to be confessed most glorious and holy; because He delights in the welfare of His creatures, and makes religion so desirable a mystery, and enjoins such admirable things as would make all transcendently blessed and good and perfect, were they perfectly observed.

He designs that all should be amiable whom we are commanded to love, and that we should be not only prone to love but actually full of it. And the reason why He constitutes love as the sovereign law is because, as our Saviour saith, *There is none other greater commandment;* none more blessed or divine or glorious, none more conducive to our bliss, His pleasure, the perfection of His kingdom. Removing the law of love, it is impossible to put another law in its place which can answer the designs of His wisdom and goodness, or comply with the exigencies of our estate and condition. It is as easy to change the nature of God, and devise another deity as good and convenient, as to invent a better law than this, which is plainly of all other the most divine and holy.

If we ascend up into heaven and take a perfect account of all the operations and effects of love as they appear in glory, we may first give ourselves the liberty of wishing, and consult what of all things possible is most to be desired. Had we a power to choose, what kind of creatures would ourselves be made? Could we desire to be anything more great and perfect than the image of God? In the full extent and utmost height of its nature, it is the resemblance of all His blessedness and glory. To have beings without power, or power without operations, will never make us like God, because by an infinite and eternal act of power He is what He is. Actions are so necessary that all felicity and pleasure is continually founded in some act or other, and no essence is of any value but as it employs itself in a delightful manner. What law, then, would we have to regulate our actions by? Since actions are of different kinds—some good, some evil, some hurtful, some honourable, and some delightful, some base and odious, some are miserable and some are glorious—we would choose such a law to guide our actions by as might make them honourable and delightful, and good and glorious. All these are, with wisdom and blessedness, shut up in love.

And by love it is that we make ourselves infinitely beautiful and amiable and wise and blessed, while we extend that delightful and blessed affection to all objects that are good and excellent; so that on this side we have all that we can desire—essences, laws and actions that most tend to our full and complete perfection. If, on the other side, we look after objects for this affection, and desire to have some creatures most excellent, and fit for their beauty to be beloved, what creatures can we wish above all other, that can be made to satisfy and please us? Can anything be more high and perfect than the similitude of God?

God is love, and His love the life and perfection of goodness. There is no loving goodness so sweet and amiable as that alone; none so wise, none so divine, none so blessed. What laws can we desire those creatures to be guided by, but the laws of love? By love they are made amiable and delightful to us; by love they are made great and blessed in themselves. All honour and praise, benevolence and goodwill, kindness and bounty, tenderness and compassion, all sweetness and courtesy and care and affability, all service and complacency, are shut up in love. It is the fountain of all benefits and pleasures whatsoever. All admiration, esteem and gratitude, all industry, respect and courage are shut up in love; and by love alone doth any object of ours sacrifice itself to our desire and satisfaction. So that on that side our wishes are completed too, while the most high and blessed and glorious creatures love us as themselves. For thereby they are as much our felicity as their own, and as much take pleasure and delight therein. As for God, His way is perfect; like curious needlework, on either side complete and exquisite.

All that we can fear or except [1] against is His omission in forbearing to compel His creatures to love, whether they will or no. But in that liberty which He gave them, His love is manifested most of all. In giving us a liberty, it is most apparent; for without liberty there can be no delight, no honour, no ingenuity or goodness at all. No action can be delightful that is not our pleasure in the doing. All delight is free and voluntary by its essence. Force and aversion are inconsistent with its nature. Willingness in its operation is the beauty of the soul, and its honour founded in the freedom of its desire. Whatsoever it does not desire and delight in, though the matter of the performance be never so excellent, the manner is spoiled and totally blasted. Now, can we compel another to desire or delight in anything? The soul in itself hath an inclination to, or an aversion from, every object. The ingenuity [2] and worth of the soul is expressed in the kindness of its own intention. In the freedom of its desire to do what is excellent, in the delight it taketh to love, its goodness is founded.

Now, though God infinitely hated sin, yet He gave us an irrevocable power to do what we pleased, and adventured the hazard of that which He infinitely hated, that, being free to do what we would, we might be honourable and delightful in doing, freely and of our own accord, what is great and excellent. For without this liberty, there can be no love; since love is an active and free

[1] Complain.

[2] Sincerity.

affection, that must spring from the desire and pleasure of the soul. It is the pleasure of a lover to promote the felicity of his object. Whatsoever services he is compelled to do, he is either merely passive in them, or cross unto them. They are all void of the principal grace and beauty that should adorn them, and make them pleasant and satisfactory. Men may be dead, and moved like stones; but in such cases there is no love; neither do they act of themselves, when they are overruled and forced by another. For this cause hath it pleased God, in order to our perfection, to make the most sublime and sovereign creatures all free; wherein He hath expressed the greatest love in the world, as we may see by all the displeasures and pains it hath cost Him, through our abuse of so illimited and great a perfection. But where His love is most highly and transcendently expressed, there are we most prone to suspect it, nature is so cross [1] and disorderly.

There can be no wisdom without a voluntary act, for in all wisdom there is counsel and design. Where no consultation or election precedes, the best operation in all the world is blind and casual. Fortune and chance must have no hand in that which wisdom effecteth; no more than force and necessity must have in goodness, where all the kindness ought to be in the intention of the benefactor. There is something in it which I cannot explain. It is easily conceived, but will never, I think, in words be expressed. The will has a mighty hand in all the divinity of perfect goodness. It is the mind of the doer that is the principal object of all our desire and expectation.

Having for these causes made His creatures free, He has forfeited their choice and secured their determination, as far as was possible. He hath done all that can be devised to make them love us, and left nothing undone, but only that which was absolutely necessary, that they might love. They could not love us, if they were not left to themselves to do it freely. And, their ability being provided for, nay, an inclination given to make them willing, He has strictly commanded and enjoined them to love; by nature allured them, and ordered us so that we might be fit to be beloved. He hath made it sweet and rational to love; given them His own

[1] Contrary.

example, and solemnly protested that He will accept of no love to Himself but what is accompanied with love to His friends and servants; engaged them to love, or be eternally miserable. And if, for all this, they will not love, the fault is none of His. All that He has done to secure their love to Himself, He has done to secure their love to us; and is as much or more concerned in their love to us than in that which Himself requireth and expected. Nay, He hath made it impossible for them truly to love themselves without doing of it; and if they will neither love God nor themselves, we may well be despised for company. He infinitely desires their love, and would take infinite pleasure in the operation. There is no way to make themselves honourable and delightful to God, but only by loving us, as his soul requireth. And by all these inducements and causes are we ourselves stirred up to love, freely to exert the power of love to others in like manner.

That which yet further commendeth this love of virtue unto us is that it is the only soul of all pleasure and felicity in all estates. It is like the light of the sun, in all the kingdoms and houses and eyes and ages; in heaven and earth, in the sea; in shops and temples, in schools and markets, in labours and recreations, in theatres and fable. It is the great daemon of the world, and the sole cause of all operations. It is evidently impossible for any fancy, or play, or romance, or fable to be composed well and made delightful, without a mixture of love in the composure. In all theatres, and feasts, and weddings, and triumphs, and coronations, love is the soul and perfection of all. In all persons, in all occupations, in all diversions, in all labours, in all virtues, in all vices, in all occasions, in all families, in all cities and empires, in all our devotions and religious actions, love is all in all. All the sweetness of society is seated in love; the life of music and dancing is love; the happiness of houses, the enjoyment of friends, the amity of relations, the providence of kings, the allegiance of subjects, the glory of empires, the security, peace and welfare of the world is seated in love.

Without love, all is discord and confusion. All blessings come upon us by love, and by love alone all delights and blessings are enjoyed. All happiness is established by love, and by love alone is all glory attained. God knoweth that love uniteth souls, maketh men of one heart in a house, fills them with liberality and kindness to each other, makes them delightful in presence, faithful in absence; tender of the honour and welfare of their beloved; apt to obey, ready to please; constant in trials, patient in sufferings; courageous in assaults, prudent in difficulties, victorious and triumphant.

All that I shall need to observe further is, that it completes the joys of heaven. Well, therefore, may wisdom desire love; well may the goodness of God delight in love. It is the form and the glory of His eternal kingdom. And therefore it is that the Apostle saith, *Charity never faileth; but whether there be prophecies, they shall fail; whether there be tongues, they shall cease; whether there be knowledge, it shall vanish away. For we know in part, and we prophesy in part; but when that which is perfect is come, that which is in part shall be done away. For now we see through a glass darkly, but then face to face; now I know in part, but then shall I know as also I am known. And now abideth faith, hope and charity, these three; but the greatest of these is charity.*

CHAPTER XX

Of Prudence. Its foundation is charity, its end tranquillity and prosperity on earth, its office to reconcile duty and convenience,[1] *and to make virtue subservient to temporal welfare. Of prudence in religion, friendship and empire. The end of prudence is perfect charity*

CHARITY is that which entereth into every virtue, as a main ingredient of its nature and perfection. Love is the fountain and the

[1] Expediency.

end of all, without which there can be no beauty nor goodness in any of the virtues. Love to one's self, love to God, love to man, love to felicity, a clear and intelligent love, is the life and soul of every virtue; without which humility is but baseness, fortitude but fierceness, patience but stupidity, hope but presumption, modesty but simpering, devotion but hypocrisy; liberality is profuseness, knowledge vanity, meekness but a sheepish tameness, and prudence itself but fraud and cunning. For, as all other virtues, so is prudence founded on charity. He that is not good can never be prudent, for he can never benefit himself or others. For the designs of prudence are to secure one's self in the exercise of every virtue, and so to order the discharge of one's duty as neither to hurt a man's self in his life, estate, honour, health or contentment, nor yet to fail in the attainment of that worth and beauty which will make our lives delightful to others, and as glorious to ourselves as beneficial and delightful.

Prudence hath an eye to every circumstance and emergency of our lives. Its design is to make a man's self as great and glorious as is possible and, in pleasing all the world, to order and improve all advantages without incurring the least inconvenience; to reconcile our devotion, obedience and religion to our interest and prosperity in the world; to shun all extremes, to surmount all difficulties, to overrule all disadvantages, to discern all opportunities, and to lay hand on all occasions of doing good to ourselves. Its office is to consult and contrive and effect our own welfare in every occurrence that can befall us in the world, and so to mingle all virtues in the execution of our duties that they may relieve and aid and perfect each other, in such a manner as at once to be pleasing to God, profitable to His creatures and to ourselves; to take heed that we do nothing out of season, nor be guilty of any defect or excess or miscarriage. All the virtues are united by prudence, like several pieces in a complete armour, and disposed all like soldiers in an army that have their several posts and charges; or like the several orders and degrees in a kingdom, where there are variety of trusts and services to be done, and every man has his office assigned by the king, and knows his own work and is fitted for the same. For, as no one man is sufficient for all, the same person cannot be chief priest in the temple, and general in the army, and admiral at sea. So neither can every virtue serve for all purposes, but there must be several virtues for several ends. As the king ordereth and directeth all his officers and subjects in their several places, if they do their duty in their own sphere, the great end is attained by all, which no one of them alone was able to effect. So here, one virtue supplies the defects of another; and though every one of them moves in his own precincts, and does not at all intermeddle with another's charge, yet the work is done as effectually as if any one virtue did it alone.

While all the virtues conspire to supply what is wanting in each other, prudence is the general overseer and governor of all; which, while every single virtue is ignorant of what the others are doing, fits and proportions the subservient ends to which every one of these directeth its care and labour and skill, to the great and last end of all, the entire perfection and glory of the kingdom. So that, here upon earth, prudence seemeth to be the king of virtues, because we have such a multiplicity of concerns and affairs to look after that it is impossible for any one virtue but prudence alone to attend them all.

This discovereth the excellency of virtue, and detecteth a very great error to which we are liable, while we are prone imprudently to expect more from any virtue than it is able to perform. We are apt to believe that in every virtue there is an infinite excellency; and this great expectation of ours is a good opinion of virtue, yet turneth not seldom to its disgrace and infamy. For when we look upon any single virtue and see it so defective that it scarce answereth one of many ends, because we find ourselves deceived in our expectation of its perfection, and the service of that virtue so curt and narrow, which we thought to be infinite, we are distasted [1] at its insufficiency, and prone to slight it as a poor inconsiderable business, infinitely short of our hopes and expectations; nay, and to be discouraged from the practice of it, because we find it attended with many difficulties and inconveniences, which it is not able to remedy or answer. Thus, we are deterred from liberality for fear of the poverty to which it exposeth us; from meekness, because it encourageth all people

[1] Disgusted.

to trample us under feet; from holiness, because it is scorned and hated in the world; from fortitude and courage, because of the perils and hazards that attend it; from self-denial because of the displeasures we do to ourselves in crossing our appetite. Nay, sometimes men are so wicked as to hate to be obliged, for fear of the inconveniences of gratitude, and are much prejudiced against fidelity and love and truth and constancy. For all these virtues can answer but one exigence, for which they are prepared, especially in our daily conversation with men; and a mistake in one of them doth expose us to more inconveniences than its benefit is worth.

This is the offence; and the truth is, no virtue is of any value as cut off from the rest. We may as well expect all beauty in a nose divided from the face, or an eye plucked out of the head, all perfection in an ear or a tongue cut off, all serviceableness in a hand or foot dismembered from the body, as a full and perfect security from any one virtue whatsoever. If one were sufficient, the rest would be superfluous. Man's empire and dominion would be a very narrow thing—at least, a very empty and shallow thing—if any one virtue were enough for his felicity. As his exigencies and concerns are innumerable, so are his cares and endowments, his honours and pleasures, his offices and employments, his virtues and graces. His offices and his virtues must be at least so many as will serve to regulate all his concerns. And if any be so comprehensive as to cure many exigencies at the same time, his virtues are the greater in force and extent, but the fewer in number. Their perfect sufficiency is to be measured by the ends for which they are prepared; and their beauty consists, like that of an army with banners, in the proportion and symmetry of the entire body, the mutual supplies and succours they afford to one another, the unity of such a great variety of things in order to the attainment of the same great and ultimate end, the full and complete number of offices and inferior ends, and the extreme providence wherewith they are reducible to one supreme end, which is most high and excellent.

It is enough for the ear if it can hear well, though it is no more able to see or taste than a stone. It is enough for the eye to see well, though it is no more sensible of noise than a rock or a tree.

The office of the tongue is to taste well, of the nostril to smell well, and there is no defect in any of these, because they are every one sufficient for its own immediate end; and also tempered and united together, that the rest are supplies to make up the defect of every single sense and organ; and all together perfectly subservient to the whole man, for whose sake they were prepared, that he might enjoy the benefit of them all. The eye sees for the ear, and the tongue, and all the rest of the members of the body. The foot supports and carries the eye, the hand defends and feeds the eye, the ear instructs and counsels the eye. The nostrils smell for the eye, and the tongue tastes and talks for the eye; which the eye cannot do for itself, because it was made to need the assistance of the rest. The eye directs all these in lieu of their services, and is of far greater value than if a man had no other member but an eye alone. For the eye is the light of all the members, and great in its relation to the whole man. It sees for the ear and the hand and for all, and is to all these after some measure beneficial, but without these would be to no purpose.

There is an infinite excellency in every virtue, but it is to be sought in its relation to all the rest. It is good for nothing in its place but for that particular end to which it is assigned. In attaining that end, it is subservient to all other virtues and, while it serves all, is aided by all. The other virtues remedy the inconveniences to which this doth expose us and, being all joined together, carry us safely and securely to our last end. Because the influence of every one passeth through all, every single virtue is pleasing to God and a means, in its place, of our whole felicity.

The beauty of all the virtues is to be sought in prudence, for there they meet in an entire body. Their correspondence and convenience, their symmetry and proportion, their unity and variety, their full and perfect harmony, make up the features of the soul and complete its graces; just as the diversity of members perfects the body. Knowledge gives light to love, but love gives warmth and feeling to knowledge. Love may, perhaps, like a separate soul, dwell in heaven alone; and yet even then it must include all knowledge and righteousness and wisdom and holiness; for if love know not how to guide itself, it will never attain its end, nor be a perfect virtue. But here upon earth, 'tis like the soul in the body; it must eat, and drink, and see, and hear; has a thousand works to do, and therefore standeth in need of many virtues. Love without goodness is perhaps a thing impossible, because it always designs well; but love without wisdom is a common thing, for such is all that mistakes its end. Love without discretion is a mischievous thing; love without prudence a helpless thing; love without courage a feeble and cowardly thing; love without modesty an impudent and troublesome thing; love without the fear of God is lust and wantonness. And if the most great and glorious of all the virtues stands in need of all its companions, the less and inferior must needs be lame and maimed without the residue, especially without the superior.

Upon this account it is that so much care and study goes to the making up of a virtuous man. All kinds of virtues must concur to complete his perfection. The want of any one denominates a vice and makes him vicious. Nay, the want of any one destroys the form and essence of the rest. Virtue is not virtue but in order to felicity. If it hath lost its force, it hath lost its nature. As a little poison turns the best meat from nourishment into poison, so doth one vice, cherished and allowed, corrupt and vitiate all the virtues in the whole world. Hence it is that the philosophers say, all the virtues are linked together in the golden chain of prudence; and that a thing is made good by all its causes, evil by the least defect. For as one tooth wanting in a clock makes all the other wheels and materials useless, though the frame be never so elaborate and curious, so doth the absence of the smallest virtue make void and frustrate all the residue.

A man of a kind and bountiful disposition, that is loose and intemperate, may ruin his estate and die like a prodigal and vainglorious fool. A stout, courageous person that is proud and debauched will be little better than a soldierly ruffian, and live, if not like a thief for want of honesty, yet like a swaggering hector for want of discretion. A man endued with all kind of learning may be morose and covetous, and by one vice lose all the benefit of his education. A religious votary that is splenetic and revengeful brings a disgrace upon his whole profession. But he that is wise and learned, and holy and just, and temperate and courageous, and kind and liberal, and meek and humble, and affable and cheerful, and prudent and industrious, shall be serviceable and honourable and delightful to others, profitable to himself, and always triumphant. Especially if he be so discreet and prudent as to make all these virtues move like stars in their courses, and knows how to apply and manage their excellencies in their due and proper places upon all occasions. For they are so many, different in nature, that some of their influences will hit every business; and all of them together pass a grace and lustre upon each other, so divine and heavenly that they will make their owner venerable in the eyes of the world, and correct the malignity of the most injurious and censorious. Which moved our Saviour to exhort us to be *wise as serpents, innocent as doves;* and occasioned that of the Apostle, *He that will love life and see good days, let him refrain his tongue from evil, and his lips that they speak no guile; let him eschew evil and do good; let him seek peace and ensue it. For the eyes of the Lord are over the righteous; and who is he that will harm you, if ye be followers of that which is good?* The only sure way to live happily here upon earth is to join all kind of virtues together, and to let them work in season according to their several natures.

What the efficacy of prudence is may be seen in friendship, in the regiment of states and kingdoms, in the rule and government of private families. He that is fitted for all these is an excellent person.

It is the office of prudence, in all estates, to find out the temper of those with whom we are to deal, and so to suit the exercises of all virtues with their several humours as may make their operation consistent with our own repose and their benefit, without infringing our duty.

In friendship it often falleth out, by reason of the spiritual sickness of those to whom we relate, that we must either make shipwreck of fidelity and a good conscience, or run the hazard of losing our friend, by displeasing that we may be profitable to him. There is no duty so necessary as that of free and faithful reproof; no duty so nice [1] as this. A good man knows it is incumbent upon him, and yet is very averse from the discharge of it. It is as troublesome to himself as to the person that needs it. 'Tis difficult

[1] Delicate.

to be done well, and so unpleasant to both. Here prudence comes in, and deviseth expedients for all inconveniences, and with a strange facility scatters all doubts and fears.

Three things it discovers to be necessary in the foundation of the business, three in the superstructure and three in the conclusion. He that reproves well must show a great respect and tenderness to the person, a necessity of the discharge of that duty, his averseness to it, and how nothing but his perfect love could make him undertake it. The foundation of the success is laid by these provisions. In the superstructure, he must consider whether it be best to be done merrily or severely, by a brief hint or a strong enlargement, according to the temper and degree of the person. He must choose out the best opportunities, and consult the honour of him he reproveth. And if he be displeased and grow angry at the liberty, he must in the close of all bear it patiently, surmount it with courtesy and pursue him with kindness. He that rules his own passion is master of another man's; he must needs win him and melt him; for no man thus dealt with is so very a beast as to be angry long. Or the mischief is, when he that reproveth miscarrieth in some of these rules, especially the last; for there are few so prudent as not to be exasperated with the afront that is put upon their kindness and fidelity, when they are injured for their good will; few so discreet as to consider which way their patience and meekness are to be made the instruments of amity and happiness.

In the management of empires and kingdoms, prudence hath a vast and mighty province to reign in. A good king, when he designs the extirpation of vice and the establishment of righteousness, meets with many rubs and obstacles in his way, all which are easily and sweetly by prudence removed. His great encouragement is the beauty of religion and the assistance of God; for he knows very well that equity and piety are such glorious things that, though few practice them as they ought to do, yet all admire them.

Godliness and honesty need nothing but to be maintained and assented by the prince. When they are once countenanced by authority, all the enemies of religion are confounded and dare not lift up their face against it. Wise and holy men may easily be exalted, and are more capable of exaltation than others. As they are more faithful when they are in power, they will be more grateful to the prince and more obliging to the people, and in all respects more able to serve them both. The good will secure the throne and exalt the kingdom. Prudence, in such a work, knows where to begin and where to end; by what steps and degrees to proceed; what instruments to use; how to oblige, and how to awe; whom to oblige and awe; where to remit the rigour of the law, and where to be severe. The truth is, prudence consists most in attempting the business; for it will go on, and is ever waited with success when undertaken. A king that is so wise as to design and endeavour the reformation of his nation must needs be prudent. God has assured him, *The throne is established by righteousness. When it goeth well with the righteous, the city rejoiceth; and when the wicked perish there is shouting. By the blessing of the upright the city is exalted, but it is overthrown by the mouth of the wicked.*

In families, the force of prudence is prodigious. Some men, by the assistance of this virtue, live more happily upon a mean estate than others upon thousands. They have more respect among their servants, more honour among their neighbours, more plenty at home, more authority abroad, more peace and comfort everywhere, than men forty times above themselves in state and grandeur. Its first care is to be wary in the choice of servants; for they that are good act well by nature, and have little need of force and compulsion. Its next business is to oblige them; which is done by a religious example which instills a reverence, a strict prohibition of all debauchery, a sweet and affable behaviour, a plentiful provision for their comfortable subsistence; a prudent connivance at smaller faults, a distribution of rewards as well as punishments for the encouragement of their virtues, a meek and gentle reproof of their faults, a kind acknowledgment of their good deserts (which is a cheap and easy kind of payment, yet more obliging than any dry gift of gold or silver). A prudent man will demean [1] himself in his family, as to make himself cordially beloved of all; so ordering his affairs that the services of those about him shall be like preferments. By which means it will come to pass that he shall have his choice of servants, because it will be esteemed a blessing to be with him; and in the next place, their

[1] Behave.

service will be mingled with respect and love. They will be faithful as well for his sake as their own. In the midst of all this, his prudence will guide him to take a strict account, and to make all his servants see it is impossible to cheat him. Thus in all affairs prudence happily demeans itself; and of this gift especially is that of Solomon to be understood, *A gift is as a precious stone in the hand of him that hath it; whithersoever it turneth, it prospereth.*

For the foundation of all kind of prudence, you must remember that he that winneth souls is wise. Men's hearts are the stars by whose influences the affairs of the world are regulated. They are, as our Saviour called them, good or evil treasures, out of which proceed murders, adulteries, thefts, slanders, etc., or praises, honours, preferments, riches, pleasures, all kind of gifts and benefits. And the prudent man's main business is to make himself entirely beloved by all the world, which can never be without great fidelity, courage, goodness, prudence and dexterity. Flattery and base compliances make a man odious.

The last end of prudence is eternal happiness and glory, to which it moveth by crooked meanders and windings-out as occasion requireth. It is a strange virtue, for it is conversant amongst terrene and inferior objects, and yet a far more difficult virtue than wisdom itself. Wisdom is a high and heavenly virtue, but its rules are always fixed and its objects stable; whereas prudence hath no set and stated rules but, in all occasions, is to mould and shape itself, it knows not which way, till it comes to action. Its paths are in the deep and mighty waters, among storms and tempests.

CHAPTER XXI

Encouragements to Courage. Its nature, cause and end. Its greatness and renown. Its ornaments and companions. Its objects, circumstances, effects and disadvantages. How difficulties increase its virtue and triumphs. How subservient it is to blessedness and glory

LOVE and prudence are the parents of courage. A feeble hen,

a timorous mother, will sacrifice their lives for their young ones. And he that forgetteth all his own interests divests himself, together with them, of his fears and, despising death first, easily slighteth all other things. Even a coward by nature is made more bold and confident by skill at his weapon; and he that is always assured of the victory can never be afraid of the encounter or the enemy. He that is dexterous at the use of all virtues, and knows how to apply them so as ever to come off more honourably, will laugh at the trial of his own innocence, and make a game of difficulties and terrors.

Valour is a right and strong resolution of the soul, whereby it dare encounter with any difficulty and trouble, for virtue's sake. It is the armour of the soul against all impressions of fear. Its effect is an equal and uniform stayedness of mind, against all dangerous and terrible accidents. It containeth magnanimity, patience, constancy, invincible resolution, boldness and industry in its nature. Its cause is the love of virtue, and the sense of anything that is base and vile, a high ambition and love of glory. Its end is the preservation of a man's person and honesty, the conquest of all opposition in the way to bliss, the destruction or subjection of enemies, triumph and conquest, the establishment of peace, the attainment of liberty and glory. Its attendants are prudence, justice and temperance. The principal ornament and grace of valour is worth and goodness. Its aids and encouragements are infinite; it groweth great and high by making use of all the causes of hope and confidence. Conflicts and dangers are the element in which it lives. It owes its whole being to them, for without causes of fear there could be no courage in all nature. The knowledge of God is the root of divine valour, and fidelity to His laws its commendation. The assurance of His love, and all those things that serve to beget and confirm it, are subservient to it. It draws in strength and encouragements from all obligations and rewards from all great and holy examples, from the knowledge of its own sublimity, from the greatness of felicity, from the omnipotence and omnipresence and providence of the deity, from His truth and goodness, and from all those things wherein He has manifested His love above the heavens.

Of all the virtues in greatest estimation, this is the most renowned; for its prerogative is so great that it is simply called virtue, virtue being the word to express and signify valour among the Latins; because the force and efficacy that is in it is most visible and apparent, and by that all other virtues are secured, vindicated, exercised and made useful. It is styled *manhood* among the English, with a peculiar emphasis, as if the essence of a man was founded in courage; because his vigour is emasculated and his dignity lost, that is effeminate and timorous; for he is scarce a man that is a coward.

What a glorious and incomparable virtue this is appeareth from the baseness and ineptitude of its contrary. A coward and an honest man can never be the same; a coward and a constant lover can never be the same; a coward and a brave man can never be the same. Cowardice and wisdom are as incompatible for ever as love and wisdom were thought to be of old. A coward is always despicable and wretched, because he dares not expose himself to any hazard, nor adventure upon any great attempt, for fear of some little pain and damage that is between him and an excellent achievement. He is baffled from the acquisition of the most great and beautiful things, and nonplussed with every impediment. He is conquered before he begins to fight. The very sight of danger makes him a slave. He is undone when he sees his enemy afar off, and wounded before the point of the sword can touch his shadow. He is all ways a terror and burden to himself, a dangerous knave and a useless creature.

Strange is the vigour of a brave man's soul. The strength of his spirit and his irresistible power, the greatness of his heart and the height of his condition, his mighty confidence and contempt of danger, his true security and repose in himself, his liberty to dare and do what he pleaseth, his alacrity in the midst of fears, his invincible temper, are advantages which make him master of fortune. His courage fits him for all attempts, renders him serviceable to God and man, and makes him the bulwark and defence of his king and country.

Let those debauched and unreasonable men that deny the existence of virtue contemplate the reality of its excellency here, and be confounded with shame at their prodigious blindness.

Their impiety designs the abolishment of religion and the utter extirpation of all faith and piety, while they pretend the distinction between virtue and vice to be merely feigned for the aweing of the world, and that their names have no foundation in nature, but the craft of politicians and the tradition of their nurses. Are there no base fellows nor brave men in the world? Is there no difference between a lion and a hare, a faint-hearted coward and a glorious hero? Is there nothing brave nor vile in the world? What is become of these Rodomontados wits! Where is the boasted glory of their personal valour, if there be no difference, but courage and cowardice be the same thing?

How empty these self-conceited but shallow ranters are is evident by their short and narrow measures. They place all gallantry and worth in valour; all the virtue of a man they think seated in this. They forget that policy and learning, and prudence and gratitude, and fidelity and temperance, and industry and compassion and bounty, and affability and courtesy and modesty, and justice and honesty are virtues, and that in every one of these there is something fitting a man for the benefit of the world. Nay, they have lost the notion of virtue, and know not what it is. Those things by which a man is made serviceable to himself and the world they think not to be virtues, but imagine chimeras which they cannot see, and then deny they have any existence. A man is capable of far more glorious qualities than one of them; and his courage itself may be raised to far higher ends and purposes than buffoons and thrasonical [1] heroes can dream of.

It is to be noted here that any one of those things that are called virtue, being alone, is not a virtue. It is so far from aiding and setting us forward in the way to happiness that oftentimes it proveth a great and intolerable mischief, and is never safe but when it is corrected and guided by the rest of its companions. To stir no further than courage alone, what is courage in a thief or a tyrant or a traitor, but like zeal and learning in a pernicious heretic?

You may note further that goodness is a principal ingredient in the excellency of this virtue, though it be distinct in its nature from the being of courage. A brave man will expose his life in an

[1] Boastful.

honest cause, for the benefit and preservation of others, though not for the damage or destruction of any. He will slight his own safety and despise his repose, to make himself a saviour and a benefactor. A true courage holdeth virtuous actions at such a price that death, imprisonment, famine, dishonour, poverty, shame, indignation, all allurements and temptations are nothing, compared to the performance of heroic deeds. He exceedeth all constraint, and walketh in the glorious liberty of the sons of God.

The last note which I shall offer to your observation of this occasion is this, for the illustration of the reason and excellency of God's dispensations. The great end for which God was pleased, not to seat us immediately in the throne, but to place us first in an estate of trial, was the multiplication of our virtues. For had we been seated in the glory of heaven at the first, there had no such virtues as patience and courage and fidelity been seen; no faith or hope or meekness, no temperance or prudence or self-denial in the world; which virtues are the very clothes and habits of the soul in glory. The graces and beauties of the soul are founded in the exercise of them.

Actions pass not away, but are fixed, by the permanent continuance of all eternity; and, though done never so long ago, shall appear before the eye of the soul for ever in their places, be the glory of their author, the lineaments and colours of his beauty; seen by God and His holy angels, and delightful to all that love and delight in worthy things. Our life upon earth being so diversified, like a sphere of beauty so variously adorned with all sorts of excellent actions, shall wholly and at once be seen as an entire object, rarely and curiously wrought; a lively mirror of the nature of the soul. And all the elements of which it is compounded, all the parts that conspire in its symmetry, all the qualities, operations and perfections that contribute to its glory, shall afford wonder and pleasure to all spectators; while every soul shall be more concerned in its actions than in its essence (indeed, its essence, however considerable, is of little or no value in comparison of its operations); every virtue being the natural offspring and production of the soul, in which its vigour principally appeareth, an effect discovering the nature of the cause, and the sole occasion of its shame or glory. For if the essence of the soul be all power, and its power exerted in its operation, the soul must needs enter into its actions and consequently be affected with all that befalls its operations. All acts are immortal in their places, being embalmed, as it were, by eternity, till the soul revive and be united to them. Then shall it appear in its own age, and in eternity too, in its last life enjoying the benefit of its first. And in that sense is that voice from heaven to be understood, which commanded the Divine to write, *Blessed are they that die in the Lord, from henceforth; yea, saith the Spirit that they may rest from their labours; and their works do follow them.* For the glory of the place is nothing to us, if we are not endued with those glorious habits which will make our souls all glorious within. We must be glorious and illustrious ourselves, and appear in actions that will beautify the throne to which we are exalted.

That these actions may be great and amiable, manifold and excellent, is the desire of every soul, the natural wish and expectation both of reason itself and of self-love.

How glorious the counsel and design of God is for the achieving of this great end, for the making of all virtues more complete and excellent, and for the heightening of their beauty and perfection, we will exemplify here in their perfection of courage. For the height and depth and splendour of every virtue is of great concernment to the perfection of the soul, since the glory of its life is seated in the accomplishment of its essence, in the fruit it yieldeth in its operations. Take it in verse, made long ago upon this occasion:

For man to act as if his soul did see
The very brightness of eternity;
For man to act as if his love did burn
Above the spheres, even while it's in its urn;
For man to act, even in the wilderness,
As if he did those sovereign joys possess,
Which do at once confirm, stir up, enflame,
And perfect angels, having not the same—
It doth increase the value of his deeds,
In this a man a seraphim exceeds.

To act on obligations yet unknown,
To act upon rewards as yet unshown,
To keep commands whose beauty's yet unseen,
To cherish and retain a zeal between
Sleeping and waking, shows a constant care,
And that a deeper love, a love so rare
That no eye-service may with it compare.

The angels, who are faithful while they view
His glory, know not what themselves would do
Were they in our estate! A dimmer light
Perhaps would make them err as well as we,
And in the coldness of a darker night
Forgetful and lukewarm themselves might be.
Our very rust shall cover us with gold,
Our dust shall sparkle [1] while their eyes behold
The glory springing from a feeble state,
Where mere belief doth, if not conquer fate,
Surmount, and pass what it doth antedate.

The beatific vision is so sweet and strong a light that it is impossible for anything that loves itself, and sees the face of God, to turn away to any vanity from so divine and strong a blessedness. To love God in the light is a cheap and easy thing. The love that is showed in a more weak estate to an absent object is more remiss, perhaps, and black in appearance, but far deeper, if, in the lover's weakness and its object's absence, it be faithful to the death; constantly solicitous and careful to please, laborious and industrious, wakeful and circumspect, even and immutable, and freely springing from its own desire, not out of bare pleasure but humble obedience to the laws of its benefactor. All the courage which it shows in such occasions is more full of mystery and divinity than is imaginable; far more moving and full of virtue, while it struggles with impediments, disadvantages and difficulties than if, without any such occasion of showing its virtue, it did smoothly and peaceably proceed in the highest rapture.

Add to that the mysteriousness of its beauty in all the varieties

[1] 1675 sprinkle—emended by Dobell and Margoliouth.

of its operations, and the different sweetnesses that still appear in all its several effects upon new occasions. The very representations of love upon the stage, in its conflicts and agonies, produces another kind of sense in the spectator than that of embraces. It is more tender and endearing, touches the soul, of its beloved especially, in a more vigorous and lively manner. It makes all fruitions afterward more precious. By fidelity, courage and immovable perfection it maketh the lover more honourable, and effects far more serious alterations in the soul—solid joys and tender compassions, moving and bleeding resentments [1]; all which end in satisfactions heightened with more perfect complacencies.[2]

Thus you see courage in the root made more glorious by a person's exposure and abasement. In the fruit and exercise it is otherwise to be considered. Where there is no evil to be endured, or no strength to be resisted, there can be no courage or virtue at all. Where the conflict is more sharp, the victory is more pleasant and the success of the fight is far more honourable. Where a giant is to fight with a gnat or a dwarf, the disproportion of his strength takes away the pleasure of its trial and a glory of the combat. There is no room or occasion for its exercise. And though it might, without any trial, be known to Him that sees all things in their hidden essences, yet without its exercise it remaineth unexerted, is wholly vain, especially when there is no occasion for it in nature. The pleasure of the spectacle springeth from its operation.

To see a seraphim surmount one of our difficulties, in the midst of all his strengths and advantages, is no more than to see a giant destroy a gnat or subdue a grasshopper. But in man there is a certain degree of strength that makes him a fit match for the appointed encounter. In the estate of innocency, indeed, his enemies and difficulties were very few; just as many as were needful for the trial of his obedience, gratitude, fidelity. All the hardship he was to undergo was to cross his appetite and, though he did not as yet see which way it was reserved for him, to be so courageous as to hope well, so grateful to God as to dare to confide in Him, rather let go the knowledge that he might gain by eating it than break His commandment. All other

[1] Sentiments. [2] Pleasures.

duties were his pleasure and felicity. Here lay his trial, and his obedience should have been crowned with infinite reward, all which would in some measure have risen out of the duty discharged by him. For by this resignation and self-denial he had manifested his obedience, and acquitted himself, and showed his love and his prelation [1] of his Maker's pleasure above all other concerns; wherein he had been approved, and wise and holy, and well-pleasing to God. He would have put the crown upon God's works in accomplishing the end for which he was made, and had been very delightful to all the angels. He had been crowned with glory and honour in all their complacency.

If that were too little, because he had then no enemy but his appetite, the dimness of his sight maketh up the mystery. If his clarity was too great, and there was no proportion between his strength and the temptation, that proceeded of the tenderness of God's love, which feared to adventure him too far, and had rather something of honour should be endangered than his soul lost, or thrust upon the hazard of too great a temptation. When the angels fell, the devil was let loose upon man, for the increase of his honour and dominion; yet, like a dog on his chain, so far and no farther. He had but one way, and that was to persuade our first parents to do what was forbidden. Persuade he might, and try his skill to deceive, but he could not compel, nor otherwise afflict or hurt him in the least. He had not power so much as to diminish the least hair of his head. Yet so gracious was Almighty God that, upon this trial of his prudence and courage, the exercise of these virtues had been infinitely pleasing to His eternal love; because He infinitely delighted in the welfare and preservation of what was so precious to Himself, as a soul is that is beloved. In that complacency [2] Adam had found little less than infinite glory. It did not become the tenderness of God's love to expose him to any severer trial.

For there are certain periods and fit bounds
Which he that passeth all his work confounds.

But when Adam fell, and brought more hazards and difficulties upon himself, God might justly leave him to them, for his greater trial and more perfect glory.

[1] Preference. [2] Delight.

Now we are more blind and weak by nature, yet infinitely beloved and more precious; for the price of the blood of the eternal Son of God is laid upon the soul as an addition to its interior value. We are, even in our corruption, to grapple with sin and hell and death, and sickness and poverty and fear, and all the devils and afflictions in the world; nay, which is worse than all, with our own errors, lusts and passions, more near and bitter enemies. A poor clod of earth is to overcome all the world; to fight, as the Apostle speaks, *with principalities and powers, with the rulers of the darkness in this world, with spiritual wickedness in high places;* and to return laden with victories and trophies into the kingdom of heaven. Nor is the combat so unequal, but that there is a mighty hope and assurance of triumphing, though Lucifer and his angels are to be trampled under feet. For under the disguise of this apparent clod, there lies concealed a mighty, great and celestial personage, a divine and glorious creature, miraculous and mysterious, even the image of the deity, that can derive strengths and succours from all eternity. And being aided by the conduct of so great a captain as our Lord Jesus Christ, who has taught us by His example not to fear, because He has overcome the world, we may safely sing, *O death, where is thy sting? O grave, where is thy victory?* and challenge all the powers of heaven, earth and hell to the combat; which for one single person to do against all the creation is the most glorious spectacle which the world affords.

Who shall separate us from the love of Christ? Shall tribulation, or distress, or persecution, or famine, or nakedness, or peril, or sword? As it is written, for thy sake are we killed all the day long, we are accounted as sheep to the slaughter. Nay, in all these things we are more than conquerors, through Him that loved us. For I am persuaded that neither death, nor life, nor angels, nor principalities, nor powers, nor things present, nor things to come, nor height, nor depth, nor any other creature shall be able to separate us from the love of God, which is in Christ Jesus our Lord.

To be courageous is the easiest thing in the world, when we consider the certain success which courage, founded on goodness, must needs attain. For he that makes his fortitude subservient only to the excess of his love has all the powers of heaven and earth on his side, and the powers of hell, that are already subdued, are the only foes that are to be vanquished by him. To dare to be good is the office of true and religious valour. And he that makes it his business to oblige all the world, he whose design it is to be delightful to all mankind, has nothing to overcome but their error and bitterness; which by meekness and kindness, and prudence and liberality, will easily be accomplished. For they all love themselves, and cannot choose but desire those that are kind and serviceable to them, and must, so far forth as they love themselves, honour and delight in their benefactors. So that courage, thus guided by prudence to the works of charity and goodness, must surely be safe and prosperous on earth; its admirableness and its beauty being a powerful charm, an invincible armour.

CHAPTER XXII

Of Temperance: in matters of art, as music, dancing, painting, cookery, physic, etc.: in the works of nature, eating, drinking, sports and recreations; in occasion of passion, in our lives and conversations. Its exercise in self-denial, measure, mixture and proportion. Its effects and achievements

PRUDENCE giveth counsel what measure and proportion ought to be held in our actions; fortitude inspires boldness and strength to undertake; but it is temperance doth execute what both of them design. For temperance is that virtue whereby the actions of prudence and power are moderated, when they come to be exerted.

It is the opinion of some that, as patience respects[1] afflictions, so temperance is wholly taken up in moderating our pleasures,

[1] Concerns.

and hath no employment but in the midst of prosperity. But since there are certain bounds which fear and sorrow ought not to exceed, temperance hath its work in the midst of calamities and, being needful to moderate all our passions, hath a wider sphere to move in than prosperity alone. Its province is more large and comprehensive, including all estates and conditions of life whatsoever.

Others there are that admit of its use in all conditions, but confine it to one particular employment, even that of enlarging or bounding the measure of every operation; but in real truth it has another office, and that more deep, perhaps, and more important than the former. For actions are of two kinds, either mixed or simple. Where the work is single and but one, it is expressed in nothing else but the measure of the action, that it be neither too short nor too long; too remiss, nor too violent; too slow, nor too quick; too great, nor too little. But where many things are mixed and meet together in the action, as they generally do in all affairs of our lives, there its business is to consider what and how many things are to enter the composition, and to make their proportion just and convenient. As in preparing medicines, the skill whereby we know what is to be put in and what left out is of one kind, and that of discerning how much of every ingredient will serve the turn, of another. The skill of mingling is like the virtue of prudence; but the actual tempering of all together exhibits the virtue of temperance to the life, because it reduces the skill to its operation. Its end is the beauty and success of our endeavours.

Of what use and value temperance is in our lives and conversations we may guess by its necessity, force and efficacy on all occasions.

The fit mixture and proportion of the four elements in all bodies is that upon which their nature, form and perfection dependeth. Too much of the fire, too much of the water, too much of the air, too much of the earth, are pernicious and destructive. There is an infinite wisdom expressed in the mixture and proportion of every creature.

Beauty and health, agility, repose and strength depend upon the due temperament of human bodies. The four humours of choler, melancholy, phlegm and blood are generally known; but there are many other juices talked of besides, by the discreet and accurate mixture of which the body of a man or beast is perfected. Some great inconveniences always follows the excess or defect of these. Disorder and disproportion go hand in hand, and are attended by sickness and death itself.

In matters of art, the force of temperance is undeniable. It relateth not only to our meats and drinks, but to all our behaviours, passions and desires.

> All music, sauces, feasts, delights and pleasures,
> Games, dancing, arts, consist in govern'd measures;
> Much more do words and passions of the mind
> In temperance their sacred beauty find.

A musician might rash [1] his fingers over all his strings in a moment, but melody is an effect of judgment and order; it springs from a variety of notes, to which skill giveth time and place in their union. A painter may daub his table [2] all over in an instant, but a picture is made by a regulated hand, and by variety of colours. A cook may put a tun [3] of sugar or pepper or salt in his dishes, but delicates are made by mixture and proportion. There is a temperance also in the gesture of the body, the air of the face, the carriage of the eye, the smile, the motions of the feet and hands; and by the harmony of these is the best beauty of the world either much commended or disgraced. A clown and a courtier are known by their postures. A dancer might run into extremes, but his art is seen in the measure of his paces, and adorned with a variety of sweet and suitable behaviours. A physician may kill a man with the best ingredients, but good medicines are those wherein every simple hath its proper dose, and every composition a fit admixture of good ingredients. A poem, an oration, a play, a sermon, may be too tedious, or too dull, or too feeble and impertinent; but all its faults are avoided by a fit temperance of words and materials.

[1] Run, dash.
[2] Board, canvas.
[3] Cask.

Temperance everywhere yields the pleasure, and excess is as destructive as defect in any accomplishment whatsoever, virtue being seated in the golden mean. It is by an artificial limiting of power that everything is made as it ought to be, complete and perfect. All kinds of excellence in every sort of operation spring from temperance. A curious picture, a melodious song, a delicious harmony, by little invisible motions of the pen or pencil, or by ductures [1] scarce perceivable in the throat or fingers, finisheth the work, where art is the only power of performing.

We know that upon men's actions far more does depend than upon dancing and painting; their wisdom and virtue, their honour, life and happiness. And therefore more care ought to be exhibited in the actions of which their conversation is made up and accomplished. In their meats and drinks and recreations, it is apparent that without temperance there can be no success or order. The best wine in the world makes him that is lavish in the use of it a sot. The most wholesome and delicious meat upon earth by excess of eating, may turn to a surfeit. If sports and recreations take up all a man's time, his life is unprofitable. Their end is lost and their nature changed; for instead of recruiting, they consume one's strength; and instead of fitting a man for it, devour his calling.

An exact hand over all our passions and a diligent eye to extravagant actions tend much to our welfare, repose and honour. Loose and impertinent laughter, excessive cost in apparel, a lascivious wandering of the eyes, an ungoverned boldness which turns into impudence, an extremity of fear which degenerates into baseness, a morose and sour disposition, anxiety and needless care, immodest and violent strivings after things we too eagerly desire, inordinate love, too keen and bitter resentments,[2] a fierce and raging anger, a blockish stupidity, a predominant humour of melancholy, too much sloth and too much activity, too much talk and too much silence—all these are diligently to be ordered and avoided. For upon the right temperament of these we are made acceptable and amiable; and, being so, are full of authority, and can do, within the compass of virtue and reason, all that

[1] Movements.
[2] Sentiments.

we desire among our friends and companions, for our own good or the benefit of others. And by this means also we shall be admitted to the society and friendship of great men, where a nod or a word is able to prevail, more than the strength of oxen and horses among the dregs of the people. But, for lack of tempering these ingredients aright and as we ought, we become odious and insupportable, lose all esteem and interest, are rejected and trampled under feet, as vicious and deformed.

Here you may observe that all the qualities and dispositions in nature are ingredients and materials in our lives and conversations, and for the most part it is their excess or defect that makes the miscarriage, when we err in the mixture. There is a certain mixture of gravity and cheerfulness, remissness and severity, fear and boldness, anger and complacency, kindness and displeasure, care and carelessness, activity and idleness, sorrow and joy, forwardness and reservedness, nay, of envy, pride and revenge in every man's life, as well as of selfishness and flowing courtesy, plainness and policy—at least the grounds of these things, which are neither virtues nor vices in themselves, yet make conversation transcendently virtuous, when they are wisely tempered and united together.

I do not look upon ambition and avarice, nay, nor upon envy and revenge, as things that are evil in their root and fountain. If they be, temperance has a strange virtue in its nature, for, as chemists make antidotes of poisons, so doth this virtue turn the matter of all these into a quintessential perfection. Nay, selfishness and pride itself escape not its influence. A little touch of something like pride is seated in the true sense of a man's own greatness, without which his humility and modesty would be contemptible virtues. In all baseness of mind there is a kind of folly and cowardice apparent; and more veneration follows an humble man that is sensible of his excellency. An airy humour, without something of the melancholy to ballast it a little, would be light and trifling; and a melancholy humour, without something of air and jovialness in it, too sour and disobliging. Anger without softness is like untempered steel, brittle and destructive; and a pliant humour without some degree of stiffness, too near to flattery and servility. Anger is the matter and fuel of courage, and its appearance afar off puts a majesty into meekness, that makes it redoubted. A sorrowful humour, neatly allayed with a mixture of sweetness, begets a tenderness and compassion in the spectator, that turns into a deeper and more serious love. A little selfishness puts our companions in mind of our own interest, and makes them perceive that we understand it, which lends a lustre to our self-denial, and renders our liberality more safe and precious. Plainness without policy is downright simplicity, and policy without plainness void of honesty. The one makes us crafty and renders us suspected; the other exposes us and makes us ridiculous; but both united are venerable and prudent. By the appearance of revenge in its shady possibility, a man that never does other than actually forgive does oblige for what is past, yet threaten and discourage from the like offences. All these are the subjects of temperance. A little spice of jealousy and emulation are advantageous, in the midst of our security and resignation. They give a relish to our confidence in, and prelation [1] of, others; and make our security and civility taste of our love to the person we prefer, and of our love to virtue. There is not one humour, nor inclination, nor passion, nor power in the soul that may not be admitted to act its part, when directed by temperance.

Nor is it unlawful to alter the natural complexion by care and study. I know very well that the complexion of the body can hardly be changed by the strongest physic, and that choler and phlegm and abundance of blood will, where they are, have their natural course without any remedy. But the humours of the soul are more tractable things; they are all subject to the will in their operations; and though they incline, yet they cannot act but by consent and permission. I know furthermore that custom and habit is a second nature. What was difficult at first becomes at last as easy in its exercise as if it were innate; and that the soul of a virtuous man does in process of time act by a new disposition. I know further that all virtuous operations are free and voluntary, and that the office of virtue is to correct and amend an evil nature. Let no man therefore be disgusted, because a made-up man is artificial and not natural; for when the con-

[1] Preferment.

versation is sincerely guided to a good end, the more free and voluntary it is, it is the more noble; the more industry and desire a man expresses in attaining all these measures and perfections, they are the more virtuous; and the probity of his will is to be the more accepted. For virtues are not effects of nature but choice, which, how free soever it may appear, is as stable as the sun, when founded upon eternal principles. It secures any friend in the good and amiable qualities he desires in his beloved, as much as nature itself could do, though they depend upon the will, which is capable of changing every moment. This of temperance in the government of our humours.

I shall add but one note more, and that is, that a wise man discards the predominancy of all humours, and will not yield himself up to the empire of any; for he is to live the life of reason, not of humour. Nor will he have any humour of his own but what he can put off and on, as he sees occasion. He will cleave eternally to the rules of virtue, but will comply in his humour so far as to make his conversation sweet and agreeable to every temper. Religion and charity, as well as courtesy and civility, prompt to this; and where these concur with his reason and favour his interest, he may well do what St. Paul taught him, *become all things to all men, that he might gain some.* And this encouragement he hath; a man, by sacrificing his own, may comply with the satisfaction of all the world, and find his own far more great and honourable and sweet and amiable in the end, far more high and blessed in the love and esteem he shall obtain thereby, than if he had gratified his first inclination without any respect to the prelation [1] of others. It will bring him to the fruition of pleasures far greater than those he despised.

Temperance in the full composition and use of virtues is far more sublime, and more immediately approacheth the end of virtue, than any temperance in meats and drinks. It is resident nearer the throne of felicity, and seateth us by her. You may see its task as it is prescribed in prudence. But for example's sake, we will instance it in meekness, which of all the virtues is the most weak and naked. A meek spirit receiveth its temper, its encouragement, strength and facility from the union and con-

[1] Preferment.

currence of all the virtues. Knowledge is its light, and love the principle of its life and motion. Wisdom guideth it to the highest end. Righteousness is a great incentive thereto, while it teacheth us to esteem the favour of God, and the excellency of those souls whose value makes us tender of their repose, and prone to honour them with a due esteem, as well as to desire their peace and salvation. Holiness maketh us to delight in our duty. Goodness inclines us to sacrifice our own, to the welfare of others. Mercy leads us to pity their infirmities, and more to compassionate their misery than to be provoked with their distemper. Justice makes us to pay our Saviour's love and merits what we owe to Him. All these establish the habit of meekness in our souls. Fortitude does several ways conspire thereunto, for it makes us to adventure upon any trouble that we can fall into thereby, and puts a lustre upon us in the act of meekness. Patience habituates the soul to afflictions, and makes our sense of injuries easy. Repentance minds us of other employments than anger and revenge, even a contrite sorrow for our own offences. Humility gives us a sense of our own unworthiness, and a willingness to be yet more low than our enemies can make us. It inclines us also to confess that we have deserved far worse and more bitter evils, and to despise ourselves; which when we truly do, no injuries or wrongs can move us. Faith carries us up to higher enjoyments. Hope hath respect to the promised reward. Our love towards God enflames us with desire to please Him; charity to our neighbour is prone to forgive him. Prudence teacheth us to expect no figs from thorns, nor better entertainment from briars and brambles, but rather to right ourselves by improving their wrongs, and to turn their vices into our virtues. Magnanimity despiseth the courtship of worms, and scorneth to place its rest and felicity in trifles. Liberality is industrious to find out occasions of obliging and conquering. Contentment is fed by higher delights, and beautifies our meekness by a cheerful behaviour. Magnificence carries us to the most high and illustrious deeds, and by very great and expensive methods to multiply our favours and benefits on our beloved; for all are our beloved, whether friends or enemies. Temperance itself takes off the stupidity and sluggishness of our meekness, puts activity and vigour into it, that it may not be a sheepish but heroic virtue; nay, adorns, secures and perfects it by the addition and exercise of all these; and by giving to every other virtue its form and perfection, makes them more fit and able to aid and assist us here. It moderates our passions, and puts a better dose of life into our consideration. If there be any other virtue, it is not so remote but that it may lend us its helping hand, and be subservient to the perfection of our love and meekness. Which, however simple it may appear in solitude, is very strong and irresistible, amazing, as far from contempt as the sun is from darkness; when it is animated with courage, and made illustrious by love, enriched with liberality and made bright by knowledge; guided by wisdom to the highest end, and by prudence to well-known and advantageous, though inferior, purposes. When the soul appeareth neither foolish nor cowardly, nor base nor soft, but high and magnanimous in its operation, meekness is redoubted.

In the throne of glory, all the acts of faith and hope and repentance shall be for ever perfected, or swallowed up in fruition. The fruit of all occasional and transient virtues shall remain; the divine virtues shall be so firmly united that in their act and exercise they shall be one for ever. By knowledge we shall see all that the light of heaven and eternity can reveal. By love we shall embrace all that is amiable before God and His holy angels. By wisdom we shall use the most glorious means for the attainment and enjoyment of the highest end, which is God in all His joys and treasures. In the use of those means we must actually enjoy all blessedness and glory. Righteousness and holiness, and goodness and charity, shall, with all the rest, be the lineaments and colours of the mind, the graces and beauties of the blessed soul. They shall shine upon its face, and itself shall be glorious in the perfection of their beauty, as God is. Its goodness shall make it a fountain of delights to all the other creatures. It shall be all humility, yet all enjoyment; amazed at its own nothingness and vileness, yet ravished with wonder and the height of its felicity. For the lower it is in its own eyes, the more great doth the goodness of God appear, and the more transcendently sweet is its adoration and satisfaction. By its gratitude it sacrifices itself eternally to the deity, and taketh more pleasure in His glory than its own. It is all godliness and contentment.

All these virtues are exercised together in the state of glory, not so much by our own temperance as by the infusion of His most heavenly grace, who fills us with His own fullness and perfection by way of reward; and, causing us to enter into His eternal rest, maketh us to cease from our own works, as He also did from His, by inspiring us with his own wisdom, life and strength, and actuating all our powers by His own for ever; that we, by virtue of His grace infused, may live in the image of His eternal moderation, and attain the extremity of bliss and glory, which He hath (exceeding His almighty power) by an exquisite and mysterious temperance in all His operations divinely attained.

CHAPTER XXIII

Of Temperance in God. How the moderation of Almighty Power, guided in its works by wisdom, perfecteth the creation. How it hath raised His own glory and our felicity beyond all that simple power could effect by its infiniteness

IF moderation hath such happy effects in men, where the strength is small, the wisdom little, the matter base, the occasion low, as in divers instances it is manifest it hath, how glorious must this virtue be, where the power is almighty, the wisdom infinite, the subject-matter perfect, the end and the occasion most divine and glorious!

It would seem a strange paradox to say that almighty power could not exist without infinite wisdom; but it is infinitely true, for the wisdom and power of God are one. No blind power can be almighty, because it cannot do all that is excellent. That power would without wisdom be blind is as evident as the sun; the want of that being as great an impediment to its operations as the lack of eyes is to a man upon earth; which so eclipseth and darkeneth his power that he cannot perform those excellent works to which light is necessary. There is no blind power in God, and therefore no power distinct from His understanding. *By His wisdom He made the heavens, by His understanding He established the earth. By His knowledge the depths are broken up, and the clouds drop down the dew.*

Wisdom is the tree of life, which beareth all the fruits of immortality and honour. Inartificial violence will never carry it. There is a mark to be hit, and that is in everything what is most fair and eligible. It may be missed as much by shooting over it as by falling short of it. Naked power cannot tell what to propose as its aim and object. Only that which is able to contrive is able to effect its desire, in the work it conceiveth most fit and excellent for its power to perform.

It is a stranger paradox yet, that power limited is greater and more effectual than power let loose; for this importeth that power is more infinite when bounded than power in its utmost liberty. But that which solveth the riddle and removeth all inconvenience [1] is our assurance of this, that God can do nothing but what is wise, and that His wisdom therefore is all His power. And of this it followeth, that nothing is possible with God but what is infinitely excellent; for to do anything less than the best is unwise and, being so, is contrary to the nature of wisdom, which is His power.

The will of God is His wisdom. By the mere motion of His will He created all things; and therefore it is His power. His power and His wisdom meet in His will, and both are the same. By His word He made the worlds, and His eternal word is His eternal wisdom.

All this I speak because it is the office of wisdom to propose the most excellent end, and to pursue it by the most efficacious means; and because the wisdom of God will be found one with His eternal moderation.

The utmost end of all that is aimed at is indeed illimited. It is the best and greatest thing that infinite and eternal wisdom could conceive; but, being out of all measure high and excellent, in includeth innumerable virtues, that are shut up in bounds for their greater perfection. Whereupon it followeth that God hath

[1] Difficulty.

attained a more excellent effect than if He had made any one thing singly infinite.

His love being infinite and eternal, in sacrificing itself in all its works for its object's welfare, became an infinite and eternal act; which was not contented unless, in all its works, it added art unto power, and exerted its wisdom in all its productions. Had it made one infinite, some are of opinion it had exceeded itself; at least, done all that was possible, both for itself and for its object; and that one infinite, being so created, must be its only object. For more than infinite what can be? We are apt to think that nothing can be beside. But to show that God is infinitely more than what we conceive, while we think Him infinite, and that we infinitely wrong Him while we limit His essence to one single infinity, who is every way infinite—in Himself, in all His works, in all His ways, in all His counsels, in every one of His perfections—He hath made everything either infinite or better than so. For by variety of effects He hath attained an end in the beauty and correspondence of all His productions, far more amiable and divine than any one effect is capable of being. All things by a kind of temperance are made and ordered in number, weight and measure, so that they give and receive a beauty and perfection, everything to and from all the residue, of inestimable value, in relation to the goodness and love of their Creator.

I doubt not but God, would His wisdom have permitted such a thing, could have made an infinite object. For wherever God is, He is able to act; and His omnipresence is infinite wisdom and power which, filling immensity, is able to exert itself beyond all the bounds of space in an infinite manner all at once. If it do so, it cannot rest in a less attainment than one that answers the measures of its operation. If it did, that attainment would be infinitely defective; for infinite wisdom could certainly conceive one infinitely better. But this I will aver, that God hath wrought abundantly more than if He had made any one single effect of His power infinite. He hath wrought a work that pleaseth Him infinitely better, and so will it please us, when we are wise as He is.

Had He made any one single infinite, it must be either corporeal or spiritual; be it either, there is room enough in His understanding and omnipresence to receive it. Empty space is an infinite object in His understanding. But for the glory of His moderation, it is evident that He hath attained a far greater and more perfect end.

Had he made an infinite object of a spiritual nature, it must be a spirit endued with illimited power, to see His omnipresence and eternity. And had He made no more than only this, it is to be feared that the spectator would be displeased for want of objects, in preparing which the love of God should have glorified His wisdom and goodness for its fruition.

If you say, the omnipresence and eternity of God had been filled with that creature, it is evident that spirits fill no room, though they see all things; and that it had been much better if objects had been prepared for its enjoyment.

Had he prepared any one corporeal object for the fruition of that creature, any corporeal object if infinite in its dimensions would be wholly useless, nay, pernicious and destructive; for it would exclude all other beings to which it might be serviceable, out of place, and have nothing whereto to be beneficial.

If you say it would be beneficial to God, or to that spectator, or that intelligible power, that spirit for whom it was made, it is apparent that no corporeal being can be serviceable to a spirit but only by the beauty of those services it performeth to other corporeals, that are capable of receiving them; and that therefore all corporeals must be limited and bounded for each other's sake. And for this cause it is that a philosophical poet [1] hath said:

As in a clock 'tis hindered-force doth bring
The wheels to ordered motion by a spring,
Which ordered motion guides a steady hand
In useful sort at figures just to stand,
Which, were it not by counter-balance stayed
The fabric quickly would aside be laid
As wholly useless: so a might too great,
But well proportioned, makes the world complete.
Power well-bounded is more great in might

[1] i.e. Traherne.

Than if, let loose, 'twere wholly infinite.
He could have made an endless sea by this,
But then it had not been a sea of bliss.
A sea that's bounded in a finite shore
Is better far because it is no more.
Should waters endlessly exceed the skies
They'd drown the world, and all whate'er we prize.
Had the bright sun been infinite, its flame
Had burnt the world and quite consumed the same.
That flame would yield no splendour to the sight,
'Twould be but darkness, though 'twere infinite.
One star made infinite would all exclude,
An earth made infinite could ne'er be viewed.
But all being bounded for each other's sake
He, bounding all, did all most useful make.
And which is best, in profit and delight,
Though not in bulk, He made all infinite.
He in His wisdom did their use extend,
By all, to all the world from end to end.
In all things, all things service do to all,
And thus a sand is endless, though most small,
And everything is truly infinite,
In its relation deep and exquisite.

This is the best way of accommodating things to the service of each other, for the fruition of all spectators.

Moderation is not so called from limiting and restraining, but from moderating and ruling. If reason require that a thing should be great, it is the part of temperance to make it so. Where reason requires, it is a point of moderation to enlarge and extend power; nay, to stretch it out to the utmost of its capacity, if wisdom order it, is but equal. To moderate almighty power is to limit or extend it, as reason requires. Reason requires that it should be so limited and extended as most tends to the perfection of the universe.

If it be more wise, and more tends to the perfection of the universe, that millions of intelligible spirits should be created, and every one of them be made infinite in understanding, it shall be done; if not, temperance forbears. If sands and atoms tend more to the perfection of the world than angels, there where they do so sands and atoms shall be made, and angels there where they tend more to the perfection of the world. So that everything is best in its proper place. Were there no sands or atoms, there would be no universe; for the earth, the sea, the sky, the air, all bodies consist of these, either united or divided. If they had been left unmade, and angels had been created in their places, there had been no visible world at all.

To make visible objects useful, it was necessary to enshrine some spirits in corporeal bodies, and therefore to make such creatures as men, that might see and feel, and smell and taste and hear, and eat and drink, by their bodies, and enjoy all the pleasures of the world by their souls. And by their souls, moreover, know the original and end of all, understand the design of all, and be able to celebrate the praises of the Creator. For by this means pure essences abstracted from all corporeity might enjoy the world, while they delight in the glory of its uses, and especially in those complete and amiable creatures for whom it was prepared.

It was expedient also to make their bodies finite, that they might converse together; but their inward intelligence of endless reach, that they might see the holy angels, delight in them and by their love be delightful to them; that they might also be able to search into the depth of all things,and enjoy eternity; nay, that they might be fit recipients for the infinite bounty and goodness of God, which is infinite in its communications.

That they should be subject to His laws and depend upon Him was necessary in like manner. For by that distinction an infinite difference was between Him and them; that disparity being laid in the foundation. Though the benefits they receive are altogether infinite, the distance is still the more infinite between them; for the greater the bounty is, the greater the obligation. The love and service they owe is infinite, and so is the gratitude.

To see all His glory is to be able to admire it, and to adore it with infinite amazement and joy; which is to be completely just unto it, and perfectly blessed.

There is but one thing more, wherein almighty power was,

by wisdom infinite, to restrain itself for the perfection of His kingdom; and that is, to create them free that were made to enjoy it. Not to determine their wills by a fatal necessity, but to make their esteem and fruition of God and His works their duty, and to leave them to themselves for the more free and voluntary discharge of their duty. For by that means, it would make them capable of rewards and punishments, in the righteous distribution of which the nature and the glory of a righteous kingdom consisteth.

Thus did God, by infinite moderation and by a sublime and transcendent temperance prepare His kingdom, and make everything exquisite in His whole dominion, to the praise of His glory and the satisfaction of His infinite and eternal reason; the similitude of which reason being the essence of the soul, all these things fall out for our glory and satisfaction also.

Now if God Himself acquired all His joys by temperance, and the glory of His kingdom is wholly founded in His moderation, we may hope that our moderation and temperance in its place may accomplish wonders, and lead us to the fruition of His, by certain steps and degrees; like those that are observed in the womb towards manhood, and in the school of our childhood towards perfect learning.

Too much rain or too much drought will produce a famine; the earth is made fertile by a seasonable mixture of heat and moisture. Excess of power may overwhelm, but moderation is that which perfecteth and blesseth the creation.

Almighty power is carried far beyond itself, or really is made almighty, by virtue of that temperance, wherein eternal wisdom is eternally glorified.

If anything be wanting to the full demonstration of the perfection of God's kingdom, it is the consideration of His delay; for we are apt to think, He might have made it eternally before He did. But to this no other answer is necessary (though many might be made) than that all things were from all eternity before His eyes, and He saw the fittest moments wherein to produce them; and judged it fit, in His wisdom, first to fill eternity with His deliberations and counsels, and then to beautify time with the execution of His decrees. For were there no more to be said but this, His empire is eternal, because all possibilities, nay, and all impossibilities, are subject to His will. But if it be confessed that eternity is an everlasting moment, infinite in duration but permanent in all its parts, all things past, present and to come are at once before Him, and eternally together. Which is the true reason why eternity is a standing object before the eye of the soul, and all its parts, being full of beauty and perfection, for ever to be enjoyed.

If any man be disposed to cavil further, that God might at the very first have placed angels and men in the state of glory, the reply is at hand: that God very well understandeth the beauty of proportion, that harmony and symmetry springs from a variety of excellent things in several places, fitly answering to and perfecting each other; that the state of trial and the state of glory are so mysterious in their relation that neither without the other could be absolutely perfect. Innumerable beauties would be left, and many transcendent virtues and perfections be abolished with the estate of trial, if that had been laid aside; the continual appearance and effect of which is to enrich and beautify the kingdom of God everlastingly. That God loveth man far more than if He had placed him in the throne at first, and designeth more glory and perfection for him than in that dispensation he could have been capable of; all which springeth from the restraint of His power in some occasions, that it might more fully be exerted in the perfection of the whole and, of all things that were possible to be made, might end in the supreme and most absolutely blessed.

Therefore upon the whole matter we may conclude with Solomon, *Happy is the man that findeth wisdom, and the man that getteth understanding. For the merchandise of it is better than the merchandise of silver, and the gold thereof than of fine gold. She is more precious than rubies, and all the things thou canst desire are not to be compared with her. Length of days is in her right hand, and in her left hand riches and honour. Her ways are ways of pleasantness, and all her paths are peace. She is a tree of life to them that lay hold upon her, and happy is every one that retaineth her. The Lord by wisdom hath founded the earth; by understanding hath He established the heavens. My son, let not them depart from thine eyes. Keep sound wisdom and discretion.*

Wisdom is the principal thing; therefore get wisdom and, with all thy getting, get understanding. For the same wisdom which created the world is the only light wherein it is enjoyed.

CHAPTER XXIV

Of Patience. Its original. How God was the first patient person in the world. The nature and the glory and the blessed effects of His eternal patience. The reason and design of all calamities. Of patience in martyrdom. The extraordinary reward of ordinary patience in its meanest obscurity

PATIENCE is a virtue of the third estate. It belongs not to the estate of innocence, because in it there was no affliction; nor to the estate of misery, because in it there is no virtue; but to the estate of grace it appertains, because it is an estate of reconciliation, and an estate of trial, wherein affliction and virtue meet together. In the estate of glory there is no patience.

This is one of those distasteful virtues, which God never intended. It received its bitterness from sin, its life and beauty from God's mercy. If we dislike this virtue, we may thank ourselves, for we made God first to endure it. And if all things are rightly weighed, no creature is equal to God in sufferings. We made it necessary for the eternal Godhead to be incarnate, and to suffer all the incommodities of life, and the bitter torments of a bloody death, that He might bear the penance of our sins, and deliver us from eternal perdition.

The corporeal sufferings of our Saviour are not comparable to the afflictions of His spirit. Nor are there any sufferings or losses so great as those we cast upon the Godhead. He infinitely hateth sin, more than death, and had rather be crucified a thousand times over than that one transgression should be brought into the world. Nothing is so quick and tender as love, nothing so lively and sensible in resenting.[1] No loss is comparable to that of souls, nor any one so deeply concerned in the loss as God Almighty; no calamity more piercing than to see the glory of His work made vain; to be bereaved of His desire, and frustrated of His end in the whole creation. He had rather we should give Him the blood of dragons or the cruel venom of asps to drink than that we should pollute ourselves or His kingdom with a sin. Nay, it were better (if without a sin it could be done) that the whole world should be annihilated than a sin committed. For the world might be created again with ease, and all that is in it be repaired with a word; but a sin once committed can never be undone; it will appear in its place throughout all eternity, yet is so odious, and so infinitely opposed to the holiness of God, that no gall or wormwood is comparable thereunto.

To see his beloved blasted, his love despised and his son rebellious; to see the most amiable law in the world broken, His kingdom laid waste and His image defaced; to see all His labour marred and spoiled, His benefits slighted and His infinite goodness abused and undervalued; all obligations imposed and all rewards prepared in vain, is worse than to see one's palace on fire as soon as it is builded, or one's wife smitten with leprosy and one's only beloved son run mad. For a child to trample on his father's bowels is nothing in comparison. He therefore that feels what he made God to endure, what grapes of Sodom and clusters of Gomorrah he offered to His teeth; how evil a thing and bitter it is, to forsake God; how the Scripture saith, *He was grieved at the heart,* when He saw the corruption and impiety of the earth; and how the sorrow inflicted was so sore as to make Him *repent that He had made man* in the world—he surely will be more concerned at the evil he hath done than at any evil he can otherwise suffer; and his godly sorrow, as Moses' rod did eat up all the rods of the Egyptians, will devour all other sorrows whatsoever.

To consider that God was the first patient person in the world must needs sweeten the bitterness of patience, and make it acceptable unto us. To consider that we alone brought it upon ourselves, and may thank ourselves for the folly of its introduction

[1] Feeling.

must make us, out of very indignation against ourselves, contented to suffer, and in pure justice quietly to digest it. But to consider yet further, that God, by bearing our offences with patience, took off the trouble of them from us and, by refusing to ease Himself of the greatness of His displeasure in pouring it back again on our own heads, digested it so as to turn our eternal torments into transitory woes—nay, into His own agonies and pains on the cross—this will help our reason to rejoice at *our light afflictions which are but for a moment;* especially since they *work out for us a far more exceeding and eternal weight of glory.*

The first impression of that abominable mischief, which occasioned patience in God, made it a calamity but not a virtue. Detestation and grief in themselves are but sufferings, and mere sufferings have no virtue, nor so much almost as action in them. If His detestation and grief had broken out in impatience, we had all been destroyed; anger and fury had poured down upon us. That which made it a virtue was the great and mighty continence whereby it was kept in and governed for all our benefit. For it was full of goodness and compassion and mercy and love; and that was indeed the virtue of patience, in which so much magnanimity and government did appear, so much wisdom and steadfastness and immutability. And upon this virtue of that act whereby He restrained His displeasure, the whole kingdom of grace, and the glory of His mercy and love, and the blessedness and exaltation of His church is founded. It depended upon it, and from His patience it proceeded.

Patience, then, is that virtue by which we behave ourselves constantly and prudently in the midst of misfortunes and troubles; that virtue whereby we do not only forbear to break out in murmurings and repinings, or support ourselves from sinking under afflictions, or suppress our discontentments and refrain from anger and disquiet; but whereby we retain our wisdom and the goodness of our mind, notwithstanding all the confusions and disorders that would disturb us, and demean [1] ourselves in a serene and honourable manner, surmounting the pains and calamities that trouble us and that would otherwise overwhelm us; while we move in a quick and vigorous manner under our burden, and by

[1] Behave.

a true courage improve our afflictions, and turn them into the spoils of invincible reason.

It is an easy observation, that troublous times are the seasons of honour, and that a warlike field is the seed-plot of great and heroical actions. Men that live in quiet and peaceful ages pass through the world as insensibly as if they had been all their days asleep. Hazards and calamities and battles and victories fill the annals with wonder, and raise great men to an eminent degree of fame and glory. It is St. Chrysostom's opinion, that a man shows far greater bravery that grapples with a disease or surmounts his evil fortune, or behaves himself with courage in distress, bears the burning of his house, or the loss of his goods, or the death of his children, with an equal spirit; in the midst of all calamities retains his integrity with humility and patience, and blesses God, cheerfully submitting with resignation to His will, and shows himself constant in all estates, than he that in the midst of a prosperous condition buildeth houses and temples, shineth in the exercise of bounty and magnificence, and obligeth all the world, without any other expense than that of his moneys. A pelican that feeds her young ones with her blood is a more noble bird than an eagle, that fills her nest with ravine, though taken from the altar; for though that of a sacrifice be the more sacred food, that of one's own blood is more near and costly.

Times of affliction are seed-times for a future harvest. We are made perfect through sufferings; though the way be mysterious and the manner almost incomprehensible, whereby the sufferings we endure conduce to our perfection. Consider the patience of Job, how great a spectacle his sufferings made him to God, angels and men, and how glorious he became by his patience to all generations.

This virtue has an appearance, by reason of its objects and materials, so cross [1] to its disposition that, if anything be difficult in all nature to be understood, patience is one, it being a thing of the most deep and obscure value. Its nature and effect seem contrary to each other. It raises a man by depressing him; it elevates by overwhelming, it honours by debasing, it saves by killing him. By making a man little and nothing, it magnifies

[1] Contrary.

and exalts him. No act of love is attended with such bleeding circumstances as that of cruel resolution, in exposing ourselves to all calamities that can befall our souls, for our beloved's sake. It is the glory of the Good Shepherd that *he lays down his life for the sheep.* And for this very cause is our Saviour honoured by God and men, *because being in the form of God he made himself of no reputation, but took on himself the form of a servant,* and died the most cursed death of the cross, for the sake of the world. *Wherefore,* saith the text (that is, *for which very cause*) *God also hath highly exalted him, and given him a name which is above every name; that at the name of Jesus every knee should bow, of things in the heaven, things in the earth and things under the earth.*

Nor is this gift of God so purely arbitrary but that it has a foundation in nature. Angels and men do not bow their knees only because they are commanded, but because they see reason to incline them to bow their knees. There is something in our Saviour's nature, action and merit that deserves it at their hands. The wonderful love wherewith He loved us is the root, the soul and glory of His passion. It is wonderful as it made Him willing to become death and sin and a curse for us. But the height of our ecstasy is in the reality of His passion, and in the full accomplishment of all its purposes.

It is the virtue of love which is infused into patience, and the chief elixir of its nature is founded in the excellency of a spirit that suffers for another's sake. This therefore we ought ever to remember, that patience, when it is a virtue, springs from love; and that this love is chiefly towards God and next that to our neighbour. When we suffer anything for God's sake, or for our neighbour's good, we suffer in a wise and virtuous manner. And the honour which follows such a suffering is the crown of glory which it shall for ever wear. It is a vain and stupid thing to suffer without loving God or man. Love is a transcendent excellence in every duty, and must of necessity enter into the nature of every grace and virtue. That which maketh the solid benefit of patience unknown, its taste so bitter and comfortless to men, is its death in the separation and absence of its soul. We suffer, but love not. Otherwise, love to the person for whose sake we suffer is its own support and comfort. It makes the action to be valuable, and infuses a sweetness into all the affliction it can make us endure; a sweetness answerable to the welfare and pleasure which is either caused or secured to our object thereby. Our own growth in the approbation and esteem of the person we love is the desirable greatness which we covet to attain; which can no way be confirmed and increased so perfectly as by suffering for him. For our fidelity, sincerity, reality, vigour, life and industry can never be made so fair and apparent as when we pursue our love, and are carried by it to the utmost extremities of death and misery; and labour through all disasters, persecutions and calamities to obey and honour and please and glorify the object which, in times of quiet, we pretend [1] to love. In an easy and prosperous estate, there is little difference between friendship and flattery; but he that sticks firm in calamity is a friend indeed. The trial of love consists in the difficulties it endures for its beloved.

And for this cause it is that God will expose us to so severe a trial; Himself ordaining some trials in the beginning, but permitting more, when we brought them upon ourselves. Many also He suffereth to come, which we daily bring upon our own heads by our own folly. Some He inflicteth perhaps Himself, for the chastisement of our sins or the medicine of our souls; to abate our confidence and to excite our care; to awaken us out of our lethargy, and to quicken our sense both of our miserable condition and our need of His favour; to humble our rebellion, to heal and purge our corruptions, to moderate our passions, to heighten our penitence, to abate our pride, to increase our ardour in devotion and prayer; to make our subjection to and dependence upon Him clear; to stir us up to a more strict examination of ourselves in our thoughts, words and deeds, lest some Jonas or other should lie in the ship, that continues the tempest upon us; to enkindle our compassion towards our afflicted brethren, and to enflame us with more perfect zeal and love towards God. It is like wormwood that embitters the nipple, to wean us from the world, and augment our desire *to be dissolved and to be with Christ;* to make us groan after our eternal rest, and long for *the glorious liberty of the sons of God.*

[1] Profess.

Sometimes He suffereth tribulations and trials to come upon us by the perverseness of men who, being left at liberty in their dominion over the world, are the principal authors of all the troubles and disorders in it. To know the several springs and sources of affliction is very expedient; for our patience and contentment much dependeth upon it. A confused apprehension makes us blind, but a clear sight distinguisheth between the will of God and the corruption of nature; which in ourselves and others is the principal cause of all our disturbances.

Be it by which of all these occasions it will, or for which of all these ends it can befall us, it is evermore to increase our conquest, and to make us like the King of Sufferings, pure and perfect. And the consideration of God's over-ruling power and providence therein, which makes all these things to work together for our good, begetteth a grateful admiration in us, as well as a sense of our dependence on His goodness; which increaseth the fear of God in our souls, and animates us with great wonder that He should put His hand to touch the vile and evil offspring of our sin, and turn all into good, and make it to rest in our exaltation and glory by His wisdom and mercy.

Concerning God's end in bringing and permitting all these evils, the scripture is very frequent. It was one of Job's contemplations, *What is man, that thou shouldst magnify him, and that thou shouldst set thine heart upon him, and that thou shouldst visit him every morning, and try him every moment?* Man is magnified by his trials. It was David's observation, *The Lord is in his holy temple; the Lord's throne is in heaven. His eyes behold, his eyelids try the children of men. The Lord trieth the righteous; but the wicked and him that loveth violence his soul hateth.* It was Daniel's prophecy, *And some of them of understanding shall fall, to try them, and to purge and to make them white, even to the time of the end.* God Himself expresseth His own resolution, *I will bring part of them through the fire, and will refine them as silver is refined, and try them as gold is tried. They shall call on my name, and I will hear them. I will say, It is my people; and they shall say, The Lord is my God.*

The meaning of all which places is, not as if God did stand in need of all these trials to know what is in us; for He knoweth what is in man from all eternity; before these trials come, *He searcheth the heart and trieth the reins,* and discerneth the thoughts and purposes of the soul. He seeth every inclination in the seed, every grace in the secret habit of the mind, and every virtue in the root. They lie in the seed, but yet He seeth a mighty difference between quiet habits and effectual operations; for they differ as much as the root and the blossom, or the blossom and the fruit. For virtues to lie asleep in the soul, and for virtues to be actually and fully perfected, is as great a difference as for a vine to be of a generous kind and prone to bear, but to remain without fruit, or for a vine to bring forth and to be really laden with all the bunches of grapes that beautify it. The excellency of its nature is vain, if its fruit be never brought to perfection.

There is a glory in the work which the silent habit is uncapable of. It is the life and vigour of the exercise in which all the brightness consisteth. Even diamonds in the quarry are dull and dim; they receive not their full lustre and price till they are cut and polished. God hath placed our trial in sharp and bitter achievements; because the love that is expressed in agonies and conflicts acquires other kind of beauties, that produce more violent and strong effects in the mind of the spectator, and touch the soul of the beloved with more quick and feeling compassions, than any love expressed in ease and pleasure can pretend to.

And since all our felicity consists in the violence of God's love, His great and perfect sense of our beauty and honour, His full and complete delight and complacency, all that which affects His soul with more feeling and tender resentment,[1] must be very dear and precious to us, because it maketh us more dear and precious to Him. We live in Him more effectually, and feel ourselves rooted in His love, and crowned with His complacency [2] more abundantly, by how much the more His affection bleedeth and His pity, which embalms love, is stirred up to receive us. And therefore is it that St. Peter saith, *We are in heaviness for a season through our manifold temptations, that the trial of our faith, being much more precious than of gold that perisheth, though it be tried with fire, might be found unto praise and honour and glory at the appearing of Jesus Christ.*

[1] Sentiment. [2] Pleasure.

For, as we have before observed, love is more effeminate in a condition of repose, where all is sweet and easy to ourselves. There can be no fidelity, no patience, no fortitude, no actual sacrificing of all our contentments and joys to our beloved; no victory over death and hell and the grave; no endearments springing from the same, no prelation[1] of our object above ourselves; no loss of honour, riches, liberties and lives for our object's sake; and the more this is actually done, the more of necessity must be the following joy of glory. And for this cause doth St. Peter further exhort us, *Beloved, think it not strange concerning the fiery trial which is to try you, as though some strange thing happened unto you; but rejoice, inasmuch as ye are partakers of Christ's sufferings; that, when his glory is revealed, you may be glad also with exceeding joy. If ye be reproached for the name of Christ, happy are ye, for the spirit of glory and of God resteth upon you. On their part he is evil spoken of, but on your part he is glorified.*

This he speaketh, I confess, of the persecutions, imprisonments and flames of the martyrs, that were God's friends and the champions of His truth in the world, that in vindication of His glory endured the brunt and received all the arrows of His enemies in their bosom; but no man has cause to be discouraged. For where the greatness of the cause is wanting, and the apparent glory of the consequence unseen, as for the most part it is in all our common and ordinary afflictions, there to submit to the will of God—where there is so much baseness as in poverty; in sickness, where there is so much unprofitableness; in private losses and calamities, where there is so much obscurity—merely because it is God's pleasure, and because in other things He hath infinitely obliged us and prepared infinite and eternal joys, this hath a peculiar grace in its nature that, in ordinary occurrences, makes our patience more rare and extraordinary.

There are a thousand things that may be said on this theme, which for brevity I must pass. All I shall observe further is this: that as the scriptures open the design of patience and unveil the face of its mysterious nature, so doth reason show its invincible height and magnanimity. Patience is a virtue whose element is in miseries. It owes its being to pains and calamities; were

[1] Preferment.

there no miseries, there could be no patience. Evils are its playfellows; it feeds upon sorrows, thrives by disadvantages, grows rich by poverties. It must needs surmount all opposition, for the more it endures, the greater it is. It is impossible for calamity to hurt patience; it is made perfect by sufferings. The more patient a man is, his patience is the greater; and the greater his patience is, the more strong and mighty his soul is. Nothing can quell him, or discourage or overcome him that is complete in patience. He dareth all things, because he can endure them. All his martial and heroical virtues are knit together in patience. Fortitude itself cannot win the field without it. The most valiant soldier is but useless if he cannot endure hunger and cold, and heat and rain, the incommodities of a march and lying on the ground; while he that endures all things marches on, and gets into the field where fidelity, love and loyalty are tried; and cannot be hindered from the full and perfect exercise of all these, because he can bear anything that is evil, he can do anything that is good. He will fight the good fight with alacrity, and at last most certainly attain the crown of righteousness and the King's favour.

CHAPTER XXV

The cause of Meekness is love. It respects the future beauty and perfection of its object. It is the most supernatural of all the virtues. The reasons and grounds of this virtue in the estate of grace and misery. Its manifold effects and excellencies. Of the meekness of Moses and Joseph

MEEKNESS is a virtue of the third estate, as well as patience. Patience regards calamities, meekness wrongs. The injuries that we receive from others are its proper objects. It springs from love, and tends to its continuance and preservation. It hath something peculiar in its nature, because it gives immutability to goodness, and makes our worth not to depend on other men's deservings, but our own resolutions. It is fed by charity and, like a grateful offspring of a parent so amiable, helps in its greatest extremity to preserve it from extinction. For all love by nature dies into distaste, when its object hath offended; because approbation, which is the first step to esteem, and esteem itself, which is a degree to love, have no other object but something that is amiable and fit to be beloved. And again, everything that is divested of all its excellence is common, if not odious, and lost to our affection, till meekness comes in to rescue and save both our love and it from its dismal period. Its end is the recovery of what has offended; hope and possibility are the foundation of its exercise. Prudence is the guide by which it is conducted to the satisfaction of our desire in the restitution of amity between us and our adversary.

Where there is no hope that the beauty of what we love may be regained, meekness hath lost its virtue, and with that its existence. For if it be impossible that an evil person should ever be reclaimed, it is to no purpose to be meek. He that can never be delightful more is utterly useless; meekness, therefore, which derives its solidity and power from its end, is in such cases utterly abolished. For this cause it is that we are to esteem our Saviour's blood the ground on which it stands; since all nature, without His incarnation, death and passion, could never restore a sinner to the possibility of becoming just and amiable. This virtue of meekness respects the future beauty and perfection of an object that is now deformed. It must needs be of transcendent excellency, since the practice of meekness is acquired by the price of our Saviour's blood, and the first step to its exercise did cost the death of the eternal God.

It is a transcendent virtue, because the means of introducing it are wholly supernatural. It carries us above all the rules of nature, above all the principles of reason, and in that is supernatural. For by reason we are to be just and good towards all that are innocent, and kind to all those to whom kindness is due; but it is not by nature either just or rational that we should love any creature that is evil; and how God came to do it is an infinite wonder. Though now, since He hath first loved us who are so vile, nothing is more natural than that we should do as we are done unto—imitate Him, and love those whom our Creator loveth; with pity and benevolence at first, that we may hereafter do it with full complacency.[1]

That human nature is infinitely exalted by the incarnation of the Son of God is confessed by all those that believe the article of our Saviour's incarnation. That the earth, how base soever it seem, is the bride of heaven, its own quiet, and the embrace of the skies (that make it the centre of all their revolutions) sufficiently demonstrate; though few have observed that the sun and moon and stars dance attendance to it, and cherish it with their influences, while the earthly globe is crowned with the fruits of all their secret endeavours. That the angels desire to look down into those things which are done upon earth, the very scriptures witness. And yet, for all this, it would seem a new doctrine to affirm that there are works done here upon earth that are by nature above the heavens. Yet all the operations of the Holy Ghost and all the good works of holy men, especially the meekness and patience of the saints (which are founded on the greatest miracle in all eternity, the love of God to sinners, and His stupendous humiliation and passion for them) are set upon a higher basis than all nature, except that of the deity, can afford unto us. Which note I make for our greater encouragement to the works of meekness. They are all in nature like the effects of our Saviour's love to the greatest offenders. Reason itself is now exalted above all its former heights, and there is reason, since our Saviour's death, for the doing of that which no reason, before He designed to forgive and die for us, could lead us to do.

That God by the greatness of His love may condescend to such indignities as are infinitely unworthy of Him we see by the examples of kings and queens and other high and delicate personages, that suffer their children to play with their beards and the tresses of their hair, which other persons dare not so much as approach, for the reverence of their majesty. I have oftentimes admired[2] at the mean offices to which parents stoop, and the familiar boldness they permit to their little ones, to play with their sceptres and crowns, and eyes and lips, with their breasts

[1] Delight.
[2] Wondered.

and jewels; and sometimes to pinch and hurt, nay, and to defile them too, being unmindful of their state, and far from all anger and indignation. But the free pardon and desire of the return of vicious and debauched children is a nearer instance and resemblance of God in His gracious dispensations, who suffers all nature still to attend us, though we continually profane His name and injure His eternal goodness by our manifold transgressions.

This example of God, who died for sinners in the person of His Son, and prayed for His tormentors in the very act of their cruelty and rage against Him, should prevail with us to esteem all those whom He owneth for His children as our own bowels, and to be as meek and condescending to all mankind as parents are to their children; the reasons of which duty are thus variously offered to our consideration.

To labour after those principles only that establish our repose in the estate of bliss and innocency is utterly impertinent [1] to our present condition.

> Were all the world a paradise of ease
> 'Twere easy then to live in peace.
> Were all men wise, divine and innocent,
> Just, holy, peaceful and content,
> Kind, loving, true and always good,
> As in the golden age they stood—
> 'Twere easy then to live
> In all delights and glory, full of love,
> Blest as the angels are above.
>
> But we such principles must now attain,
> (If we true blessedness would gain)
> As those are which will help to make us reign
> Over disorders, injuries,
> Ingratitudes, calamities,
> Affronts, oppressions, slanders, wrongs,
> Lies, angers, bitter tongues;
> The reach of malice must surmount, and quell
> The very rage and power of hell.

[1] Irrelevant.

No man but He that came down from heaven, and gave His apostles power to handle vipers and drink any deadly thing without harm, was able to reveal the way of peace and felicity to sinners. He and only He, that made them able to trample Satan under feet, and taught them how to vanquish all the powers of darkness, was worthy to make known this glorious mystery of patience and meekness, by which, in despite of all the corruptions and violences in the world, the holy soul of a quiet man is armed and prepared for all assaults; and so environed with its own repose that in the midst of provocations it is undisturbed, and dwells as it were in a sanctuary of peace within itself, in a paradise of bliss, while it is surrounded with the howlings of a terrible wilderness. Nothing else can make us live happily in the world; for among so many causes of anger and distaste, no man can live well but he that carries about him perpetual antidotes and victories.

There are two things absolutely necessary to felicity; outward security and inward contentment. Meekness is as it were the bulwark of security which, though it be as soft as wool, is able with more success to repel the violence of a cannon-bullet than the rough temper of a stone wall. Contentment springs from the satisfaction of desire in the sight and fruitions of all treasures and glories. And as the sun is surrounded with its own light, the felicity of the enjoyment becomes its own fortress and security. For he that is thoroughly happy has so much work to do in contemplation and thanksgiving that he cannot have while [1] to be concerned with other men's disorders. He loves his employment too well to be disturbed, and will not allow himself the thoughts of revenge or anger.

In two things meekness is greatly profitable to a man's self, possession and triumph. He that permits the tumult of this world to enter into his soul, and suffers the temple of the Holy Ghost to be defiled with rage and anger, makes it an unfit habitation for the blessed Spirit. Doves will not dwell in pigeon-houses disturbed, or haunted with vermin; nor can felicity be enjoyed but by serene and quiet thoughts that are full of tranquillity. For *where envying and strife is, there is confusion and every*

[1] Time.

evil work. But the wisdom that is from above is first pure, then peaceable, gentle and easy to be entreated, full of mercy and good fruits. And the fruit of righteousness is sown in peace, of them that make peace; which must of necessity precede fruition, as triumph followeth.

Were I for my life to interpret that text of our Saviour, *The meek shall inherit the earth,* I should in the first place say that every knowing man may enjoy the beauty and glory of the whole world, and by sweet contemplations delight in all the abundance of treasures and pleasant varieties that are upon earth, especially since, by the ordinance of nature, all men are to be his peculiar treasures. This he might do, I say, did all men love him, and fill the world with glory and virtue. But since all is confounded by their perverseness and disorder, his fruition is utterly lost, unless he will forgive all injuries, and by the virtue of meekness maintain the quiet of his own soul in the midst of their distempers. The meek man is not fretted nor disturbed, but may enjoy all still; and the unspeakable joy which all the glories of God's kingdom do afford him shall make him more meek, and able also to pacify and rule, and heal the minds of his enemies, and even by the love of sinners to recover his right and ancient fruitions.

To be able to live at quiet, and enjoy the felicity of heaven and earth, notwithstanding all the attempts of our enemies, makes them mad when they see they cannot fret us; and so by consequence a greater revenge is seated in meekness than in revenge itself. For our repose is their punishment and torment that hate us. Their vexation falleth on their own head, when they see they miss of their aim and cannot molest us. But it is a joy to see ourselves seated in a throne of repose, clean out of their reach; it breeds a kind of triumph and ovation in the soul. The secret conscience of its own power is a glory and satisfaction unimaginable.

He that masters his own passion is master of another man's, and seldom falls into those broils and inconveniences that are the destruction of ungoverned and hasty spirits; which made Solomon say, *He that is slow to anger is better than the mighty, and he that masters his spirit than he that taketh a city.*

He that troubleth his own house shall inherit the wind. He that is nice[1] and exquisite in exacting all faults shall never be beloved. They are disobliging, angry, testy men that are hated; and the revengeful that do frequently fall into mischief. But to be kind to the unthankful and the evil, and to deal with all men better than they deserve, is the way to be beloved by the worst of men, and admired by the best.

Meekness is the retreat of goodness, and the only force in the rear of liberality. He that does one injury after forty kindnesses blots out the memory of all his courtesies; and he that revenges an injury seems to do one. For he that did the wrong seems innocent to himself, because he felt it not; and, seeming innocent, takes the revenge as an undeserved injury, and is lost for ever. Now, some injuries we must expect from our best friends, which are always lost for want of meekness. So are all the benefits we do, unless we will forgive as well as give. But an injury forgiven is forgotten by him that did it, and the friendship continues at the expense, and to the honour and comfort, of the pardoner, as if no offence had ever been committed. Nay, if afterwards he comes to see the candour of his abused friend, he that did the injury loves him better than before, because he pardoned him the wrong.

Meekness, as it preserves friendship between two, makes goodness invincible and unalterable in one. He shall not be good long whose goodness dependeth on others' merits. He is a miserable weak man that is of an exceptious[2] humour. He is a trouble to his own flesh, and subject to the power of every wasp, whether he shall be good or no. He is quickly stopped in his career of virtue, and easily turned out of the way, that is apt to be infected with another's malice. He carries no antidotes about him, and for want of a preservative is in danger of the contagion. Meekness is a means of the health of the soul. A passionate man, being all over sore, is covered with hot and angry boils, which cannot be touched.

It preventeth much mischief in families. An occasion of anger is like a spark of fire; it is of great consequence where it falleth. If it falls into barrels of gunpowder, it blows up the world; if

[1] Scrupulous.
[2] Irritable.

into green wood or watery places, it does no harm. Penitent tears and the verdure of humility prevent such flames and extinguish the quarrel. If wild-fire[1] be thrown, I will put it out with my foot, and not, by throwing it back, give my enemy the advantage of retorting it upon me. A soft answer pacifieth much wrath, but virulent speeches are a firebrand tossed to and fro, of them that love death.

By revenge, a man at best can but preserve himself, by killing his enemy; but meekness well managed destroys the enmity, preserves the person, and turns the enemy into an excellent friend.

Meekness is not the way to peace and repose and victory only, but to honour and glory. As it is the strength, *it is the glory of a man to pass over a transgression.* He that is lightly angered is quickly lost, and a fickle friend is not worth a farthing. A straw and a feather shall forfeit all the obligations in the world, in some tempers. Nay, he that is revengeful is a dangerous person, and *with an angry man thou shalt not go.* He has the plague upon him, and is prohibited company. All this is dishonourable. But a man that is a resolved and stable friend, that cannot be altered, that will not change, though he be wronged, but forgive and pity, and continue to serve and love his friend, though he shows him some dirty tricks; he that will surmount all by invincible kindness, he is a solid and weighty friend, a rare treasure and exceeding precious. Neither my errors nor misfortunes are able to change him that loveth me purely because he will love me. When his excellency is found out, he will more highly be esteemed, not only by his friend but by all that see him and note his fidelity.

Injuries well forgiven are the highest obligations in the world; especially if a man has been injured after many benefits. A friend that will so oblige is more to be preferred than the gold of Ophir.

Meekness brings a man into respect with his servants and into power with his neighbours. *Anger resteth in the bosom of fools;* but meekness hath always this advantage, it is attended with wisdom and other virtues, as goodness and courage. A man that is prudent in affairs and zealous of good work, faithful in

[1] Inflammable substance used in battles.

retaining secrets, and so full of love that he is prone to do all manner of good with industry, and is courageous to expose himself to any hazard for the benefit of his neighbours, shall keep his servants in awe, and yet be beloved of them. He shall be able to do among his neighbours what he pleaseth. He shall, when well known, become the father of all their families. They will entrust their wives and children in his hands, as I have often experienced; their gold, their bonds, their souls, their affairs, their lives, their secrets, houses, liberties and lands; and be glad of such a friend in whom to be safe, and by whom to be assisted. But though you have all the virtues in the world, the way to the use of them is blocked up without meekness; for your neighbours are few of them wise or good and, if you will be provoked by injuries, you will upon forty occasions so distaste [1] them that they will never trust you. You will look as like a trifler, a knave or a fool as one of them, and be as very [2] a madman. He that will not do good but to deserving persons shall find very few to do good to. For he shall not be acquainted with good men, and from doing good to others he excludes himself. But if all his other virtues are beautified by meekness, such a man will be like an angel, and live above all his neighbours, as if he were in heaven; so that meekness is his real exaltation. And this made our Saviour to cull out that blessing for the meek, *the meek shall inherit the earth.* Even here upon earth, the meek are they that are most blessed.

To do good to an innocent person is humane, but to be kind and bountiful to a man after he has been injurious is divine. Philanthus gave laws and countries to the Parthenians, and was disgraced and banished; but he did them good after the injury, and was made their god, as Justin recordeth.

The very nature of the work encourageth us to its exercise, because it is God-like and truly blessed. But there are many other considerations moving us unto it.

> Mankind is sick, the world distemper'd lies,
>   Oppress'd with sins and miseries.
> Their sins are woes; a long corrupted train

[1] Displease. [2] True.

Of poison, drawn from Adam's vein,
Stains all his seed, and all his kin
Are one disease of life within.
They all torment themselves!
The world's one Bedlam, or a greater cave
Of madmen, that do always rave.

The wise and good like kind physicians are,
That strive to heal them by their care.
They physic and their learning calmly use,
Although the patient them abuse.
For since the sickness is, they find,
A sad distemper of the mind,
All railings they impute,
All injuries, unto the sore disease
They are expressly come to ease.

If we would to the world's distemper'd mind
Impute the rage which there we find,
We might, even in the midst of all our foes,
Enjoy and feel a sweet repose;
Might pity all the griefs we see,
Anointing every malady
With precious oil and balm;
And while ourselves are calm, our art improve
To rescue them, and show our love.

But let's not fondly our own selves beguile;
If we revile 'cause they revile,
Ourselves, infected with their sore disease,
Need other's helps to give us ease.
For we more mad than they remain,
Need to be cut, and need a chain
Far more than they. Our brain
Is craz'd, and if we put our wits to theirs
We may be justly made their heirs.

But while with open eyes we clearly see
  The brightness of His Majesty,
While all the world, by sin to Satan sold,
  In daily wickedness grows old,
  Men in chains of darkness lie,
  In bondage and iniquity,
    And pierce and grieve themselves!
The dismal woes wherein they crawl enhance
  The peace of our inheritance.

We wonder to behold ourselves so nigh
  To so much sin and misery,
And yet to see ourselves so safe from harm!
  What amulet, what hidden charm
  Could fortify and raise the soul
  So far above them, and control
  Such fierce malignity?
The brightness and the glory which we see
  Is made a greater mystery.

And while we feel how much our God doth love
  The peace of sinners, how much move,
And sue, and thirst, entreat, lament and grieve
  For all the crimes in which they live,
  And seek and wait, and call again,
  And long to save them from the pain
    Of sin, from all their woe,
With greater thirst as well as grief, we try
  How to relieve their misery.

The life and splendour of felicity,
  Whose floods so overflowing be,
The streams of joy which round about His throne
  Enrich and fill each holy one
  Are so abundant, that we can
  Spare all, even all to every man,
    And have it all ourselves,
Nay, have the more! We long to make them see
  The sweetness of felicity.

While we contemplate their distresses, how,
  Blind wretches, they in bondage bow,
And tear and wound themselves, and vex and groan,
  And chafe and fret so near His throne,
  And know not what they ail, but lie
  Tormented in their misery,
    Like madmen that are blind,
In works of darkness nigh such full delight;
  That they might find and see the sight.

What would we give, that they might likewise see
  The glory of His majesty!
The joy and fullness of that high delight,
  Whose blessedness is infinite!
We would even cease to live, to gain
  Them from their misery and pain
    And make them with us reign.
For they themselves would be our greatest treasures
  When sav'd, our own most heavenly pleasures.

O holy Jesus, who didst for us die,
  And on the altar bleeding lie,
Bearing all torment, pain, reproach and shame,
  That we, by virtue of the same,
  Though enemies to God, might be
  Redeem'd and set at liberty;
    As thou didst us forgive,
So meekly let us love to others show,
  And live in heaven on earth below!

Let's prize their souls, and let them be our gems,
  Our temples and our diadems,
Our brides, our friends, our fellow-members, eyes,
  Hands, hearts and souls, our victories,
  And spoils and triumphs, our own joys!
  Compar'd to souls, all else are toys.
    O Jesus, let them be
Such unto us as they are unto thee,
  Vessels of glory and felicity!

How will they love us, when they find our care
Brought them all thither where they are!
When they conceive what terror 'tis to dwell
In all the punishments of hell,
And in a lively manner see,
O Christ, eternal joys in thee!
How will they all delight
In praising thee for us, with all their might!
How sweet a grace, how infinite!

When we understand the perfection of the love of God, the excellency of immortal souls, the prize and value of our Saviour's blood, the misery of sin and the malady of distempered nature, the danger of hell and the joys of which our sorest enemies are capable, the obligations that lie on ourselves, and the peace and blessedness of so sweet a duty, compassion itself will melt us into meekness; and the wisdom of knowing these great things will make it as natural to us as enjoyment itself, as sweet and easy as it is to live and breathe. It will then seem the harshest and most unnatural thing in the world to forbear so fair, so just, so reasonable, so divine a duty.

Nor is it a small comfort that the more vile our enemies are, the more price and lustre is set upon our actions. Our goodness is made by their evil the more eminent and conspicuous. We improve their injuries and turn them into benefits; we make a virtue of necessity, and turn their vices into graces; make them appear more abominable and vile, if they continue obstinate; and the greater their perverseness is, the more great and honourable is our virtue. It was the praise of Moses, that *the man Moses was the meekest man upon all the earth;* yet one passionate expression lost him so much in the esteem of God that it hindered his entrance into the land of Canaan. How great an instrument he was nevertheless in the conduct and felicity of the Jews, and how much he profited the whole nation by his meekness, sacred story doth record. How Joseph also dealt with his brethren, how he saved all the family of Israel in the root by his meekness, and by meekness purchased an everlasting name of glory and renown, all Christian ages and nations understand, where his praises are celebrated to this day; and the benefit thereof is spread abroad and propagated throughout all generations for evermore.

CHAPTER XXVI

Humility is the basis of all virtue and felicity in all estates, and for ever to be exercised. As pride does alienate the soul from God, humility unites it to Him in adoration and amity. It maketh infinite blessedness infinitely greater, is agreeable to the truth of our condition, and leads us through a dark and mysterious way to glory

MEEKNESS respecteth others' faults, humility and penitence our own; but humility is more large than penitence, and is a distinct affection of another nature. Penitence is an exercise of the affection of sorrow, and that only for sin. Humility is an acknowledgement of all our vileness; it respects our original out of nothing as well as our guilt; our weakness and unworthiness, our dependence upon another's will, our debt and obligation, the duty of obedience and allegiance which we owe, and all the naked truth of our condition. It confesseth our homage, and is sensible of our smallness and subjection. All that a man hath received it distinguisheth from what he is of himself, and its fruits or effects are suitable to its nature. It is the virtue by which we think basely of ourselves, and behave ourselves in a lowly and submissive manner. It makes us soft and pliant as wax, susceptible of any form that shall be imposed on us by our benefactor, and prone to gratitude. It is accompanied with a high and mighty sense of benefits received, and made noble by the honour which it inclines us to return to God and man for all the goodness which they show unto us. It is of incomparable use in our felicity, because it magnifies our esteem of all our happiness and glory.

It is not through ignorance or want of good will that we speak nothing of vices, the woeful deformity of which, being exposed to view near the excellence of virtue, would put a greater lustre on all their brightness; but the abundance of matter which virtue itself doth afford forbids us to waste our time and paper in the description of their contraries; the glory of their nature being so full and perfect in itself that it needeth not the aid of those additional arts, which labour to set off the dignity of imperfect things by borrowed commendations. And besides this, the mischief and inconveniency of every vice is so great and manifold that it would require a distinct and entire volume to unfold the deformity of their destructive nature, so fully as their baseness and demerit requires. It is sufficient therefore to observe that pride is of all other things most odious to God; because it puffeth up the soul with self-conceit, is forgetful of its original, void of all gratitude and prone to rebellion. Is it not an odious and abominable thing, for a creature that is nothing in himself to fly in his Creator's face, and to usurp a dominion over itself to the apparent wrong of its sovereign Lord; to rob its benefactor of all the glory of His bounty, to renounce and deny all dependence upon Him, and to forswear its homage and allegiance; to ascribe all its glories to itself, and abhor all sense of honour and gratitude; to look upon itself as the sole original and author of all its greatness, and to be dazzled so with the brightness of its condition as to forget the true fountain of it, the goodness and the love of Him that first raised him to all that treasure and dominion; to dote on its own perfections without any reflection on the bounty of Him that gave them!

All this is to act a lie, and to be guilty of apparent falsehood. It is as full of fraud and injustice as is possible, and as full of folly as it is of impiety. For pride aimeth at the utmost height of esteem and honour, and is fed by its own beauty and glory, yet foolishly undermineth and blasteth the person it would advance with the greatest baseness and shame imaginable. It devours the beauty which ought to feed it, and destroys the glory in which it delighteth. The higher, the greater, the more perfectly glorious and blessed the person that is exalted, his ingratitude (which is the dregs of baseness) is the more black and horrid, and provokes the greater detestation. It forfeits and renounces all the delight which the goodness of its Lord and Benefactor affordeth; it cuts off the soul like a branch from the root that gave it life and verdure. It tends all to division, alienation and enmity. It turns that complacency,[1] which is its only bliss, into wrath and indignation; and whereas it delights in nothing more than appearing highly amiable in the eyes of all spectators, it falleth into contempt and extreme disgrace before all the creatures in heaven and earth, that look upon it and behold its unworthiness. No toad has so much deformity or poison or malignity as pride in its nature. It is the ruin of all that is great, and turns the brightest of the seraphims into the most abominable of devils.

Now, if pride be so pernicious, and be by nature (though a mere fantasy) so destructive, what shall humility be, which is full of truth and reality! How forcible, how divine, how amiable, how full of truth, how bright and glorious, how solid and real, how agreeable to all objects, how void of error and disparity, how just and reasonable, how wise and holy, how deep, how righteous, how good and profitable, how mightily prone to exalt us in the esteem of God and man! How agreeable to all its causes and ends, how fit and suitable to all the circumstances of man's condition! I need not say more; it bears its own evidence, and carries causes in it that will justify our Saviour's words, *He that humbleth himself shall be exalted.* He that is puffed up has but a counterfeit glory, but humility is full of solid glory. Its beauty is so amiable that there is no end of counting its proportions and excellencies. The wise man that saw into the nature of things very clearly said, long before our Saviour was born, *Pride goeth before a fall, but before honour is humility.* He that exalteth himself must needs be humbled, because the colours are envenomed wherewith he painteth his face, which in a little time is discerned, and at the very first instant the painting begins to turn into a canker.

The amiableness of humility appeareth by its excellency; on these two the greatness of its beauty and success is founded. It is so agreeable to all the principles of nature and grace and glory, to all the desires of angels and men, to all the designs of God

[1] Joy.

Himself, and to all the interests and concerns of the soul, that it cannot but be the most advantageous virtue in the whole world.

It is strange that a man should look with the same eye upon two objects so infinitely distant and different from each other; but at the same time he seeth God and Nothing, heaven and earth, eternal love and dust to be his originals. Self-love and justice, wisdom and goodness, joy and gratitude have the same objects, but look upon them in a several manner, and are very differently affected with them. Humility regards all objects, high and low, good and evil; but with a peculiar remark and notice of its own. It takes them in another light, and discerns them all with another kind of sense. It is in some manner the taste of the soul. Their truth appeareth to the eye of knowledge; their goodness is apprehended by the life of love; the perfection of their serviceableness to the most perfect end is discerned by wisdom; the benefit which all spectators receive is the delight of goodness; the incomprehensible depth and mysterious intricacy of their frame and nature is the peculiar object of our wonder and curiosity. They help our faith as they show a deity, and the truth of all religion and blessedness. As they are the gifts of God, they are the provocations of gratitude, and as they are aggravations of sin, they are respected by repentance. As they are the means of our glory and our proper treasures, they are the objects of contentment. But humility looks upon them in relation to its unworthiness, compares them with itself and its own deserts, and admires the disproportion that is between them. It useth them all as grounds of a deeper and profounder lowness in the esteem which it ought to have of itself, and as the incentives to love and gratitude, which it pays in the depth of a most profound acknowledgment and adoration.

This habit or affection of the soul is not inconsistent with its joy and glory (as by some foolish people, that are by ignorance and errors far from God, is generally supposed), but highly conducive and subservient to its perfection. It gives us the tenderest and greatest sense; it passes through all things, embraceth the poles, and toucheth all extremes together. The centre itself is but the middle of its profundity. It hath a nadir beneath it, a lower point in another heaven on the other side opposite to its own zenith. In its own depth it containeth all the height of felicity and glory, and doubles all by a mystery in nature. It is like a mirror lying on the ground with its face upwards; all the height above increaseth the depth of its beauty within, nay, turneth it into a new depth. An inferior heaven is in the glass itself, at the bottom of which we see the sky, though it be not transplanted, removed thither. Humility is the fittest glass of the divine greatness; and the fittest womb for the conception of all felicity; for it hath a double heaven. It is the way to full and perfect sublimity. A man would little think that by sinking into the earth he should come to heaven. He doth not, but is buried, that fixeth and abideth there. But if he pierceth through all the rocks and minerals of inferior world, and passeth on to the end of his journey in a straight line downward, in the middle of his way he will find the centre of nature; and by going downward still, begin to ascend, when he is past the centre. Through many obstacles full of gross and subterraneous darkness, which seem to affright and stifle the soul, he will arrive at last to a new light and glory, room and liberty, breathing-space and fresh air among the antipodes; and by passing on still through those inferior regions that are under his feet, but over the head of those that are beneath him, finally come to another sky; penetrate that, and leaving it behind him, sink down into the depth of all immensity. This he cannot do in his body, because it is gross and dull, and heavy and confined; but by a thought in his soul he may, because it is subtle, quick, airy, free and infinite. Nothing can stop or exclude it, oppress or stifle it. This local descent through all the inferior space and immensity, though it brings us to God, and His throne, and another heaven full of angels, on the other side of the world, yet is it but a real emblem of the more spiritual and mysterious flight of humility in the mind.

We all know that the way to heaven is through death and the grave, beyond which we come to another life, in eternity; but how to accommodate this to the business of humility few understand. By this virtue we are inclined to despise ourselves, and to leave all the garish ornaments of earthly bliss; to divest ourselves of the splendours of temporal prosperity, and to submit to all afflictions, contempts and miseries that a good cause can bring upon us. In the eyes of other men we are beneath their feet, and so we are in our own, till we are gone a little further; but on the other side of all this bareness, we find a better life in communion with the deity. *Forasmuch then,* saith St. Peter, *as Christ hath suffered for us in the flesh, arm yourselves likewise with the same mind; for he that hath suffered in the flesh hath ceased from sin; that he no longer should live the rest of his time in the flesh, to the lusts of men, but to the will of God. For the time past of our life may suffice us to have wrought the will of the Gentiles, when we walked in lasciviousness, lusts, excess of wine, revellings, banquettings and abominable idolatries; wherein they think it strange that ye run not with them to the same excess of riot.* There is a motion from vice to virtue, and from one degree of grace to another, by which we leave the fantastic world, with all its shows and gauderies; and, through many afflictions and persecutions, come to the real and solid world of bliss and glory.

What hand humility hath in leading us through all afflictions and in facilitating the way of pressure and calamity, I need not observe. I shall note the error which men incur by their weariness and haste, who, because they do not immediately see the bliss of humility and patience, if they do not curse yet they boggle at all calamity. These men ought to be informed that the middle of the way is not the place of rest and perfection. They must pass through all these things to the further regions of clarity and glory. Men are not to stick in calamities themselves; but if humility lead them to suffer all indignities with patience, it must lead them further, to the bottom of their estate and condition; to the true light, and to the clear and perfect sight of their own vileness; in which they shall see their original, their misery, their sin, their glory; their God and themselves, their bliss and their forfeiture, their recovery and their Saviour; their hope and despair, their obligations in the height of eternal love and bounty, and their shame and confusion in the depths of their apostasy and ingratitude; their infinite demerit, and God's infinite mercy; the riches of free grace, and their own unworthiness; and in all these, *the length and breadth and depth and height of the love of God, which passeth knowledge, that they might be filled with all the fulness of God.*

Humility makes men capable of all felicity. All deep apprehensions and great resentments,[1] all extents and distances of things, all degrees of grace and virtue, all circumstances that increase the guilt of sin; all adorations, prostrations, admirations, debasements, thanksgivings, praises, exaltations, are founded in humility. All the fullness of all estates, all honour and obedience, all devotion and worship, all the beauty of innocence, all the deformity of sin, all the danger of hell, all the cost of our redemption, all the hatred of our stupidity and perverseness, all the hope of heaven, all our penitence and grief, all our fear and expectation, all our love and all our joy are contained in humility. There they are expressed, there they are exercised. There they are enlarged and beautified in like manner. There they grow deep and serious and infinite; there they become vigorous and strong; there they are made substantial and eternal. All the powers of the soul are employed, extended and made perfect in this depth of abysses. It is the basis and foundation of all virtue and gratitude whatsoever. It is in some sort the very fountain of life and felicity itself; for as nothing is great but in comparison with something else, so nothing is sweet but what is new and eternal.

All life consists in motion and change. The pleasure of acquiring is oftentimes as great, and perhaps always greater, than that of enjoying. The long possession of that which we have always had takes away the sense, and maketh us dull. Old and common things are less esteemed, unless we rub up our memories with some helps, to renew them and our senses together. Gifts are always sweeter in the coming than in the abiding with us. And if what I observe in the course of nature be of any force, there is no possibility of enjoyment, at least, no perfection in fruition, without some relation to the first acquisition. Old things are apt to grow stale and their value to be neglected, by their continuance with us. I have noted it often, in the joy that young heirs have, when they first come to their estates; and the great felicity which lovers promise to themselves, and taste also when they meet together in the marriage-bed; the pleasures of which all pass off by degrees, not solely by reason of our dullness and stupidity, but far more from a secret in the nature of things. For

[1] Feelings.

all delight springs from the satisfaction of violent desire. When the desire is forgotten, the delight is abated. All pleasure consists in activity and motion; while the object stands still, it seemeth dead and idle. The sense of our want must be quick upon us, to make the sense of our enjoyment perfect. The rapture proceeds from the convenience [1] between us, the marvellous fitness that is in such objects to satisfy our capacities and inclinations. The misery and vacuity must needs be remembered to make the convenience live, and to inspire a sense of it perpetually into us. The coming of a crown and the joy of a kingdom is far more quick and powerful in the surprise and novelty of its glory than in the length of its continuance. We perceive it by the delight which lovers taste in recounting their adventures. The nature of the thing makes the memory of their first amours more pleasant than the possession of the last.

There is an instinct that carries us to the beginning of our lives. How do old men even dote into lavish discourses of the beginning of their lives? The delight in telling their old stories is as great to themselves as wearisome to others. Even kings themselves, would they give themselves the liberty of looking back, might enjoy their dominions with double lustre, and see and feel their former resentments,[2] and enrich their present security with them. All a man's life put together contributes a perfection to every part of it, and the memory of things past is the most advantageous light of our present condition. Now, all these sparkles of joy, these accidental hints of nature and little rays of wisdom, meet together in humility.

We recount the ordinary discoveries of the inclination of nature because humility is, if I may so speak, the rendezvous of their perfection. All the stirrings of grace and nature, all the acts of God and the soul, all His condescensions and beginnings to advance us, all His gifts at their first coming, all the depths and changes of our condition, all our desires, all our primitive and virgin joys, the whole story of our creation and life and fall and redemption, in all the newness of its first appearance; all our wants and dangers, exigencies and extremities, all our satis-

[1] Accord, agreement.
[2] Sentiments.

factions and delights, are present together in our humility; and are so infinitely near and present thereunto, so sweet and vigorous in their mixture, so strangely powerful in their influence, that they inspire our hearts, enter our thoughts and incorporate with our souls; and are as near and sweet as our present condition, be it never so blessed. All put together is far more sweet than our present condition. A great part of our felicity and glory is in it, while we take it into our conceptions here, and apply it to our souls in an humble manner; but it will be much more our felicity in heaven. It is of so much concernment that a great divine in our English Zion hath said, The greater part of our eternal happiness will consist in a grateful recognition, not of our joys to come, but of benefits already received.

Now look into the office and work of humility. I will not tell you how here upon earth it shunneth all strife and contention about places, and all the mischiefs consequent thereto; nor of the unity and peace and honour it produceth. These are all but temporal benefits. It has ten thousand other walks and circuits and periods of revolution. I will tell you how it behaves itself in paradise and heaven.

Humility, by leading us to the bottom of our condition, sets our original before our eyes, considers that eternal abyss of idleness and vacuity out of which we were taken, that miracle by which we were made of nothing. How destitute we should have been in ourselves, had not God created the world, had He not been pleased to communicate Himself and His glory to us! How weak and unable we were to devise or desire any felicity, yet how infinitely necessary the preparation of it after we were created! How great our desires and expectations were, how sore and urgent our wants and necessities; how much we needed infinite wisdom and almighty power to fill immensity with the omnipresence of their glory, and to fill their omnipresence with effects and treasures! How gracious and good God was, to do all this for us without our asking; and how justly David's rapture may be taken up by the soul, *The king shall joy in thy strength, O Lord, and in thy salvation how greatly shall he rejoice! Thou preventeth him with the blessings of goodness, thou settest a crown of pure gold upon his head. His glory is great in thy salva-*

tion; honour and majesty hast thou laid upon him. For thou hast made him most blessed for ever; thou hast made him exceeding glad with thy countenance!

We might have been made, and put, in the condition of toads, who are now created in the image of God, have dominion over all His works and are made capable of all eternity. The infinite condescension of God is the amazement of the soul. The depth of its low estate increaseth the height of its exaltation. All that it wanteth in itself it findeth in the goodness of its benefactor; and the joy of being so beloved is greater than that of having all these things of ourselves for ever. For the love of God alone, and His goodness in giving, is our last and best and proper felicity. Hereupon follows the extinction of all envy, regret and discontentment; the sacrificing of ourselves, the annihilating of ourselves, the lowliness of ourselves and the exaltation of God, and the adoration of God, and the joy of adoring the greatest of all other; the amity and friendship between God and His creature, the unity of both and their happiness for ever. Without this humility of looking into the bottom of our first condition, all this is impossible. And for this cause is humility an eternal virtue, in all estates for ever to be enjoyed—I might have said, exercised.

Thus in the estate of sin and misery, all the odiousness of our guilt, all our despair and deformity, all our shame and misery, all the necessity of hating God and being hated of Him, comes before the eyes of a humble soul, with all the mercies and condescensions of eternal love in the work of redemption.

And in the state of glory itself, all the particular sins, neglects, rebellions, apostasies and villainies we committed against God, after all His mercy and goodness in the death of His Son; how infinitely base we were in despising all His bounties and glories; how infinitely those offences made us unworthy of heaven and the eternal glory we now enjoy; how marvellous and incomparable His love was, in pursuing us with so much long-suffering and patience; how amiable He is, and how vile and unworthy we are in all this, it is the office of humility to feel and ponder. Thus, you see its work and you may easily conjecture its eternal reward. All things are in it, in the utmost height and depth of resignation and contentment enjoyed.

I need not observe that sweetness of conversation, that civility and courtesy that springs from humility. The meek and lowly are the same men; the kind and the charitable, and the affable and the good, are all of them humble, and so are all they that prefer others above themselves, and render themselves amiable by loving their inferiors and giving place to their equals. At least they imitate humility, as complimental courtiers do for their advantage. And it is no small token of its excellency that the greatest enemies of humility and virtue are sometimes forced to fly to it for succour; as those that well know they can never thrive nor prosper in the world without esteem, not gain esteem without covering their vices under the mask of virtue. All the advantages and effects of this will be enjoyed eternally.

CHAPTER XXVII

That contentment is a virtue. Its causes and its ends; its impediments, effects and advantages. The way to attain and secure contentment

THOUGH we have not named it in our first distribution of virtue into its several kinds, yet the commendation which contentment hath in scripture imports it to be a virtue; so does the difficulty of attaining it, and the great and mighty force it is of, in our lives and conversations. *Having food and raiment,* saith the Apostle, *let us therewith be content; for godliness with contentment is great gain;* where he fitly noteth that godliness is the original of true contentment, and that the gain of so great a virtue is inestimable. The truth is, it is impossible to be happy or grateful without it.

A discontented mind is exceeding prone to be peevish and fretful, and throws a man into all the indecencies of avarice, ambition, envy, treason, murder, contention, turbulence, murmuring, repining, melancholy and sourness, angers, baseness and folly; into all the malevolence and misery which can disorder the soul or disturb the world. Suspicion, unbelief, enmity against God, fear and cowardice, barrenness in good and praiseworthy employments, weariness and complaint, hatred of retirement, spiritual idleness and ignorance are its companions; followed by debaucheries and all the sorts of vile and wicked diversions. For man is an unwelcome creature to himself till he can delight in his condition; and while he hates to be alone, exposeth himself to all kind of mischiefs and temptations, because he is an active creature, and must be doing something, either good or evil.

True contentment is the full satisfaction of a knowing mind. It is not a vain and empty contentment, which is falsely so called, springing from some one particular little satisfaction that, however momentary it be, does for the present delight our humour; but a long habit of solid repose, after much study and serious consideration. It is not the slavish and forced contentment which the philosophers among the heathen did force upon themselves; but a free and easy mind, attended with pleasure, and naturally rising from one's present condition. It is not a morose and sullen contempt of all that is good. That negative contentment, which passed of old for so great a virtue, is not at all conducive to felicity, but is a real vice; for to be content without cause is to sit down in our imperfection; and to seek all one's bliss in one's self alone is to scorn all other objects, even God Himself and all the creation. It is a high piece of pride and stiffness in a man, that renders him good for nothing, but makes him arrogant and presumptuous in the midst of his blindness, his own slave and his own idol, a tyrant over himself and yet his only deity. It makes a man to live without God in the world, and cuts him off from the universe. It makes him incapable either of obligation or gratitude, his own prison and his own tormentor. It shuts up the soul in a grave, and makes it to lead a living death, and robs it of all its objects. It mingles nature and vice in a confusion, and makes man fight against appetite and reason. Certainly that philosopher has a hard task, that must fight against reason and trample under foot the essence of his soul, to establish his felicity!

Contentment is a sleepy thing!
If it in death alone must die,

A quiet mind is worse than poverty,
    Unless it from enjoyment spring.
That's blessedness alone that makes a king!
Wherein the joys and treasures are so great,
They all the powers of the soul employ,
  And fill it with a work complete,
    While it doth all enjoy.
True joys alone contentment do inspire,
Enrich content, and make our courage higher.
  Content alone's a dead and silent stone;
    The real life of bliss
  Is glory reigning in a throne
    Where all enjoyment is.
The soul of man is so inclin'd to see
Without his treasures no man's soul can be
    Nor rest content uncrown'd.
      Desire and love
Must in the height of all their rapture move,
  Where there is true felicity.
Enjoyment is the very life and ground
Of life itself; whose pleasant motion is
      A form of bliss;
All blessedness a life with glory crown'd.
Life! Life is all; in its most full extent
Stretcht out to all things, and with all content.

The only reason why a wise and holy man is satisfied with food and raiment is because he sees himself made possessor of all felicity, the image of the deity, the great object of His eternal love, and in another way far more divine and perfect, the heir of the world and of all eternity. He knows very well that, if his honour be so great as to live in communion with God in the fruition of all His joys, he may very well spare the foul and feeble delights of men. And though the law be not so severe as to command him to be content without food and raiment, yet if for God's sake he should, by the wickedness of men, be bereaved of both, he may well be patient, nay, and die with glory. And this indeed is that which maketh contentment so great a virtue.

It hath a powerful influence upon us in all estates; to take off our perplexity, solicitude and care, and to adorn our lives with liberty and cheerfulness, by which we become acceptable and admirable to the sons of men. It makes us prone to be kind and liberal, whereby we become obliging and full of good works; for it delivers us from all servile fear, and gives us courage and confidence in God. For well may we dare to trust Him in such little matters, who has manifested His friendship and bounty in such infinite good things, and made it impossible for us to be miserable, if we are pleasing to Him. An intelligent and full contentment elevates the soul above all the world, and makes it angelical. It instils a divine and heavenly nature, enflames the soul with the love of God, and moves it to delight in devotion and prayer. The sweetness of his thoughts and the beauty of his object draws a lover often into solitudes; and a royal man in a strange country, especially when he has heard tidings of his father's death, and the devolving of his crown and throne on himself, desires to be alone, that he may digest these affairs in his thoughts a little. He delights in being retired, because he can find nothing worthy of himself in company. Magnanimous souls are above garlands and shepherds; and there is no greatness of soul like that which perfect contentment inspires.

But that which above all other things makes me to note the virtue of contentment is its great influence, efficacy and power in confirming our faith. For when I see the beauty of religion, I know it to be true. For such is its excellency that, if you remove it out of the world, all the things in heaven and earth will be to no purpose. The business of religion is the love of God, the love of angels and men, and the due esteem we owe to inferior creatures. Remove this love, this charity, this due esteem, this delight that we should take in all amiable objects; life and pleasure are extinguished. I see nature itself teaching me religion; and by the admirable contexture of the powers of my soul, and their fitness for all objects and ends; by the incomparable excellency of the laws prescribed, and the worthiness and beauty of all the objects for which my powers are prepared, see plainly, that I am infinitely beloved; and that all the cross [1] and disorderly

[1] Perverse.

things that are now upon earth are mere corruptions and depravations of nature, which free agents have let in upon themselves. All which, since they are reducible to the government of reason, and may by wisdom be improved to my higher happiness, I am sure I am redeemed, and that there is some eternal power that governs the world with so much goodness for my felicity, since I myself was not able to do it. That all ages are beautified by His wisdom for my enjoyment, I hope in like manner, nay, I see it plainly. And of all these joys the cross of Christ is the root and centre.

I confess it is difficult to gain this high and divine contentment, because its measure and value is infinite. Nay, there are other causes, both temporal and eternal, that may seem to be impediments. One was a business which David did experience, the prosperity of the wicked. They live in so much splendour, pomp and grandeur, have so much respect and reverence paid unto them, and reign as it were in the high esteem of all that are round about them, in such a manner that a poor good man is hardly looked upon among them. His condition seemeth servile, and he is little regarded. David triumphed over it: *Truly God is good to Israel, even to such as are of a clean heart. But as for me, my feet were almost gone, my steps had well nigh slipped. For I was envious at the foolish, when I saw the prosperity of the wicked; for all the day long have I been plagued, and chastened every morning.*

Whether it be through nature or corruption, I cannot tell—at least, I will not stand to dispute it; but it is somewhat grievous to see men of the same mould with ourselves so highly magnified, and ourselves slighted and unable to appear with equality among them; because the true greatness of our souls is hidden, oppressed and buried, as it were, in the meanness of our condition. But yet we have excellent company—David and the prophets, Christ and His apostles and all the martyrs, that are now so glorious. And, if you please, you may consider what these great men do when the show is over. We, when we come abroad, are weak and despised, and they when they are alone. A virtuous man is great within, and glorious in his retirements; is honoured also among men in truth and reality. The rest make an outward show, and are honoured in ceremony. We are accepted in the eyes of

God and His holy angels, and they are condemned. Their life is a dream, and ours is eternal. We expatiate over all the world with infinite joy and wonder in our solitudes, and they are nothing when they return to themselves.

That wherein the greatest difficulty of all doth consist is the boundless desire and ambition of the soul, whereby we are tempted to envy anything that is above us, and for ever to be displeased unless our glory and blessedness be eternal. I do not mean immortal only, but of everlasting extent and infinite beauty. We soar to the best and highest of all that is possible and, unless in all ages and kingdoms our satisfaction be complete and our pleasure exquisite, we are prone to be tormented with the perfection of our desires. But God having given Himself and all His kingdom and glory to us, there is no room for complaint. All His power being glorified by His wisdom and goodness for our advancement, we need nothing but a clear sight of the face of truth, and a lively sense of our condition, to ravish and transport us into ecstasies and praises.

The happiness of a contented spirit consists not alone in the fruition of its bliss, but in the fruits and effects it produceth in our lives. It gives us many advantages over sin, temptation, fear, affliction, poverty, sickness, death and all other casualties to which we are obnoxious,[1] by reason of our frail and fickle condition. But all these I shall pass over, and only mention two, which are worth our care and desire: security and power.

As there is a vain and empty contentment, so there is a rash and foolish security. For a man to wink at all hazards to which he is exposed, and without any consideration of what may befall him, to give himself up to his ease and pleasure, is as great madness as it is for a general environed with enemies to sleep without his guards, or to be totally negligent of his camp and his army. But when he has conquered all his enemies, then to be filled with melancholy fears and panic terror is as great a weakness as a man of worth can be capable of. Even in the midst of them, when he has surveyed all their strengths and made full provision for their incursions, he may take his rest with liberty, provided he be moderate and wary in his proceedings. This last is our con-

[1] Liable.

dition. We must not live as if there were no sickness and death in the world. We must remember there are calamities of every kind, and fortify ourselves with principles and resolutions against them; *put on the whole armour of God,* which is called sometimes *the armour of light,* and stand prepared for all assaults whatsoever. When we have so done, as it is a terrible thing to be surprised, so it is a glorious thing with open eyes to see and know all the evil that is in death, imprisonment, persecution, shame and poverty, famine, banishment, pain and torment; and yet to be secure in the midst of our fruitions.

There is a worthless and there is a divine security. It is a poor business for a man to be secure that has nothing to lose. A beggar sings upon the road, without any fear of thieves. But to be full of gold and jewels, yet safe from danger; to be secure in a palace of delights, in the midst of a kingdom and in the possession of all its glory—this is a valuable and sweet security, a safety enriched with solid enjoyments. Much more is it here upon earth to have the bliss and security of angels. Among wolves and tigers and bears and dragons, among thieves and murderers, bloody men and devils, among dead men's bones, and graves and sepulchres; when showers of arrows fall round about us, and hell is beneath us; this is something more than to be secure where no danger is near, no calamity possible. It is a kind of triumph in security, and hath a peculiar glory in it which the very security of heaven is incapable of. And yet poor frail man, obnoxious [1] and liable to all these destructions, is safe among them all, when he is gotten into the heart of God's kingdom and surrounded with felicity. Its very beauties are its strengths. He knows himself beloved of the eternal God, and that the King of Terrors is but a disguised bugbear; a dark and doleful passage to the ignorant, but to him a bright and transparent way to the King of Glory. This blessedness is of a stable, incorruptible nature, which nothing can destroy. It digesteth all kind of evils, and turneth them into nourishment. There is a wisdom above us, and a wisdom within us, that maketh *all things work together for good to them that love God;* and nothing is able to hurt us but ourselves.

Now for power which felicity giveth: there is an intrinsic

[1] Exposed.

power in the enjoyment itself, for which felicity is to be admired, in comparison of which all other powers are but poor and feeble. To speak with the tongue of men and angels, to move mountains or turn them into gold, to raise the dead, to command the sun, are common things, the power of creating worlds is but vain, without the power of enjoying them. All honour, pleasure and glory are shut up in felicity. Had we a power of creating and enjoying all worlds, it were infinitely short of the power of enjoying God, because He is infinitely greater and higher than all; the creating power is superfluous to us, because all is most exquisite and perfect already. The fool's wishing-cap and the philosopher's stone are but trifles; all things that are not gold are better than gold. Felicity giveth us the power of enjoying all, even God Himself; all angels and men, and all worlds, nay, all their riches, splendours and pomps in their places; which is the most amiable and desirable, the most sweet and profitable power of all other.

But when we are contented, there is another power worth the having, which felicity giveth us. It enables us to despise the menaces and angers of men; it setteth us above their reach, and inspires us with a comely boldness to dare to do anything that is good, as well as with ability to dare to suffer anything that is evil. He that is secure, and he that hath enough, is independent, and bold as a lion. And besides all this, he has a certain lustre in his actions, that gives him authority and power over others, to intercede and prevail in his requests, to live in honour and good esteem, and to make many subservient to his best occasions. He is great in heaven, and whatever he asks of his eternal Father in His Son's name, with wisdom and piety, shall not be denied him. He can touch the hearts of millions, by his Father's meditation: *for the hearts of kings are in the hands of the Lord, to turn them as the rivers of water*. He made his people to be pitied of all them that carried them away captive, and gave them favour in the sight of the Egyptians. And this secret alone is of more value than we can well describe.

To receive power from heaven to be virtuous, to delight in virtue, to be irresistible and invincible in the practice of it, is a very divine and glorious privilege. Felicity itself is the fountain of this power, and the knowledge of its greatness that which enflames us with the love of it. Felicity is excellent not only as it is the end of virtue, but the encouragement of it. He that is content has a great advantage above all other men, because he moves with greater ease, and passeth through all difficulties with greater pleasure. A general of an army, that works with the common soldiers in the trenches, does the same work, but with more honour and less labour. He is not servile in it, as the rest are, but his pleasure is to do it for all their encouragement. He does it in the quality of a prince, and with less molestations; he has higher incentives and more sublime rewards. Yet he does it too with greater merit and acceptance. A man that sees and knows the glory of his high and heavenly estate does all things triumphantly. The sweetness of his bliss alters the very nature of his fights and battles. He does all things in the light, without groaning and reluctancy. He marches on with dancing and melody, and cheerful looks and smiles and thanksgivings; whereas they that are discontented move heavily, and are in all their proceedings lame and maimed.

The way to attain the felicity of contentment is to attain felicity, that we may be contented. True felicity is the source of contentment and of all virtue. It is never to be gotten but by digging after knowledge, as for hidden treasures. Praying for it is a good way, but prayer without industry is a mere mockery. Industry, on the other side, without prayer is loose presumption. For a man to pray to God to make his field fruitful without ploughing and sowing is madness; and to expect it all from his own labour, without God's blessing, impiety. But God never yet said to any of the seed of Jacob, *Seek ye my face in vain.*

When contentment is gotten, it must be secured by the same means by which it was obtained. Care in fencing is as necessary as care in ploughing; and there is labour too, but sweet and delightful labour, even in reaping the harvest. But all the work is reduced into narrow room. Thou hast no charge over any other than thine own vineyard. When thou hast gotten the knowledge of felicity and thyself, the grand means of contentment is continually to enjoy it. With all thy getting, get wisdom, and with all thy keeping, keep thy heart: *for out of it are the issues of life and death.* Nothing can waste thy conscience but sin, and nothing trouble thy repose but what disturbs thy conscience. Let virtue and felicity be thy only good, and believe firmly that nothing can hurt thee but sin alone. One evil action done by thyself is more mischievous to thee than all the calamities and sufferings in the world.

CHAPTER XXVIII

Of Magnanimity, or greatness of soul. Its nature, its foundation in the vast capacity of the understanding, its desire. Its objects are infinite and eternal. Its inquiries are most profound and earnest. It disdaineth all feeble honours, pleasures and treasures. A magnanimous man is the only great and undaunted creature

MAGNANIMITY and contentment are very near allied; like brothers and sisters, they spring from the same parents, but are of several features. Fortitude and patience are kindred too to this incomparable virtue. Moralists distinguish magnanimity and modesty, by making one the desire of greater, the other of less and inferior, honours; but in my apprehension, there is more in magnanimity. It includes all that belongs to a great soul. A high and mighty courage, an invincible patience, an immovable grandeur which is above the reach of injuries, a contempt of all little and feeble enjoyments, and a certain kind of majesty that is conversant only with great things; a high and lofty frame of spirit, allayed with the sweetness of courtesy and respect; a deep and stable resolution, founded on humility, without any baseness; an infinite hope and a vast desire; a divine, profound, uncontrollable sense of one's own capacity; a generous confidence and a great inclination to heroical deeds; all these conspire to complete it, with a severe and mighty expectation of bliss incomprehensible. It soars up to heaven and looks down upon all the dominion of fortune with pity and disdain. Its aims and designs are transcendent to all the concerns of this little world. Its objects and ends are worthy of a soul that is like God in nature; and nothing less than the kingdom of God, His life and image, nothing beneath the friendship and communion with Him, can be its satisfaction. The terrors, allurements and censures of men are the dust of its feet; their avarice and ambition are but feebleness before it; their riches and contentions, and interests and honours, but insignificant and empty trifles. All the world is but a little bubble; infinity and eternity are the only great and sovereign things with which it converseth.

A magnanimous soul is always awake. The whole globe of the earth is but a nutshell in comparison of its enjoyments. The sun is its lamp, the sea its fishpond, the stars its jewels, men and angels its attendants, and God alone its sovereign delight and supreme complacency.[1] The earth is its garden, all palaces its summer-houses; cities are its cottages, empires its more spacious courts; all ages and kingdoms its demesnes,[2] monarchs its ministers and public agents; the whole Catholic Church its family, the eternal Son of God its pattern and example. Nothing is great if compared with a magnanimous soul, but the sovereign Lord of all worlds.

Mistake not these things for arbitrary flourishes of luxuriant fancy; I speak as I am inspired by felicity. God is the cause, but the knowledge of a man's self the foundation of magnanimity. Trismegistus counteth thus : *First God, secondly the world, thirdly man; the world for man, and man for God. Of the soul, that which is sensible is mortal, but that which is reasonable is immortal. The Father of all things, being full of light and life, brought forth man like unto Himself; whom He loved as His proper offspring; for he was all beauteous, having the image of His Father.* (This is in his *Pœmander*.) Again he saith, *Man is a divine and living thing, not to be compared to any beast that lives upon the earth, but to them that are above, in the highest heavens, that are called gods. Nay, rather, if we shall be bold to speak the truth,*

[1] Joy.
[2] Estates.

he that is man indeed is above them! He is infinitely greater than the gods of the heathen; and a god like unto himself, as the wise man observes, he cannot make. *At least,* saith Trismegistus, *they are equal in power; for none of the things in heaven will come down upon earth, and leave the limits of heaven; but a man ascends up into heaven and measures it. He knoweth what things are on high, and what below. And, that which is the greatest of all, he leaveth not the earth, and yet is above; so mighty and vast is the greatness of his nature! Wherefore we must be bold to say, that an earthly man is a mortal god, and the heavenly God is an immortal Man.*

This is the philosophy of the ancient heathen; wherein, though there be some errors, yet was he guided to it by a mighty sense of the interior excellency of the soul of man; and the boldness he assumes is not so profane, but that it is countenanced here and there in the holy scripture. God Himself said unto Moses, *Lo, I have made thee a god to Pharaoh.* Again, He telleth him concerning Aaron, *He shall be to thee instead of a mouth, and thou shalt be to him instead of God.* And again, concerning all the great men of the world in general, *I have said ye are gods, but ye shall die like men.* But let us see the reason of the heathen a little, on which he foundeth his great opinions.

In one place he maketh his son Tatius to say, *I conceive and understand, not by the sight of mine eyes, but by the intellectual operation,* etc. *I am in heaven, in the earth, in the water, in the air. I am in the living creatures, in plants, in the womb, everywhere.* Whereupon he asketh him, *Dost thou not know, O my son, that thou art born a god, and the son of the One, as I am?* And the ground of this question he unfoldeth in another place, thus: *Consider him that contains all things, and understand that nothing is more capacious than that which is incorporeal, nothing more swift, nothing more powerful; but, of all things, it is most capacious, most swift and most strong. And judge of this by thyself. Command thy soul to go into India, and sooner than thou canst bid it, it will be there. Bid it pass over the ocean, and suddenly it will be there; not as passing from place to place, but suddenly it will be there. Command it to fly into heaven, and it will need no wings, neither shall anything hinder it; not the fire of the sun, nor the ether, nor the turning of the spheres, nor the bodies of any of the stars; but cutting through all, it will fly up to the last and farthest body. And if thou wilt even break through the whole, and see those things that are without the world, if there be anything without* (i.e. if the world be confined) *thou mayest. Behold how great power, how great swiftness thou hast! Canst thou do all these things, and cannot God? After this manner, therefore, contemplate God to have all the whole world in Himself, as it were all thoughts or intellections. If therefore thou wilt not equal thyself with God, thou canst not understand God. For the like is intelligible to the like. Increase thyself to an immeasurable greatness, leaping beyond every body and transcending all time; become eternity, and thou shalt understand God. If thou believe in thyself that nothing is impossible, but accountest thyself immortal, and that thou canst understand all things—every art, every science, and the manner and custom of every living thing—become higher than all height, and lower than all depths; comprehend in thyself the qualities of all the creatures, of the fire, the water, the dry, and the moist; and conceive that thou canst at once be everywhere, in the sea, in the earth; at once understand thyself not yet begotten, in the womb, young, old, dead, the things after death, and all these together; as also all times, places, deeds, qualities, quantities thou mayest; or else thou canst not yet understand God.*

But if thou shut up thy soul in thy body, and abuse it, and say, I understand nothing, I am afraid of the sea, I cannot climb up to heaven, I know not who I am—what hast thou to do with God? For thou canst understand none of those fair and good things, but must be a lover of the body and evil. For it is the greatest evil not to know God. But to be able to know, and to will, and to hope, is the strait way and the divine way, proper to the good. It will everywhere meet thee, and everywhere be seen of the plain and easy, when thou dost expect or look for it. It will meet thee waking, sleeping, sailing, travelling; by night, by day; when thou speakest and when thou keepest silence. For it is nothing, which is not the image of God.

His close is most divine: *And yet thou sayest, God is invisible; but be advised; for who is more manifest than He? For therefore*

He made all things, that thou by all things mightest see Him. This is the good of God, His virtue is this; to appear and be seen in all things. This is the bottom of all other greatnesses whatsoever. God is infinitely communicative, infinitely prone to reveal Himself, infinitely wise and able to do it. He hath made the soul on purpose that it might see Him. And if the eye, that was made for the world, being so little a ball of earth and water, can take in all, and see all that is visible; if the sight of the eye be present with all that it beholdeth; much more is the soul both able to see and to be present with all that is divine and eternal.

I know very well that a man divided from God is a weak inconsiderable creature, as the eye is, if divided from the body and without the soul; but united to God, a man is a transcendent and celestial thing. God is his life, his greatness, his power, his blessedness and perfection. And as the Apostle saith, *He that is joined to the Lord is one spirit.* His omnipresence and eternity fill the soul, and make it able to contain all heights and depths and lengths and breadths whatsoever. And it is the desire of the soul *to be filled with all the fulness of God.*

Magnanimous desires are the natural results of a magnanimous capacity. The desire of *being like gods, knowing good and evil,* was the destruction of the world. Not as if it were unlawful to desire to be like God, but to aspire to the perfection in a forbidden way was unlawful. By disobedience, and by following our own inventions; by seeking to the creature, to the stock of a tree, to make us like God—that is erroneous and poor and despicable. But to know ourselves, and in the strait and divine way to come immediately to God, to contemplate Him in His eternity and glory, is a right and safe way. For the soul will by that means be the sphere of His omnipresence, and the temple of the Godhead. It will become eternity, as Trismegistus speaketh, or one spirit with God, as the Apostle. And then it must needs be present with all things in heaven, and in the earth and in the sea, as God is; for all things will be in it, as it were by thoughts and intellections.

A magnanimous soul, then, if we respect its capacity, is an immovable sphere of power and knowledge; far greater than all worlds, by its virtue and power passing through all things, through the centre of the earth and through all existences. And shall such a creature as this be contented with vanities and trifles, straws and feathers, painted butterflies, hobby-horses and rattles? These are the treasures of little children. But you will say, a man delighteth in purses of gold, and cabinets of jewels, in houses and palaces, in crowns and sceptres. Add kingly delights, and say he delighteth in arms and victories, and triumphs and coronations. These are great, in respect of playthings. But all these are feeble and pusillanimous to a great soul. As Scipio was going up to heaven, the earth itself seemed but a nut-shell, and he was ashamed of all his victories and triumphs, amazed at his madness in quarrelling and fighting about territories and kingdoms. Contracted to a star, and lost into nothing, the whole earth is but one invisible point, when a man soareth to the height of immensity, and beholdeth and compasseth its everlasting circumference, which is infinite every way beyond the heavens. It is the true and proper immensity of the soul, which can no more be contented with the narrow confinement of this world, no more rest in the childishness of all the noise of the interests of men, be no more satisfied with its earthly glories, than the sun can be shut up in a dark lantern.

It is true, indeed, it would desire to see, as the angels do, the least and lowest of all the creatures full of the glory and blessedness of God, all wisdom and goodness in everything, and is apt to complain for want of some eternal and celestial light wherein to behold them. But if all the expansions of time and eternity should be void, and all the extents and outgoings of infinity empty round about them; though things upon earth, nay, and things in the heavens, should be never so rich and divine and beautiful; yet such is the magnanimity of a great soul, that it would hugely be displeased; its loss and its distaste would be alike infinite. Infinite honours, infinite treasures, infinite enjoyments, things endless in number, value and excellency are the objects of its care and desire; the greatness of its spirit leads it to consider and inquire whether all the spaces above the heavens, and all the parts of God's everlasting kingdom be full of joys; whether there be any end or bound of His kingdom; whether there be any defect or miscarriage, any blemish or disorder in it, any vile or common thing, any remissness or neglect, any cause of complaint or deformity. As also whether all the ages of the world are divine and sacred, whether, after they are gone, they abide to their places; whether there be anything in them to entertain the powers of the soul with delight, and feed them with satisfaction; what end, what use, what excellency there is in men. Whether all the ways of God are full of beauty and perfection; all wisdom, justice, holiness, goodness, love and power? What regions eternal blessedness is seated in? What glory, what reason, what agreeableness and harmony is in all His counsels? Whether those durations of eternity, before the world is made, are full or empty, full of bright and amiable objects, or dark and obscure? Whether the government of the world be perfect; whether the soul be divine in itself; whether it be conducive to its own felicity, or to the happiness of all those in whom it is concerned? Whether the world shall end? If it shall, after what manner, whether by deluge or accident? Whether all ages and nations shall rise from the dead? Whether there shall be a general doom, or a day of judgment? Whether I am concerned in all the transactions and passages at that day? Whether all mankind shall be united into one, to make up one complete and perfect body, whereof they all are the fellow-members? What shall be after the end of the world? Whether we shall live for ever? Whether we shall see God, and know one another? Whether we shall reign in eternal glory? Whether in the confusions of hell there be any beauty, and whether in the torments of the damned we shall find any joy or satisfaction? Whether all the riches, customs and pleasures of this world shall be seen? Whether, in the world to come, any fruit shall appear and arise from them, for which they shall be esteemed to have been not in vain, but profitable in relation to all eternity? What kind of life we shall lead, and what kind of communion and fellowship angels and men shall have with each other? Whether the works of God were unworthy of His choice, or the best of all that were possible? What His laws are, as to their nature and excellency? Whether His love be really sincere and infinite? Whether there be any such thing as infinite wisdom, goodness and bounty, blessedness and glory? Such things as these are the concerns and inquiries of a magnanimous soul. And if its expectations and desires are absolutely satisfied, it will easily appear and break forth upon all occasions into the most high and magnanimous actions.

Trismegistus (or whoever else was the author of that book) saw the deep capacity of his own soul, but, if a conjecture may be made by the residue of the discourse, did not understand the end, at least not clearly, for which it was implanted. Some knowledge he had, that all things in eternity were the objects of that power, by reason of which he calls them fair and good; but that they were to be the treasures and enjoyments of the soul, I do not find him affirming. He that knows this much must needs be of our Saviour's mind, who, when all the kingdoms of the world and the glory of them were showed Him by Satan in a moment of time, despised them all; for the divine and celestial kingdom is infinitely greater, and in a far more perfect manner to be enjoyed.

He that knoweth the honour which cometh from above will despise the honour which men can pay, and in comparison of that honour which cometh from God only, esteem all the honour of this world but false and feeble. Not as if men were, in the truth of nature, vile and despicable creatures; a magnanimous man knows all others to be by nature like himself, and is apt to reverence all of his kind as sublime and celestial creatures. But he is a man of a clear and discerning spirit, and the corruption of nature makes him to slight all that is defiled. He sees that men are generally evil, deformed and blind, erroneous, perverse and foolish, poor and miserable; and that all the honour which they generally give is irrational and feigned. A little colour in the face, a gay coat, a fine horse, a palace and a coach, an exchequer full of gold, or some such light and superficial causes, are all the grounds of the respect that they pay us.

And if the glory and esteem I have
Be nothing else but what my silver gave,
If for no other ground
I am with love or praises crown'd,
'Tis such a shame, such vile, such base repute,
'Tis better starve, than eat such empty fruit.

If a king be dejected [1] from his throne, it is but poor comfort that he is admired by persons condemned to die, and praised by beggars. The dignity and power of the persons that admire us is of great consideration, in the love and delight which they take in us. They all must vanish and perish as a dream. No honour is truly great but that which is continual and endless too. A great and mighty soul can care for no honour but that which comes from wise and amiable persons, that are themselves great and honourable, most rich and powerful, holy, just, blessed and glorious. Honour from God and His holy angels, from the eternal Son of God and all His saints, is marvellous and substantial. That honour which is paid upon great and solid causes—because a man is well pleasing to God, and exalted to His throne; because he is the very image of God, and has dominion over all the creatures; because he is infinitely beloved of God, and all angels and men are commanded to love him; because he is redeemed by the blood of Christ, and made a temple of the Holy Ghost; because he is a priest and king to his eternal Creator; because he is full of goodness and wisdom, adorned with every kind of virtue and made an heir of eternal glory; because he is faithful and true, and just and holy; because he hath conquered death and hell, and sin and the grave, and triumpheth over them—this is, being paid by such persons, honour indeed; and to desire this honour is the property and virtue of a magnanimous soul.

An eagle cannot stoop at flies. An Alexander or a Caesar cannot debase or confine their souls to the pleasures of a cottage in the wilderness. Infinite hopes and infinite desires, infinite fears and despairs and sorrows, infinite joys and delights and glories, infinite adorations, praises and thanksgivings, infinite and eternal objects, are the only fit and proper concerns for the affections of a great and magnanimous soul. The very signification of the word is greatness of soul or, if you please, of mind; for a distinction may be made between the soul and mind. The soul of man is the immutable essence or form of his nature, unemployed. His power of reasoning is alive, even then when it is quiet and unactive; and this is his soul. It is one and the same in all men, and of itself equally inclined to all great and

[1] Deposed.

transcendent things; but in the most it is misguided, baffled and suppressed, and, though it be never so great, it is to no purpose. The greatness implanted by nature is not magnanimity; it is a natural disposition, not an acquired habit, as all virtue is.

A man is then said to be of such a mind, when he determines or thinks in such a manner. His mind is good that intendeth well, his mind is evil that designeth mischief. So that the mind is the soul exerting its power in such an act; and the greatest soul in the world is but pusillanimous, that mindeth little things. A great soul is magnanimous in effect, a mind applied to mighty objects. Some men have a magnanimity infused by the power of education, and are led by custom to great things, and, in a manner, by necessity; for such is their place and calling that they are frequently led to greater objects than other men. Of this sort are the most eminent rank of grandees and princes. Kingdoms and thrones, and privy councils and queens and armies, are their natural dialect. This is no virtue, for though it be not innate by nature, yet they are born to it, and it is given by fortune. Others consider what they have to do, and make an election; and though they are born in a poor and despicable estate, are not magnanimous by nature or fortune, but by choice and voluntary election. Not to satisfy the humour of a high blood, choler and fire; nor to answer the necessities of a high calling, but to discharge the office of virtue and wisdom; and this is the offspring of the will, the true and genuine virtue; which is as it is far more worthy than any of the rest, is guided to far better and more glorious objects, and more diffusely given by the bounty of God to all kind of men in all conditions.

In the poor it is more marvellous than in the great and rich. It has such an undaunted property in its nature that, though the disproportion between them and their assurance or hope or desire seem infinite, and the end which they aim at by their magnanimity is judged impossible; though their attempt appear a ridiculous madness, to them to whom the verities of religion appear incredible; yet they are no whit discouraged or disheartened at the matter, but stoutly march on, being animated by the alarum of such a trumpet, such a drum, as magnanimity is. His faith is more divine by conquering the discouragements of the world than if he met with no censure or opposition.

If you would have the character of a magnanimous soul, he is the son of eternal power and the friend of infinite goodness, a temple of divine and heavenly wisdom; that is not imposed upon by the foul and ragged disguises of nature, but acquainted with her great capacities and principles, more than commonly sensible of her interests and depths and desires. He is one that has gone in unto felicity, and enjoyed her beauties, and comes out again, her perfect lover and champion; a man whose inward stature is miraculous, and his complexion so divine that he is king of as many kingdoms as he will look on; one that scorns the smutty way of enjoying things like a slave, because he delights in the celestial way, and the image of God. He knows that all the world lies in wickedness, and admires not at all that things palpable and near and natural are unseen, though most powerful and glorious; because men are blind and stupid. He pities poor vicious kings, that are oppressed with heavy crowns of vanity and gold, and admires [1] how they can content themselves with such narrow territories; yet delights in their regiment [2] of the world, and pays them the honour that is due unto them. The glorious exaltation of good kings he more abundantly extols, because so many thousand magnanimous creatures are committed to their trust, and they that govern them understand their value. But he sees well enough that the king's glory and true repose consists in the catholic and eternal kingdom. As for himself, he *is come unto Mount Sion, and to the city of the living God, the heavenly Jerusalem, and to an innumerable company of angels; to the general assembly and church of the first-born, which are written in heaven; and to God the judge of all, and to the spirits of just men made perfect and to Jesus the Mediator of the New Covenant.* And therefore, receiving a kingdom which cannot be moved, he desires to serve God acceptably, with reverence and godly fear. And the truth is, he can fear nothing else, for God is a consuming fire. He very well understands what the Apostle saith, and dares believe him: *I cease not to give thanks for you, making mention of you in my prayers; that the God of our Lord Jesus Christ, the Father of glory, may give unto you the Spirit of wisdom*

[1] Wonders.
[2] Government.

and revelation in the knowledge of him; the eyes of your understanding being enlightened, that ye may know what is the hope of his calling, and what the riches of the glory of his inheritance in the saints; and what is the exceeding greatness of his power to usward, who believe, according to the working of his mighty power; which he wrought in Christ, when he raised him from the dead and set him at his own right hand in the heavenly places; far above all principality and power and might and dominion, and every name that is named, not only in this world, but in that also which is to come; and hath put all things under his feet. And he gave him to be head over all things in the Church which is his Body, the fulness of him that filleth all in all. Now to him that is able to do exceeding abundantly, above all that we ask or think, according to the power that worketh in us, unto him be glory in the Church by Christ Jesus, throughout all ages, world without end, amen.

A great and a clear soul knoweth that all these intimations must needs be true, for it is an amazing miracle that they should be otherwise. Infinite love and eternal blessedness are near allied; and that these should cease is contrary to all nature, in God, in the soul of man, in heaven, in earth, in the order of the universe; and contrary to all that visible glory which in the world appeareth.

CHAPTER XXIX

Of Modesty: its nature, its original, its effects and consequences

MODESTY is a comely grace in the behaviour of a man, by which he piously dissembleth his own perfections and blusheth at his praises. It springeth from a certain fear and sense of his imperfection. 'Tis the shadow of guilt, and a beautiful cover of original corruption. It is sometimes natural, and, which is contrary to all other virtues, more truly virtuous for being so. For then it is simple, genuine and real; but studied modesty is affected and artificial. Yet where nature has not been so obliging as to give the endowment, 'tis not altogether to be condemned, since it is agreeable to the best of our conditions in this world, and supplies a defect in his nature that is born without it.

It is akin to shame, yet increases the honour of him that wears it. It is the shade of virtue, yet makes it brighter. It is a tincture of humility, visible in a vermilion and deeper dye; and the more natural and easy, the more sweet and delightful. It charms the envy of those that admire us, and by seeming to extinguish our worth gives it a double beauty. It reconciles a man to the enemies of his grace and virtue, and by a softness irresistible wins a compassion in all spectators. It is a virtue which, by refusing the honour that is due unto it, acquireth more; a real counterfeit, and the only honest and true dissimulation. It is an effeminate, yet a laudable, quality; a spice of cowardice, more prevalent [1] than courage; a virtue by which we despise all meaner honours, while we are ambitiously carried to the highest glory. It seemeth inconsistent with magnanimity, yet is her youngest sister.

It hath not many objects, nor are its aims apparent, nor its ends conspicuous. It is the mother of fine and delicate resentments [2]; its strength consisteth in tenderness and fear. He that is magnanimous in one respect may be modest in another. Praises and commendations are the fuel of its nature; it feedeth upon them, while it grows by rejecting them. It delights in what it feareth; and is full of discords, but more full of harmonies. It is pleased in its displeasure, and always fighteth with its own repugnancies. It is a virtue mixed of sense and reason. Its region is in the body more than in the soul, and in all its spiritual motions it is attended with corporeal impressions. The blood and spirits dance in the veins, as if nature were delighted with its own confusions. By captivating the favour of men upon earth, it affecteth the very angels in heaven with much of pleasure. It putteth us in mind of guilt and innocency at the same time, and by confession of the one addeth lustre to the other. By making way for the acceptance

[1] Effective.
[2] Feelings.

of a man's person, it giveth more esteem, success and efficacy to his other virtues; and by this means it hath much of excellency in a little.

He that hath it not, must needs acquire something like it; and if he be elaborate in expressing it, must hide his art under the veil of nature. Though it be remote from the highest end, it may be guided to it and, when so directed, is always innocent. It is very just, for, while other virtues make it a virtue, it is a grace unto them all. You may look upon it as a tangible flame, and see it in others; but must feel it in yourself before you can understand it. It is old in children, young in middle-aged men, at last an infant. It is greatest in the beginning of our life, it decayeth in youth, in old age it vanisheth—at least, changeth its dwelling; for it ceaseth to be in the body of an aged man, and turneth into courtesy or civility in the conversation. When it dieth, it is buried in humility and liveth in its tomb; being empaled,[1] as it were, with meekness, and waiting daily for its resurrection. Much cannot be said of it precisely, but it is best commended when left to your practice. It is the only tender infant of all the virtues; like Cupid among the gods, it appeareth frequently and is much exercised in the school of Venus; but is capable of more high and more noble uses.

Modesty in apparel is commended in the scriptures. It implies moderation and chastity together. It is sometimes opposed to lasciviousness, sometimes to excess, sometimes to impudence; and is a great virtue, if for nothing else but in the exclusion of these abominable vices.

The other virtues seem to be the members and substantial parts of the body of worth; modesty like the air and mean of them all. It is the guard of the soul against looseness and pride, a virtue repressing the fumes of self-conceit, and a kind of silent restraint of all that arrogance that delights in pomps and superfluities. Though it be a little virtue, its reality is apparent; for unless it be made up with some other supplies, the want of modesty is pernicious and destructive.

It is exercised in small things, but is of long extent in the virtue of its influence; and because of the multiplicity of its uses

[1] Placed side by side.

R

and occasions, amounts to a considerable degree of goodness. It hath something like love in its nature, for it preferreth another above itself; and in that its magnetical and obliging quality much consisteth. *In honour preferring one another*: it fulfils that law, wherein our most near and tender interest is concerned. In preferring one another, there is a lovely contest, more sweet and happy than the best agreement. It is of all other the most friendly strife and kind contention.

CHAPTER XXX

The excellent nature of Liberality. Rules to be observed in the practice of it. Regard to our servants, relations, friends and neighbours must be had in our liberality, as well as to the poor and needy. How our external acts of charity ought to be improved for the benefit of men's souls. Liberality maketh religion real and substantial

Liberality, in the common use and acceptation of the word, differs from magnificence as modesty from magnanimity. There is much of liberty and freedom in its nature. For avarice is a strict and sour vice, and they that are guilty of it are called misers; but a bountiful man hath a good eye, and is as free from anxiety as he is free in disbursing. His communicative humour is much his enlargement; he knows little of confinement, care or bondage.

There are two virtues that endanger a man's welfare in this world, and they have all the temporal promises. Meekness seems to encourage our enemies to trample us under feet, because it promiseth impunity; and it is directly said, *The meek shall inherit the earth;* nay, be so far from having enemies that *the meek shall inherit the abundance of peace.* And concerning liberality, which makes a man a beggar, or at least threatens to make him so by wasting his estate, the scripture saith, *The liberal soul shall be made fat. The liberal heart deviseth liberal things, and by liberal things shall he stand.*

Men are almost in all things contrary to God. For since they tumbled out of Eden, they have lost their wits, and their heads are downwards. They think it wisdom to keep their money against a rainy day, and to lay it up for fear of poverty. But Solomon adviseth them to the direct contrary, and maketh it an argument why they should be liberal: *Because they know not what evil may come upon the earth.* We cannot put our treasures into safer hands than into God Almighty's; nor can we make any use of gold and silver, comparable to that of charitable uses. By this it is that we *lay up a good foundation against the time to come,* and oblige others to receive us into mansions here, into everlasting habitations hereafter.

My Lord Bridgeman, late Lord Keeper, confessed himself in his will to be but a steward of his estate, and prayed God to forgive him all his offences, *in getting, mis-spending or not spending it as he ought to do;* and that after many charitable and pious works, perhaps surmounting his estate, though concealed from the notice and knowledge of the world.

I have heard of a smart obliging calumny fastened on a great man of France, by one that had largely tasted of his bounty; for having been in his house honourably entertained for some space of time, and observing how much the palace was frequented by all kind of learned men, and how liberal the master of it was, especially to men of worth and virtue, he charges the man with the greatest covetousness in the world, because he turned all his riches into obligations, as if he had put all his estate and moneys to use; but to covet affections and to be rich in hearts is no deformity.

The truth is, when the ways whereby love is begotten in the soul are well examined, and the happiness of being truly beloved and delighted in is known, no man is so wise as the liberal man. He is his own end, while he thinks not of it. For nothing is more conducive to his ease and honour than the bounty of munificence which enriches his soul. There are three things which beget love—beauty, benefits and praises. They are all three shut up in goodness, which is the fountain of liberality. The beauty of the face is a silent oratory, a high style of commendation without an epistle; yet by doing benefits it prevaileth more than by any of its charms, and maketh itself great by enriching others. Love inspires it with an amiable soul; and if others are delighted with their own praises, he that is liberal in the acknowledgment of men's virtues, and giveth honour to the worthy, is full of music in his words, of a sweet and pleasing behaviour, agreeable in his deeds and fraught with the honour which he imparteth so freely.

A liberal man is clothed like the sun with the rays of his own glory, and established himself in the hearts of his neighbours, and reigns like a king by the sole interest of virtue and goodness. *Every man is a friend to him that giveth many gifts.* He may be as holy and as temperate and as wise as an angel; no man will be offended at him, because he beautifies his religion with so much goodness. He enjoys himself and his riches and his friends, and may do what he will with perfect liberty, because he delights in the felicity of all that accost him. He puts embroideries on religion by the cheerfulness of his spirit, and carries a light wherever he goes, that makes men to reverence his person and esteem his censures. He moves in a sphere of wonders; his life is a continual stream of miracles; because he is always sacrificing himself and his possessions to the benefit of the world and the comfort of others. Benefits and blessings are his life-guard, like his guardian angels always attendant on him. His house is the habitation of joy and felicity, and yields a spectacle of contentment to every beholder. His neighbours are his security, not his suspicion; and other men's houses the forts and ramparts about his own. No man will hurt him, because they extinguish their own contentment and benefit in him. They tender him as the apple of their eye, because he is a greater comfort and advantage than that unto them. The ancient custom of Paradise, so long since lost and forgotten in the world, revives in its family, where all men are entertained as brothers and sisters, at the expenses of God and nature. He taketh care, because thrift is the fuel of liberality; and is frugal, that he may be bountiful. All his aim and labour is that he may maintain good works, and *make his light so shine before men that they, seeing his good works, may glorify his Father which is in heaven.* There is a generous confidence discovered in all his actions, and a little glimpse of heaven in his behaviour; for he lives as if he were among a company of angels. All men's estates are his, and his theirs. If he had them all, he would impart them, and restore them to supply their wants; perhaps not with so much wisdom as God hath done, but with as much pleasure and contentment as his goodness can inspire, in the exercise of power so kindly and well employed. But because the designs of God are infinitely deeper than he can well apprehend, and laid all in eternal wisdom, he is pleased and delighted that his care is prevented,[1] and that God hath done that for other men, to which his own inclination would readily prompt him, were it left undone. If it were permitted him to wish whatsoever he listed, of all other things he would chiefly desire to be a blessing to the whole world; and that he is not so is his only discontentment. But for that too there are remedies in felicity; when he knows all, his desire is granted. For a life beautified with all virtue is the greatest gift that can be presented to God, angels and men; and when all secrets shall be revealed, all hidden things brought to light, his life shall be seen in its perfection, and his desires themselves be the enjoyments and pleasures of all the creatures.

There is a certain kind of sympathy that runs through the universe, by virtue of which all men are fed in the feeding of one. Even the angels are clothed in the poor and needy. All are touched and concerned in every one. Like the brazen pillars in the temple of Minerva, if one be smitten, all resound the blow throughout the temple; or like the strings of several lutes screwed up to unisons, the one is made to quaver by the others' motions. If Christ Himself be fed in the poor, much more may angels and men. At the last day we find no other scrutiny about religion, but what we have done or neglected in liberality. *Come, ye blessed of my Father, inherit the kingdom prepared for you from the foundation of the world; for I was hungry, and ye gave me meat; thirsty, and ye gave me drink; naked, and ye clothed me; a stranger, and ye took me in. I was sick, and ye visited me; I was in prison, and ye came unto me. Inasmuch as ye have done it unto the least of these my brethren, ye have done it unto me.*

[1] Forestalled.

Love, it seems, will sit in judgment on the world; and the rule of trial shall be the fulfilling of its laws. Love shall be the glory too of all the assessors; and every act of cruelty and oppression infinitely odious in all their eyes.

There was a certain king which would take account of his servants; and when he had begun to reckon, one was brought unto him that owed him ten thousand talents. But forasmuch as he had not to pay, the Lord commanded him to be sold, and all that he had, and payment to be made. The servant therefore fell down and worshipped him, saying, Lord, have patience with me, and I will pay thee all. Then the Lord of that servant was moved with compassion, and loosed him and forgave him the debt. But the same servant went out, and found one of his fellow-servants which owed him one hundred pence, and he laid hold on him and took him by the throat, saying, Pay me that thou owest. And his fellow-servant fell down at his feet and besought him, Have patience with me, and I will pay thee all. And he would not, but went and cast him into prison till he should pay the debt. So when his fellow-servants saw what was done, they were very sorry, and came and told their Lord of all that was done.

Every neglect and contempt of our fellow-brethren is injurious and grievous to God, angels and men; for there is one common principle in all nature, to hate evil deeds, and especially those of rigour and severity, when we ourselves stand in need of mercy and have received favour. This common principle of sympathy and compassion entitles us to all the good that is done to any man in the world. The love of equity and reason, and the natural inclination that carries us to delight in excellent deeds, gives us an interest in all that are performed. The beauty of the one is as sweet and blessed as the deformity of the other is odious and distasteful. And if we ourselves are infinitely obliged and live by the bounty and goodness of another, after we have forfeited the King's favour, have received it again with pardon and forgiveness, nay, with more and greater benefits; if we shall not be liberal to one another, it is a strange inequality. But the discharge of our duty will make us amiable and delightful.

That the King of Glory is so concerned in the welfare of His subjects, were there nothing else in the duty but that consideration, is an infinite encouragement. *He that receiveth you, receiveth me,* is such an obligation that, as it is all goodness in itself, so is it all motive unto us. Eternity will scarce be sufficient to fathom its depth. Do we feed God Himself in feeding the poor, and His eternal Son Jesus Christ? Are these needy persons the representatives of the Godhead, in whom we are to show all our affection, love and gratitude to the fountain of all life and happiness? How infinite ought our liberality to be, when we consider the excellency of our bliss and benefactor! Are they beloved, are they all His sons, the very express image of Himself; all disguised and concealed kings, all temples of eternal glory? What measure can confine or shut up our bowels? [1] Are the spectators so innumerable, so divine, so blessed, so nearly allied to ourselves, so rich and great and beautiful; are they so deeply concerned in the welfare of others, and does every act of charity extend to all; shall we appear in the very act itself eternally before them? What a vast ambition of pleasing all these glorious persons should be expressed in every operation of the soul! As every thought is seen throughout all eternity, and every word that is spoken here on earth heard in the utmost extents of immensity, so there is a kind of omnipresent greatness in the smallest action, for it is virtually extended through all the omnipresence of Almighty God; even as every centre wherein it can be done is eternally near, nay, and within Him in the remotest part of His omnipresence. 'Tis dilated in a moment, and fills the immensity of God with its nature. According to its kind, it affecteth all His essence in all spaces whatsoever.

Yet is there a rule for the bounding of all external acts of charity, and another for improving it. Intelligence is the light wherein alms-deeds ought to shine and attain their glory. Love is the soul of compassion, and zeal the fervour of perfection; without which, *though a man bestow all his goods to feed the poor, and give his body to be burned, it profiteth nothing.* Where this great abyss of goodness is, prudence may dispense it, as it seeth occasion. All other virtues attending upon it, it is impossible to destroy itself here upon earth, unless the case be so urgent that

[1] Compassion.

it is better to die than to live in the world; *for a good man showeth favour and lendeth;* but it is added, *he will guide his affairs with discretion.*

The first rule is, to secure the life and growth of the tree, by causing it so to bear one year that it may bring forth fruit another. It is no good husbandry to cut it down, nor any charity to make it wither and expire; and on this very account, a charitable man must preserve himself, that he may do good, by continuing longer able to do it.

He that will examine the proportions and measures of his liberality may take this rule for the second: let thy superfluities give place to other men's conveniences, thy conveniences to their necessities, thy necessities to their extremities.

A third rule is this: our riches must be expended according to the several circumstances and occasions of our lives. A liberal man will not pinch and starve his servants, for it is contrary to the nature of bounty to oppress any, to hurt any, to trample upon any. He will be good to all, and to those most that are near to him. God hateth robbery for burnt offering, or that strangers should eat the children's meat, or that beggars or riotous persons should devour the right of a man's servants. He that does brave acts abroad, but is a niggard within doors, has a glorious train spread abroad like a peacock, but stands upon black feet, and may bear that unlucky bird for his crest, which is the emblem of pride and vainglory. So is it with young prodigals, that oppress poor tradesmen by defrauding them of their debts, yet are lavish enough to the poor and needy. This is a defect with which goodness is inconsistent, and it blasteth their charity. It is better take off one hundred pound a year from one's benevolence to the poor than wrong a servant or creditor of a shilling.

The rule therefore is this: first secure the works of necessity; have food and raiment for thyself, keep out of debt. Next, render to every man his due in point of justice, and employ no man thou canst not pay; rather perish thyself than oppress another. If thou art able, and hast anything to spare, then let the miseries of the needy be supplied in the works of compassion and charity; but let not all be swallowed up here; thy neighbours and acquaintance, and friends and kindred, claim a share; and thou must secure something for the works of courtesy and hospitality. So order all, both in thy estate and life, that the kindness of God may shine in all. So doing, thy stewardship shall be acceptable to the whole world, and thy memory blessed among men and angels.

Our Saviour when He wrought His miracles, as He opened the eyes of the blind, healed the sick, cast out devils, raised the dead, gave food to the hungry, tongues to the dumb, ears to the deaf and legs to the lame, so did He give advice to the ignorant, and interpret all His design by those parables and sermons which attended His cures. Good counsel is oftentimes a greater gift than a trunk of money. While the iron is hot, it is time to strike. Good counsel is like a bitter pill, that must be gilded with liberality. If the word of God be like good seed, the heart in which it is sown is softened by sorrow, and ploughed up by affliction, and prepared to receive it by the husbandry of Providence; and the properest season that can be chosen for instruction is the time of obliging.

He that intendeth the welfare of the soul by all the good works he doth to the body is deep and perfect in charity. A wise man will improve his advantages and enrich his gifts with pious discourses. A benefactor has authority to talk what he listeth, and bribes his auditor to patience by his bounty. Since *he that winneth souls is wise,* a profound liberality will not let slip a golden opportunity, nor suffer his gift to be dark and insignificant. He will make mention of the glory of God and the love of Christ, the guilt of sin, the danger of hell and the hope of heaven, and always endeavour to make his love apparent to that God for whose sake he pities the poor and is kind towards all. Forasmuch as man hath two parts, and his body is, without the soul, but a putrid carcase, he will put life into his money, and inspire his munificence with all his reasons, that his bounty may consist of two parts in like manner, and have a soul for its interpreter. Liberality to the soul is the soul of liberality. Paradise and heaven are better to be given than gold and silver; and every good man will imitate the Apostle, who was ready not to impart the gospel of God only, but his own soul to the benefit of those for whom Christ died.

This one thing further I desire you to note. *He that soweth sparingly shall reap sparingly, but he that soweth bountifully shall reap also bountifully.* In the kingdom of heaven every man receiveth his penny, because all their joys are common and equal. Their treasures shall be the same, but they will differ in glory. The same God, the same angels, the same men, all the same objects shall be round about every man. Every man shall see and enjoy all the glory of his eternal kingdom, because every one's life and felicity shall be perfect. But yet their works follow them; and every man shall be clothed in the beauty of his own actions, virtues and graces. There may be twenty children in the same family, yet all of several features. There may be a thousand trees in the same orchard, yet all of different kinds. The same brightness and glory may be round about them, the same sky cover them, the same earth support them, the same stars serve them, the same sea, the same dew, the same air and nourishment feed them; and yet one be more fair and honourable and excellent than the other. All the world does know that a tree laden with fruits and blossoms is far more beautiful than a tree that is barren and unfruitful; and the degrees of beauty are according as the fruits are, more or less. And as the fruits they bring forth adorn them, so do their own works praise them in the gates. Heaven, as it is a kingdom of light and knowledge, is a kingdom of perfection. Righteousness and justice flourish there in their fullness, and every several degree of excellence is entertained with an answerable degree of esteem. According to the number and greatness of their virtues, every one is honoured by saints and angels.

Now lest these fruits should receive any impediment by the vices and corruptions of men, order is taken, *that we should love our enemies, bless them that curse us, do good to them that hate us, pray for them that despitefully use and persecute us;* by which means it is that a liberal man surmounts all obstacles whatsoever, lives among dragons as if he were surrounded by doves, and, though he be environed with devils, is as if he were conversant with angels; because he takes no notice of any vice in any man to stop him, but is as liberal as if all were full of worth and virtue. Nay, he is more good and more miraculous. Their vices, their provocations, their disorders cannot stain or embitter his nature; but he will be always cheerful and bright and fair, and free and perfect. To love the amiable and be kind to the beautiful is natural and easy. It is not given to the angels but to visit the faithful and the penitent. But to love the evil, to be kind and good and serviceable to the deformed and the odious, to the injurious and ungrateful, is somewhat more than angelical. We learn it not of them, but of God and of His eternal Son; who hath commanded us *to be the children of our Father which is is heaven; for he maketh his sun to rise on the evil and on the good, and sendeth rain on the just and on the unjust.* Even publicans and sinners do, in some manner as much as angels, love them that love them. In heaven they have no malignity or malice or wrong to overcome; all that they love is beauty and goodness; unless they learn of Jesus Christ, and imitate Him here on earth towards us sinners. But our duty is far greater, and our opposition more; which is intimated also in our Saviour's words: *For if ye love them which love you, what reward have you? Do not even the publicans the same? And if ye salute your brethren only, what do ye more than others? Do not even the publicans so? Be ye therefore perfect, even as your Father in heaven is perfect.*

In the close of all, I beseech you to consider this one most cogent and weighty expostulation. It is the beloved Disciple's: *If a man say, I love God, and hateth his brother, he is a liar; for he that loveth not his brother whom he hath seen, how can he love God whom he hath not seen?* Our neighbours are not only the representatives of God, but they are here upon earth, are visible, are present with us, are corporeal, as we are, and always near us. Our actions among them are palpable, and our conversation with them real. God is invisible and absent from us; He is afar off in the highest heavens, incorporeal and incomprehensible. If we are remiss and careless in our duty towards our neighbour, all our devotion towards God will be but imaginary. Our religion will degenerate into an idle and vain chimera, become a weak and feeble shadow, be seated in the fancy, and dwindle away into an airy speculation. The reality of religion consists in the solid practice of it among the sons of men that are daily with us. The difficult and serious actions of our lives abroad feed our meditation in all our retirements, and infuse a reality and strength into our devotions, which make them solid and substantial.

CHAPTER XXXI

Of Magnificence in God. Its resemblance in man. The chief magnificence of the soul is spiritual. It is perfectly expressed in the outward life, when the whole is made perfect and presented to God. God gives all His life to us, and we should give all ours to Him. How fair and glorious it may be

GOD being proposed as the pattern of our liberality and kindness by our Saviour, the nature of His bounty is fit to be considered for our information; which is great, and public, and advantageous to many. In some of His private dispensations, it walks under the notion and form of liberality, as it giveth food and raiment, gold and silver, houses and lands to particular persons. But in other effects of His eternal love, which are great and public, its nature is changed into the highest magnificence.

Magnificence is a virtue scarcely to be found but in kings and emperors. It is busied in erecting temples and triumphal arches, magnificent theatres, colleges and universities, aqueducts and palaces, royal monuments and pyramids, marts, havens, exchanges and all those other great and mighty things wherein the glory of imperial power is made conspicuous, and whereby whole nations are benefited and kingdoms adorned.

Great power, riches, wisdom and goodness must concur in the effect which is truly magnificent. It must be of great lustre and glory, as well as of public use and benefit; and as it is wrought with great labour and expense, be imparted by a great soul, and freely given to the good of the people. For magnificence implies greatness and bounty united.

The creation of the universe was a great and magnificent work, because the lustre and beauty of the world is a sublime and wonderful gift imparted to millions. The bounty of God in adorning all ages with cities and empires, for the benefit and enjoyment of all the world, is another piece of His royal magnificence. The infusion of a soul so divine and everlasting into the body of a man is an act of love transcendently greater than all the aqueducts and trophies in the world. For such a celestial presence, such a sublime and illimited power, such a vast and noble workmanship as that is—which can see and comprehend all eternity and time together, extend to all objects in all worlds, and fill immensity with life and joy, and love and knowledge, with light and beauty and glory, with adorations and praises—though its essence be invisible and all its splendour within, is (next under God) the highest object of all the admiration of men and angels. It is a being as public as the sun, the great occasion of all the ecstasies of the seraphims, the wonder and rapture of all the cherubims, the glory of God communicated to the world in so divine a creature; a miraculous effect of His eternal power, and the resemblance of His Godhead among all the creatures.

The incarnation of His eternal Son, and the giving of the Holy Ghost, was another magnificent effect of His almighty power. So was the preparation of His word, with the gifts He gave unto men in the patriarchs, prophets and apostles; adorned with all the varieties of their labours and virtues, wisdom, courage and patience, lives and examples, deaths and sufferings, oppositions and successes, miracles and revelations. The Jewish nation alone is a magnificent gift to the whole world. The Apostle phraseth the regiment of it as a matter of bounty: *Now if the fall of them be the riches of the world, and the diminishing of them the riches of the Gentiles, how much more their fulness!* And again, *When He ascended up on high, and led captivity captive, He gave gifts unto men, some apostles and some prophets.* When He presented all nations and kingdoms as a token of His love to the angels; when He gave all those glorious hosts in the heavens to the vision, service and pleasure of men; much more when He gave all these in their marvellous order and amity united, to every soul; when He filled the heaven of heavens with joys, and gave all the glory of His kingdom to one (and that one to every one) He manifested the glory of His magnificent power in that of His great and transcendent goodness. And in relation to this, we may cry out with the Apostle (more than for the mysterious regiment of a little nation, as he doth upon the account of God's dealing with the Jews): *O, the depths of the riches both of the wisdom and knowledge of God! How unsearchable are His judgments, and His ways past finding out!* For all things are yours: *whether Paul, or Apollos, or Cephas, or the world, or life, or death, or things present, or things to come, all are yours; and ye are Christ's, and Christ is God's.* Wherefore He saith, *My thoughts are not your thoughts, nor your ways my ways. For as the heavens are higher than the earth, so are my ways higher than your ways, and my thoughts than your thoughts.* You give trifles, and give them but to one; I give worlds, and give them to every one. You divide and disperse your gifts, and lessen by dispersing them; I communicate and unite my gifts, and augment by giving them. You think it impossible for one man to enjoy all things; I think it possible for innumerable millions. You think your interest is abated and your fruition endangered by the communication of your treasures to many; I know they are increased and multiplied by the number of the enjoyers. You think gold and silver to be the greatest gifts, and that nothing is yours but what is shut up within such shores and walls and hedges; I know that men are the greatest treasures and that your interest is extended beyond all worlds, and your possessions illimited.

For according to the tenor of these words, and a little before, He saith: *Thou shalt break forth on the right hand and on the left, and thy seed shall inherit the Gentiles, and make the desolate cities to be inhabited. Fear not, for thou shalt not be ashamed; neither be thou confounded, for thou shalt not be put to shame; for thou shalt forget the shame of thy youth, and shalt not remember the reproach of thy widowhood any more. For thy Maker is thy husband, the Lord of Hosts is His name.* And a little after, He saith: *Thou shalt also be a crown of glory in the hand of the Lord, and a royal diadem in the hand of thy God. Thou shalt no more be termed forsaken, neither shall thy land any more be termed desolate; but thou shalt be called Hephzibah, and thy land Beulah; for the Lord delighteth in thee, and thy land shall be married. For as a young man marrieth a virgin, so shall thy sons marry thee; and as a bridegroom rejoiceth over the bride, so shall thy God rejoice over thee.* For a son to marry with his mother is incest; it is confusion also for a child to go in into his father's wife; and yet the Church of God shall be the lawful bride of every one of all her sons. Here is magnificence! God giveth Himself, and His eternal Son, and His Holy Spirit, and His Bride, and His apostles and prophets, and all the universe to every soul! Which justifieth that saying of St. Chrysostom, *God loveth every one with all the love wherewith He loveth the whole world.* His magnificence exceedeth all limits, laws, imaginations, wishes, possibilities; and He maketh every one heir of the world, co-heir with Christ, to inherit all things; every one more than the sole end of His kingdom. For all the ornaments and riches of a bride are given with her person; her palace and attendants are her lover's upon the marriage, as well as she; and all things that magnify or make her amiable are subservient to his enjoyment, and really his, that is her husband. So that God, giving us His Church to be our Mother and our Bride, hath intended us in all the things whereby He hath benefited her in all kingdoms and ages; and hath loved us in all the love which He hath exercised towards her; and all the fruit of all His love to the whole world resteth in our exaltation.

This is the magnificence of almighty God to every soul in His kingdom. And for this it is that the Church is called the assembly of the first-born; because all her children are the perfect heirs and kings and bridegrooms, every one completely and more to his satisfaction than if he were so alone. For as God is wholly everywhere, and the more here for being in other places; and infinitely here because He is omnipresent; so does He wholly see and intend every one, as if him alone; and love him far the more, by loving every one; for His love being infinite, it is expressed towards him in all the parts of His kingdom. And the more rich and glorious He maketh all things, the more great and happy He maketh him, according to the immeasurable all-sufficiency of His infinite wisdom.

There is in the goodness of God an infinite greatness that makes it magnificent; for He gives Himself. When a queen gives herself, whether it be to a beggar, or to one of her courtiers, or to another king, if it proceed from an ardent love the gift is full of sweetness within; but it is always attended with great magnificence without. Together with herself she gives him her palace, her exchequer, gardens of pleasure, her crown and throne, her sovereignty, her nobles, attendants, and all her kingdom. God doth infinitely more. He gives Himself by loving, and with Himself gives us all His wisdom, goodness and power, by making them full objects of complacency [1]; by doing with them, for us, all that we could devise or desire or effect with them, had they been our own and seated in ourselves. His bounty in giving Himself is attended with infinite advantages, innumerable wonders of love and goodness; a care to make Himself (as a bridegroom does) exceeding amiable and glorious; a care to purify and fit His queen for Himself with all kind of greatness and beauty; a care to adorn His palace with all kind of delectable things—riches, pleasures, magnificent furnitures, perfumes, musicians, pictures, jewels, dainties, feasts, attendants, nobles, etc.; in all which He infinitely exceedeth all the monarchs of the world. His kingdom is celebrated by David with great exultation.

Now, if we would be magnificent as God is, we must have a love within our souls that is willing to impart all these incomprehensible treasures and glories to every soul, and to all His hosts; and, if it be possible, to out-do all this, to give all these worlds, nay, God Himself, and every soul, to all with greater ardour and joy and gratitude; angels and men, ourselves, to all, and all to every one. For that love which is the fountain of all is greater than all, a greater gift and a greater treasure. And that love which imitates the first is, in its place, the only desirable and excellent thing that is possible. God's love in its place is infinitely better than all; removing it, you shake and abolish all. But in such a creature He desires to be beloved. He made him free, that he might be capable of loving; for it is impossible to love by constraint or necessity; and having made him free and left him to himself, infinitely desires to be beloved of him. All His own love unto him, and all the glories of heaven and earth which are prepared for him are means for the obtaining of that end; obligations, motives, allurements, incentives of that love which God desires. If he will not return love, all are embittered and made distasteful. Infinite love infinitely desires to be beloved, and is infinitely displeased if it be neglected. God desires to take complacency [2] in all, to see the beauty of His Bride, and the

[1] Joy. [2] Delight.

accomplishment of His design in the love of His beloved. And nothing in all worlds but the love of that person can be His satisfaction, for nothing can supply the absence or denial of that love which is his end. For in its place it is the only needful and proper thing, far more desired than all that went before. All that went before was but the means; this is the thing designed and endeavoured by them; for upon this return, all the sweetness of the rest dependeth. All is made sweet and complete and delightful, if this soul doth love God in all these things; if not, they are all made vain, and His love is turned into sour displeasure. All the other things are so far from alleviating that they increase His displeasure. The glory and abundance of them is so far from making Him to despise this love that He the more desires it, because He would not have His labour vain. And his own infinite love makes Him the more to esteem the love of this creature, which is, in its place, His sovereign object, and for that very cause so beloved and admired by all angels and men. Is not then the love which man returneth a magnificent thing?

Certainly if it answers all these preparations and obligations as their end, and be looked upon as that without which all the creation is vain and frustrate, it is the most great and marvellous thing in the world, and is, in its own place, of all other things most highly desired by all angels and men; and is the greatest gift which in and by that soul can possibly be given. It is esteem of, honour paid to, and delight in, all these great and most glorious things. It contains in itself a desire to see God pleased with more than the fruition of all worlds, and of becoming itself the greatest treasure to His eternal essence, of all that is possible. And if this desire be not satisfied, all the grandeurs of His eternal kingdom are to no purpose. But *the desire satisfied is a Tree of Life*. What the sun is to the eye, that is love to the desire. God's infinite desire of our love makes it infinitely delightful to Him. David's purpose to build the temple was more accepted than Solomon's performance. And if one contrite groan be better than all sacrifices, to love God with all the soul and understanding is better than to give Him all worlds. We sacrifice all by loving Him as we ought. We see the beauty and glory of all, and offer it all up to Him with infinite desire; our selves also, with infinite gratitude. Could we make millions of worlds, infinitely greater and more perfect than this, they should all be His. No delight, no joy, no pleasure can be greater to us than to see Him reigning. He gives all to us, that we might give it all to Him. In our affection and with our love, it is most delightful. Our affections are the flames and perfumes that enrich the sacrifice. He is a Spirit, to be served in a spiritual manner; all that we *would* do, we do. Infinite desires and intentions of pleasing Him are real objects to His eye. The goodness of the soul and the greatness of His goodness consisteth in them. A will enlarged with an infinite fancy is a prodigious depth of goodness when it is all love; it would do millions of things for its object. But God is incapable of more worlds, and all that are possible He can make Himself. Our magnificence must be shown in something He cannot do, unless He were in our circumstance; and which of all things in the world He knows most fit to be done, were He in our places. He cannot be the soul of any of His creatures, but would be the soul of that soul; the joy and delight of that soul; the life and glory of that soul; and that He cannot be, unless that soul will delight in Him, and honour and love Him. It is not He must honour Himself, but that soul. His desire is that that soul would freely turn and delight in Him freely, of its own accord; would incline itself to consider His excellencies, and dedicate itself to love and honour Him. This is one way for the soul to be magnificent towards men too, who by nature delight to see God beloved and satisfied in a point of such infinite importance.

It is true, indeed, that God can be full of indignation and punish; but for love to turn into anger is no compensation for the pleasure it lost by our miscarriage; and to punish is a strange and troublesome work, in which love is extinguished, or else afflicted. Infinite love puts an infinite value on the gift; and I think it is magnificence to give a gift of infinite value.

Our magnificence towards men must be laid on a deep and eternal foundation. We must be willing to give ourselves to their comfort and satisfaction; and that we cannot do, but by imitating God in all His goodness, studying their felicity, and desiring their love with the same earnestness, to the utmost of our power; doing in all places, in all things, in all worlds, the things they desire;

supposing them to be what they ought to be, like gods themselves.

The best principle whereby a man can steer his course in this world is that which, being well prosecuted,[1] will make his life at once honourable and happy; which is to love every man in the whole world, as God doth. For this will make a man the image of God, and fill him with the mind and spirit of Christ. It will make every man that is, the representative of God and of all the world unto him. It will make a man to reverence God in all mankind, and lift him up above all temptations, discouragements and fears. It will make him to meet the love of God, angels and men, in every person. It will make a man truly glorious, by making him pleasing to God, and universally good to every one; diffusive like the sun, to give himself to all, and wise to enjoy their complete felicity. If there were but one, the case is evident; supposing more than one, his duty is to love every one the more for all their sakes. For since he must love all, and they are all to love one, and every one, he must please them all by gratifying their love to one; and by doing so to every one, they are all concerned in the welfare of one, and pleased in the love that is born to every one.

This in the state of glory shall be clear, where every one like the sun shall be clearly seen extending his love to all; though here upon earth, where our estate is imperfect, by reason of the imperfection of our knowledge it doth not appear. Our actions are limited; for being finite in our outward demeanour, they must needs be regulated by justice and wisdom.

But two things come in here to the assistance of magnificence, whereof the first is the inferior perfection of our love to all; the second is the universal satisfaction which the beauty of our outward life will afford at the last. Concerning the last, two things are fit to be considered. First, that as God has communicated the sun, by making it visible to all, and there is not a star but is seen by all nations and kingdoms; so has He communicated the soul, by making it visible to all, and there is not a thought that shall remain uncovered, nor an action but it shall be seen by all for ever. Secondly, that as God Himself is admired for His inward

[1] Followed.

love, so is He for the operations of His outward life, I mean for His works and judgments. When they saw His works finished, *The morning stars sang together, and all the sons of God shouted for joy.* The elders are represented before His throne, casting down their crowns and saying, *Thou art worthy, O Lord, to receive glory and honour and power, for thou hast created all things, and for thy pleasure they are, and were created*: where the perfection of God's pleasure in the glory of the creation is evidently discovered to be one of the joys of heaven, a great matter of their contemplation, an eternal cause of their praises. His infinite and eternal love is that by which He is *all glorious within;* all the sweetness of His essence and all the perfection of the soul is there; but yet His saints in the Church triumphant sing the song of Moses and the song of the Lamb, saying, *Great and marvellous are thy works, Lord God Almighty! Just and true are thy ways, thou King of Saints!*

His works are the substantial creatures in heaven and earth; His ways are His proceedings and dispensations among them in all ages. For all shall appear together for ever, the one being great and marvellous, the other beautified with truth and justice; so that neither of these doth swallow up the other, but both are distinct and perfect.

Our love may be infinite on the inside, and yet our life be diversified with many limited and particular actions. Now, if our life be like God's, eternally to be seen, and our actions in passing pass not away but in the sphere of our life abide for ever, our life all at once is a mysterious object, interwoven with many thoughts, occurrences and transactions; and if it be to be presented to God like a ring or a garland, we had need to be very choice in the mixture of our flowers, and very curious [1] in the enamel of so rare a token. Perhaps it is His crown, nay, our own; His and our royal diadem. It shall shine like a glory about our souls for ever. That there should be any dirt or blemish in it is inconsistent with our felicity; but it is a magnificent present, if it be enchased with jewels; I mean, with the most pure and fit elections, the most wise and just and excellent actions, the most bright and clear apprehensions, the most divine and ardent affections. The last

[1] Careful.

are like gold, the ground-work of the crown; but the work itself is a mixture of elaborate distinctions that sparkle in their lustre like gems of several cuts and colours. An imperial crown is a magnificent present from a king to a king; but a life like God's in a sphere, for which time was lent that it might be well wrought and presented before Him when made perfect, as far surpasseth the most glorious crown that did ever sit upon monarch's brows as that can be supposed to excel a dull clod of earth or a piece of rusty iron. There all obligations and laws and duties and occasions are interwoven; all our virtues and graces and vices, all our tears and devotions and prayers; our servants, the poor, the rich, our relations, parents, friends, magistrates and ministers are set and exhibited in their proper places. They appear to the life, with all our behaviours towards them; and though we did deny a poor man's request for the sake of another, and this and that and the other particular action did not at present extend to all; but the soul was fain to use much wisdom in contracting its operation for the greater advantage, in finding out its duty, in moderating its behaviour, in balacing its occasions and accounts; yet in the result of all, it will be found full of bounty and goodness to all, by taking care to be just and pleasing to all in the beauty of its conversation.

When two things it desires to do are incompatible to each other, it studies which of the two was more just and fit and necessary; which tends most to the full and final perfection of its life. The interest of a child sometimes carries it from another man, a debt of necessity is paid with that we would give for a work of charity. Yet when all is obedience, duty and love, that life is a most magnificent gift. A wife, a sister, must be respected in her place; a son, a servant, a friend, before a stranger, if the case be such that one of them only be relieved. All in the family, being made in the image of God, as well as the beggars without doors, [1] are objects of our charity. But so much goodness being in the bottom of the design, and so much prudence and justice in the denial, where his gold and silver faileth, his affection may be infinite; and the restraints he sets upon his actions be the several cuts and distinctions in the work, the very true engravings that make the

[1] Out of doors.

jewel or the crown glorious. Its matter is life itself, yet the workmanship far excels the matter, when it is as accurate and divine as it ought to be.

This great and deep thought makes every little act of life magnificent and glorious; a better gift to God, in its place, than the creation of all worlds before Him; while a man's love is really infinite towards all, and he is ready to sacrifice himself with Moses and St. Paul for the good of the world, but is fain to set a restraint upon himself for the sake of others. The very grief which true goodness conceives at the deficiency of its power, and the force that lies upon it in so ungrateful [1] a necessity, where it must be an umpire and judge between its bowels [2] and its children, is a molestation which he endures in the midst of his duty; filling all spectators with as much pleasure as him with pain. All shall be remembered, and all these things which are now so grievous shall themselves become a part of our future glory.

Remember always thou art about a magnificent work; and as long as thou dwellest here upon earth, lay every action right in its place. Let not patience only, but every virtue, have her perfect work. Let wisdom shine in its proper sphere; let love within be infinite and eternal. In the light of true knowledge it is impossible to exceed. Be right in all thy conceptions, and wise in all thine elections, and righteous in all thy affections, and just in all thy actions. Let the habits of compassion and mercy appear and break out fitly upon all occasions; and the severity of justice too, for the preservation of the world. Let all be underlaid with solid goodness, and guided with prudence, and governed with temperance; ordered with care, and carried on with courage. Lay hold on thy incentives by a lively faith, and on all the strengths of eternity by a glorious hope. Let all be sweetened with a gracious charity, fortified and secured with invincible meekness, and profitably concealed and veiled over with humility. Let thy contentment put a lustre and grace upon all. Let magnanimity and modesty appear in thy actions, magnificence and liberality act their part; let resignation to the divine will, and gratitude, come in to complete all these, and thy life be beautified with the sweet intermixture of obedience

[1] Unpleasant.
[2] Merciful inclinations.

and devotion. Thy godliness will be so divine that all angels and men will be perfectly pleased; especially when thou hast wiped out the miscarriages by the blood of the Lamb, which in a little crystal vial, pure and clear, thou oughtest always to carry about with thee. When thou hast washed away the defilements contracted in the work with the tears of repentance, those tears too He putteth in His bottles, and they will turn to jewels. There is not one drop so small but it shall turn into a precious stone, and continue for ever as it were frozen into a gem. *Many, O Lord my God, are thy wonderful works which thou hast done, and thy thoughts which are to usward. They cannot be reckoned up in order unto thee. If I would declare and speak of them, they are more than can be numbered. How precious also are thy thoughts, O God! How great is the sum of them! If I should count them, they are more in number than the sand. When I awake I am still with thee!* And with whom else can I be? For thou only art infinite in beauty and perfection: O my God, I give myself for ever unto thee!

CHAPTER XXXII

Of Gratitude. It feeds upon benefits, and is in height and fervour answerable to their greatness. The question stated, whether we are able to love God more than ourselves. It is impossible to be grateful to God without it. A hint of the glorious consequences of so doing

WHAT God has made us able to do by way of gratitude, you must see in the chapter of Magnificence. The love wherewith all these things ought to be done shall be so great in the estate of perfection, our charity and wisdom so directly intend [1] all angels and men, and especially God above all blessed for ever, our

[1] Be devoted to.

gratitude and goodness make us so zealous for their satisfaction, that no pleasure in the whole world shall be comparable to that of being delightful to them. To receive all is sweet, but to communicate all (adorned thus within the sphere of our own lives) is infinitely beyond all that can be sweet in the reception, both for our glory and satisfaction.

There is ever upon us some pressing want in this world, and will be, till we are infinitely satisfied with varieties and degrees of glory. Of that which we feel at present we are sensible; when that want is satisfied and removed, another appeareth, of which before we were not aware. Till we are satisfied we are so clamorous and greedy as if there were no pleasure but in receiving all. When we have it, we are so full that we know not what to do with it. We are in danger of bursting, till we can communicate all to some fit and amiable recipient; and more delight in the communication than we did in the reception. This is the foundation of real gratitude, and the bottom of all that goodness which is seated in the bent and inclination of nature. It is a principle so strong, that fire does not burn with more certain violence than nature study to use all, when it hath gotten it, and to improve its treasures to the acquisition of its glory.

The holiness of all the work consists in the fervour wherewith it is done; and if our love shall in heaven answer all its causes, it will be equal to all its obligations and rewards, and as infinite, in a manner, as the excellencies of its objects. The very love of God towards all things will be in it; our love shall be in all His, and His in ours. And if we love God, angels and men, all virtue, grace and felicity as they deserve, we shall so delight in excellent actions, and in appearing amiable and glorious before them, that we would not for all worlds miscarry in a tittle. And therefore every defect, even after pardon, will be an infinite disaster as well as blemish. This is one effect of gratitude in nature. And if it were not for the satisfaction of Jesus Christ, and the efficacy of faith and repentance in His blood, the least sinner in all nature would be eternally miserable, notwithstanding the advantages of Christ's blood. It is the desire of the soul to be spotless in itself; and if it be so profane as to build on these advantages, without taking care to be as excellent as it is able, it is the most ungrateful creature in the world, and is too base and dirty to appear in glory.

To talk of overflowing in the disbursements and effusions of love and goodness, till our emptiness and capacity be full within, is as impertinent and unseasonable as to advise a beggar to give away a kingdom, or a dead man to breathe, or one that is starving to give wine and banquets to the poor and needy. But when a man is full of blessedness and glory, nothing is so easy as to overflow unto others. To forbid or hinder him is to stifle and destroy him. Breath with the same necessity must be let out as it is taken in. A man dies as certainly by the confinement as the want of it. To shut it up and deny it are in effect the same. When a man hath the glory of all worlds, he is willing to impart the delights wherewith he is surrounded; to give away himself to some amiable object; to beautify his life, and dedicate it to the use and beauty of all spectators, and to put life into all his treasures by their communication. To love and admire and adore and praise, in such a case, are not only pleasant but natural and free and inevitable operations. It is then his supreme and only joy to be amiable and delightful. For the actions of love and honour belong in a peculiar manner to a plentiful estate.

Wants and necessities, when they pinch and grind us in a low condition, disturb all those easy and delicate resentments [1] which find their element in the midst of pleasures and superfluities. Hence it is that high-born souls in courts and palaces are addicted more to sweet and honourable excesses than clowns and peasants. The one spend their life in toil and labour, the other in caresses and soft embraces, amities and bounties, obligations and respects. Compliments and visits are the life of nobles, industry and care is that of the meaner people. Honours and adorations are fit for the temple, not for the market. Soft and tender affections are more in the court than in the shop or barn. There is some difference in this respect even between the city and country. But heaven is the metropolis of all perfection. God is a mighty king, and all His subjects are His peers and nobles. Their life is more sublime and pleasant and free, because more blessed and glorious. Their very palaces and treasures are infinite incentives to the works of

[1] Feelings.

honour and delight, and they cannot rest either day or night, but continually cry, *Holy, holy, holy, Lord God of hosts! Heaven and earth are full of the majesty of thy glory.* Their beauties and perfections enflame one another. Their very joys inspire them with eternal love; and as all care and labour are removed, so are all delights and ecstasies established. Ravishments and caresses, adorations and complacencies,[1] all the force and violence of love, charms, allurements, high satisfactions, all the delicacies and riches of sweet affection, honours and beauties are their conversation. Towards God, towards themselves, towards each other, they are all harmony and joy and peace and love. They fly upon angels' wings, and trample upon spices. Aromatic odours and flowers are under feet; the very ground upon which they stand is beset with jewels. Such you know were the foundations of the walls of the New Jerusalem, and the pavement of the street was beaten gold. God and the Lamb were the light and temple of it.

That we are to enjoy all angels and men by communicating ourselves unto them is a little mysterious, but may be more easily understood than a thing so obscure as the enjoyment of God by way of gratitude. That we are to love God more than ourselves is apparently sure; at least, we ought to do it; but whether it be possible is a question of importance. That we gain infinitely by His love is certain; but that we gain more by our own is prodigious! It is our duty to love Him more than ourselves, but whether it be our nature or no is doubtful. It is impossible to ascend at the first step to the top of the ladder. Even Jacob's ladder will not bring us to heaven, unless we begin at the bottom. Self-love is the first round, and they that remove it had as good take away all; for he that has no love for himself can never feel obliged. He that cannot be obliged cannot delight in God. He that cannot delight in Him cannot enjoy Him. He that cannot enjoy Him, cannot love Him. He that cannot love Him cannot take pleasure in Him, nor be grateful to Him. Self-love is so far from being the impediment that it is the cause of our gratitude, and the only principle that gives us power to do what we ought. For the more we love ourselves, the more we love those that are our benefactors.

[1] Delights.

It is a great mistake in that arrogant *Leviathan,* so far to imprison our love to ourselves as to make it inconsistent with charity towards others. It is easy to manifest that it is impossible to love ourselves without loving other things. Nature is crippled or, if it has her feet, has her head cut off, if self-preservation be made her only concern. We desire to live that we may do something else, without doing which life would be a burden. There are other principles of ambition, appetite and avarice in the soul; and there are honours and pleasures and riches in the world. These are the end of self-preservation; and it is impossible for us to love ourselves without loving these. Without loving these, we cannot desire them, without desiring cannot enjoy them. We are carried to them with greater ardour and desire by the love of ourselves. Preservation is the first, but the weakest and the lowest, principle in nature. We feel it first, and must preserve ourselves, that we may continue to enjoy other things; but at the bottom it is the love of other things that is the ground of this principle of self-preservation. And if you divide the last from the first, it is the poorest principle in the world.

'To love another more than one's self is absurd and impossible.' In nature it is so, till we are obliged, or perhaps till we see it our interest and find it our pleasure. It is a surprise to an atheistical fool that it should be one's interest to love another better than one's self; yet bears, dogs, hens, bees, lions, ants do it; they die for their young ones. Nurses, fathers, mothers do it; brides and bridegrooms frequently do it, and so do friends. All valiant heroes love their country better than themselves. Moses would have his name blotted out of the book of life, rather than the Israelites destroyed. St. Paul could wish himself accursed from Christ for his brethren the Jews; and they both learnt it of their master, *who made Himself a curse,* and even sin, for us. And it was His interest to do it!

If we are immortal and cannot but be blessed, it must needs be our interest to love Him that is more blessed than we, better than ourselves; because by that love we enjoy His blessedness, which is more than our own, and by that love it is made ours and more than ours. Is not all our glory and virtue and goodness seated in the excess of this perfect love? Do not all brave and heroical deeds depend upon it? And does not the man deserve to be burnt as an enemy to all the world, that would turn all men into knaves and cowards, and destroy the only principle which delivers them from being mercenary slaves and villains, which is the love of others? That alone which renders a man useful to the world is the love of others. He that destroyeth this would pluck up all gratitude by the roots; all worth, goodness and honour. No wonder, therefore, he should be an atheist, since nature is so base and abominable before him.

But its principles are oftentimes so generous, in truth, that they are too great for themselves. Nothing is so ordinary in the false way as that of loving others better than ourselves. Dogs have starved themselves to death upon the absence of their masters. How many fathers have gone down with sorrow to their graves, and lost all the comfort of their lives in the death of their sons! How many mothers have broken their hearts for the death of their children! How many widows have buried themselves alive for the loss of their husbands—I mean, by sequestering themselves from the delights and pleasures of the world! How many lovers dote and wax pale, and forget their meat, sleep and employment, and run mad for their mistresses! Are there no such examples, or is there no strength in examples such as these? 'But to love God better than one's self seemeth more unnatural.' Ah, vile! The more base and more wicked we! How we should love God better than ourselves is easy to unfold by the principles of self-love and self-exaltation. Take it in the manner following; and when you have seen its possibility, consider the glory of doing it, the benefit and felicity and honour that is in it. For it is all worth and pleasure, goodness and beauty, gratitude and virtue, wisdom and security, perfection and excellency. We love ourselves more in doing it than it is possible to do without it.

It is natural to all them that love themselves to love their benefactors, and all those things that are conducive to their welfare, pleasure, satisfaction. And the more they love themselves, the more apprehensive [1] they are of the benefit they receive, and the more prone to love that which occasions it. The more goodness we find in anything, the more we are prone to love it; and the

[1] Aware.

more we love it, the more to take pleasure in it. And if we find it highly convenient[1] and extremely delightful, we had not seldom rather die than part with it. We love ourselves only that we might live to enjoy that glory, or delight, or beauty or convenience that we find so agreeable. It often falls out, for want of acquaintance with delightful things, that we think nothing so powerfully sweet as to engage our soul beyond the possibility of retrieving itself; and that nothing can cleave so strangely to our minds as to be nearer and dearer than life itself. Yet oftentimes we find men of this opinion changing their mind, when they have chanced to taste some sweetness in nature they were not aware of; and then to become such miraculous converts that they love not themselves but for the sake of that delight which they have found in the world.

I make it a great question, would men sink into the depth of the business, whether all self-love be not founded on the love of other things? And whether it be not utterly impossible without it? Only the love of those things is so near and close to the love of ourselves that we cannot distinguish them, but mistake them for one and the same.

If the sun were extinguished and all the world turned into a chaos, I suppose there are few that love themselves so but they would die; which plainly shows that the love of the world is inseparably annexed with the love of ourselves; and if the one were gone, the other would be extinguished; especially if the sweetness of the air and its freedom and ease were changed into fire and torment. For then we would surely desire to die, rather than endure it; which shows that the love of ease and repose is greater than the love of our very beings, though not so perceivable till we have examined the business.

But if there be any pleasure or goodness or beauty truly infinite, we are apt to cleave unto it with adhesion so firm that we forget ourselves, and are taken up only with the sense and contemplation of it. The ravishment is so great, that we are turned all into ecstasy, transportation and desire, and live entirely to the object of our fruition. The power of infinite delight and sweetness is as irresistible as it is ineffable. And if God be all beauty and

[1] Agreeable.

delight, all amiable and lovely, truly infinite in goodness and bounty, when we see Him and taste the grace of His excellency, the blessedness and glory wherewith we are amazed possesseth us entirely, and becometh our sole and adequate concern. After that sight, it is better perish and be annihilated than live and be bereaved of it. The fall from so great a height would fill the soul with a cruel remembrance, and the want of its former glory and bliss be an infinite torment. Now, if it loved nothing but itself, it could endure all this. Rather than forsake itself, or lose or be bereaved of its essence, it would endure any misery whatsoever. Or, to speak more correct and accurate sense, it would be incapable of any passion, patience or misery, but only that which flowed from its abolition. Nothing could prejudice it but the change of its being.

That is not likely to love itself, after the way which some conceive proper to self-love, which is willing to forsake itself upon any misery, and apt to forget itself upon any great felicity. It loves itself that it might enjoy such a pleasure, but loves that pleasure so much beyond itself that it is ready to go out of itself, and is almost beside itself for the fruition of it. Loving itself only for that end, and that chiefly and for its own sake, it loves that far more than it loves itself. And there is no limit or bound; when it once begins to love anything more than itself, it may proceed eternally; and provided its object be infinitely more excellent, it will easily and greedily love it infinitely more than it can itself, and value the continuance of its own life only for the sake of that which it so infinitely esteems and delights in. It is true, indeed, it presupposes its capacity, but what would that capacity be worth, were it not for objects?

Were there no sun, it were impossible for so fair an idea to be conceived in a mirror, as is sometimes in a glass, when it is exposed to the sky. The mirror is in itself a dark piece of glass; and how so much fire and flame and splendour should come from it, while it is a cold flint or piece of steel; how it should be advanced by any art whatsoever to so much beauty and glory as to have a sun within itself, and to dart out such bright and celestial beams, no man could devise. Yet now there is a sun, the matter is easy; 'tis but to apply it to the face of the sun, and the glass is transformed. And if God dwelleth in the soul as the sun in a mirror, while it looketh upon Him the love of God must needs issue from that soul; for God is love, and His love is in it. The impression of all His beauty swallows up the being of the soul, and changes it wholly into another nature. The eye is far more sensible of the day, and of the beauty of the universe, than it is of itself; and is more affected with that light it beholds than with its own essence. Even so the soul, when it sees God, is sensible only of the glory of that eternal object. All it sees is God; it is unmindful of itself. It infinitely sees Him, but forgets itself in the rapture of its pleasure.

But we leave illustrations, and come to the reason of the thing in particular. The soul loving itself is naturally concerned in its own happiness, and readily confesseth it oweth as much love to any benefactor as its bounty deserveth. And if the value of the benefit be the true reason of the esteem, and reason itself the ground of the return, a little kindness deserveth a little love, and much deserveth more. Reason itself is adapted to the measure of the good it receiveth, and for a shilling's worth of service, a shilling's worth of gratitude is naturally paid. For a crown or a kingdom, the soul is enflamed with a degree of affection that is not usual. Now, God created and gave me myself. For my soul and body, therefore, I owe Him as much as my soul and body are worth; and at first dash [1] am to love Him as much as myself. Heaven and earth being the gifts of His love superadded to the former, I am to love Him upon that account as much more as the world is worth; and so, much more than I love myself. If He hath given all angels and men to my fruition, every one of these is as great as myself, and for every one of those I am to love Him as much as that angel or man is worth. But He has given me His eternity, His almighty power, His omnipresence, His wisdom, His goodness, His blessedness, His glory! Where am I? Am I not lost and swallowed up as a centre in all these abysses?

While I love Him as much as all these are worth, to which my reason, which is the essence of my soul, doth naturally carry me, I love Him infinitely more than myself; unless perhaps the possibility of enjoying all these things makes me more to esteem

[1] Immediately.

myself, and increases my self-love for their sake more than my own. Thus, when I see myself infinitely beloved, I conceive a gratitude as infinite in me as all its causes. Self-preservation is made so natural and close a principle, by all the hopes and possibilities to which I am created. Those hopes and possibilities are my tender concern; and I live for the sake of my infinite blessedness. Now, that is God. And for His sake it is that I love myself, and for the glory and joy of delighting in Him, I desire my continuance; and the more I delight in Him, my continuance is so much the more dear and precious to myself. Thus is God infinitely preferred by nature above myself; and my love to myself, being thoroughly satisfied, turns into the love of God, and dies like a grain of corn in the earth, to spring up in new and better form, more glorious and honourable, more great and verdant, more fair and delightful; more free and generous and noble; more grateful and perfect. The love of God is the sole and immediate principle upon which I am to act in all my operations.

Now if you inquire what advantages accrue by this love to the soul of the lover, we are lost again in oceans of infinite abundance. The strength and brightness and glory of the soul, all its wisdom, goodness and pleasure are acquired by it, founded in it, derived and spring from it; as we have before declared upon the nature of love. The solution of that one question will open the mystery, whether we gain more by His love or our own? All we gain by His love amounts to the power of loving; the act of loving we gain by our own, and all that depends upon it.

By His love, He existeth eternally for our enjoyment, as the Father of Glory, which is begotten by itself; but we do not gain all this by His love, but by our own. Some man would say, we gain our souls and bodies by the love of God, all ages and kingdoms, heaven and earth, angels and men, infinite and eternal joys; because all these were without our care or power prepared by Him and His love alone. They were prepared indeed by His love, but are not acquired or enjoyed by it. *He so loved the world that he gave his only-begotten Son,* and with Him all the laws and beauties of His kingdom; but unless we love Him, unless we are sensible of His love in all these, and esteem it, we do not enjoy our souls and bodies, angels or men, heaven or earth, Jesus Christ or His kingdom. Rather, we trample upon all and despise all, and make ourselves deformed. All these do but serve to increase our damnation and aggravate our guilt, unless we love and delight in their Author; and His love itself will eternally confound us. So that we gain and enjoy the love of God by ours.

Now, love returned for love is the soul of gratitude. In that act, and by it alone, we gain all that is excellent, and beside all these become illustrious creatures. It is more to our avail to be divine and beautiful than to see all the world full of delights and treasures. They would all be nothing to us, without our love. Nothing does so much alienate and estrange the soul from any object as want of affection. All the kingdom of heaven is appropriated and made ours by love alone. The inferior perfections of our own essence are gained by love, and by it we accomplish the end of our creation. We receive and enjoy all the benevolence of God's former love by ours; are made excellent in ourselves, and delightful to God, which can never be brought to pass any other way but by love alone. By loving Him as we ought to do, we enable Him to take pleasure in us; and this is of all other the greatest benefit. We clothe ourselves with the similitude of all His attributes, and shine in His image by love alone. Our love, as it acquires, crowns our perfections with His infinite complacency[1]: *This is my beloved Son, in whom I am well pleased,* is a voice that can be directed to none but Him only that loveth God with an eternal love. He cannot rest satisfied in any that hate or despise Him. The eternal complacency and delight of God, whereby we are crowned with eternal glory, is acquired and receives its being in a manner by love alone.

Now to love God is to desire Him and His glory, to esteem Him and His essence, to long for Him and His appearance, to be pleased with Him in all His qualities and dispositions, or, more properly, in all His attributes and perfections; to delight in all His thoughts and ways. It is to love Him in all His excellencies. And he that is not resolved to love every excellency in Him as much as it deserveth does not love God at all; for he has no design to please Him. But he that purposes to do it must necessarily love God more than himself, because he finds more objects

[1] Approval.

for his love in God than in himself, God being infinitely more excellent than he. But if this seems a grievous talk, it is not a matter of severity but kindness. We mistake its nature; the duty does not spring from any disorder in God, nor from any unreasonable or arrogant selfishness, as base and foolish men are apt to imagine, but from His excellency. It naturally springeth from the greatness of His worth; and it is our freedom, when we see His infinite beauty, to love it as it deserveth. When we do so, we shall infinitely love it more than ourselves, because it is infinitely better; and indeed shall find it so conveniently seated in the Deity for us that, could it be transposed or removed, it would nowhere else be fit for our fruition.

It is that eternal act of love and goodness that made all the kingdom of glory for us; that care and providence that governs all worlds for our perfection; that infinite and eternal act that gave us our being. That beauty is itself the Deity, and wherever it appeareth, there God is. The Godhead is the beauty in which we are all made perfect. And because we were nothing, we must be infinitely pleased that He is eternal; because it is His eternal act that gives us a being—and the act, O how divine! It is His beauty and glory. Can we choose but love that act, which is all goodness and bounty, which prepares for and gives to us infinite felicity? If we love ourselves, we must needs love it, for we cannot forbear to love the fountain of all our delights. And the more we love it, the more ardently we delight in it; the sweeter and more transporting will all our raptures be, the more feeling and lively, the more divine and perfect will our souls and our joys be. When we know God, we cannot but love Him more than ourselves; and when we do so, His blessedness and glory will be more than ours; we shall be more than deified, because in Him we shall find our perfection, and be eternally crowned. We must of necessity sit in His throne, when we see Him enjoying all His glory, because His glory is His goodness to us, and His blessedness our felicity; because in the acts of our understanding we shall eternally be with Him, and infinitely more than infinitely be satisfied in all His fruitions. That excellency which obliges us will enable us to love Him more than ourselves; and while we delight in Him for our own sakes, we shall steal insensibly into a more divine and deeper delight, we shall love Him for His, and even in point of gratitude adore His glory.

To adore and malign are opposite things; to envy and adore are inconsistent. Self-love is apt to leap at all advantages; and the more we love ourselves, the more prone we are to covet and wish whatsoever we see great and excellent in another. But He hath conquered our envy by His infinite bounty, and made us able to adore Him by the perfection of His essence. To covet the perfections of Him we adore is impossible. It is impossible to adore Him whom we would spoil and rob of His perfections; for adoration is a joyful acknowledgment of the infinite perfections of an adorable object; resting sweetly in them with acquiescence and rejoicing. It is prone to add and offer more. An adoring soul is in the act of sacrificing itself to the Deity, and with infinite complacency [1] admiring and adoring all His glories.

His glories will be inspired into the soul itself, for the healing of that envy to which it is otherwise addicted. And instead of robbery and discontentment and blasphemy and covetousness, the soul shall be full of honour and gratitude and complacency; and be glad to see in its God the full and eternal act of perfection and beauty. It was from all eternity impossible that there should be any other but He; and He from all eternity has so infinitely obliged us that, were it possible for any other to have been, it would not be desirable. He hath obliged us, and we love Him better than any other. Should we fancy or conceive another, a power from all eternity acting; should we suppose it possible that a power besides Him might have been; it must be just such a power as this is, and act in just such a manner as this hath done, or it would be displeasing. This hath done all that we can desire, all that powers infinite and eternal can do well; and therefore all possible powers are conceived in Him. He is the full and adequate object of all desires; because He is the fountain of all the most glorious things, and the sole perfect cause of all enjoyment whatsoever.

[1] Delight.

CHAPTER XXXIII

The beauty of gratitude. Its principal causes. Amity and communion are the great effect of it. The true character of a grateful person. God's incommunicable attributes enjoyed by gratitude. All angels and men are a grateful person's treasures, as they assist him in praises. He sacrifices all worlds to the Deity, and supremely delighteth to see Him sitting in the throne of glory

GOD having prepared the way to gratitude by infusing generous and noble principles into the soul, beautified the exercise of it by divers other provisions, that conspire to make it amiable and delightful. By the one He made it possible, by the other desirable.

One of the greatest ornaments of this virtue is the grateful sense of benefits received, for in it the felicity of the receiver consisteth; on it his grateful behaviour dependeth; by it he is made grateful or acceptable; and it is one of the great ends intended in the gift bestowed by the Donor, whose satisfaction ought to be regarded highly by every honest and worthy receiver. That grateful sense is the crown of the gift, the light wherein its beauty appears, the temple of honour, as it were; the womb wherein it is conceived, and findeth its life and value perfected.

Should we stand upon the explication of these, we should have little room for the fruits and effects of gratitude, which are the principal things intended in this chapter; but in short you may take this account. The greatest benefits we can receive are but abortive, or rather turn into curses, without a grateful acknowledgment of them. All gifts are but carcasses devoid of life, unless inspired with that sense which maketh them delightful. For as causes without effects are not causes, so blessings, if they bless not, are falsely reputed blessings. No benefits can be blessings, unless they are crowned with our complacency.[1] They must be conceived in the mind before they can be trans-

[1] Delight.

formed into joy; and be transformed into joys before they can produce those praises which are the music of the benefactor's soul, as well as of the receiver's. They are not conceived, unless they are quickened with the life of the receiver; nor are they reputed blessings, till they are had in reputation. An interior sense is the life and soul of every blessing; without which a whole world of delights would be but a chaos, the very kingdom of heaven but a confusion to him for whom it is prepared, and a soul among the angels but a fool in paradise. An ungrateful person bereaves himself of the pleasure that should spring from his enjoyment, for he stifles the enjoyment of the gift he receiveth. He eclipses and extinguishes his own blessedness by the dullness of his soul and the perverseness of his behaviour. He may be surrounded with causes of delight, but is not blessed, that is not full of the joys wherewith he is surrounded. When he is full of joys, he must needs overflow with complacencies [1]; which are the very elements of thanksgiving, the matter and fuel, as well as the soul, of praises. Were there nothing in a grateful sense but this, gratitude were an incomparable virtue; because all the effects of infinite and eternal bounty are by virtue of that grace applied to the soul, and enjoyed thereby, but are lost without it. That certainly must be a great virtue, by force of which we inherit all things.

As for the beauty of the receiver, it is evident that a dull and heavy complexion is the disgrace of his nature. His stupidity makes him a worthless piece of clay, that cannot be improved to any advantage. A carelessness and contempt of benefits springeth from his sottishness, which maketh him ingrateful, that is, odious; because he cannot be won by kindness, nor wrought upon by gifts. But he is more deformed, because he acts in a brutish manner, against reason, while he faileth to do what is fit and proper on such occasions. It is a base and dirty temper that cannot be enflamed with the love of a benefactor. It is incapable of high and generous sentiments; is dull and dry, insipid and untractable; as dead as a log of wood, a crabbed and knotty piece of matter, that cannot be wrought, and is only fit for the fire! But a quick and lively perceiver, a tender sense and sprightly intelligence, is all honour and delight upon the reception; all

[1] Joys.

activity, life and vigour; angelical in his nature, sweet and heavenly; apt to come up to the benefactor and answer his desires. He is rich and abundant in amiable resentments,[1] and prone to make returns suitable to the kindness wherewith he is affected. He has a strange kind of beauty lodged in his soul; there is a sweet correspondence between his nature and his benefactor's. All his inclinations are purity and praise. He is a great encouragement to the love of his benefactor; an ornament to his worth, an appendix of his honour, and a pleasure to his disposition; all life and goodness. He is capable of amity in the heights of its exercise.

A wise and worthy benefactor designs the felicity and contentment of the person to whom he imparteth his bounties; and if he were able, would do that for him which above all other things is most to be desired; not compel him to be grateful, for that would but spoil the beauty of his return; but make him capable of the best and highest resentments,[2] that he might have the joy of seeing his benefits work kindly; all which are lost and thrown away upon an ungrateful person. This God hath done. He has put brave principles and inclinations into the soul of man, and left him freely to exert them; with infinite desire to see him act freely, but generously and nobly. For by this means only is he made capable of honour; and the essence of gratitude consists in the freedom of its operation. Having so made him, and desiring nothing more than a lovely behaviour, His joy is as great as His goodness can inspire, when He sees that sweetness, which attends the operation and the work of reason, in a grateful person; and the joy which He occasions is His own joy, in the soul of His creature; of which to rob God is a kind of sacrilege, and a cruel murder committed on ourselves. For we have an inclination to delight in the joys of which we are the authors, and by a kind of echo or reflection, find the pleasure doubled which we take, and which is taken, in the communication of our bounties. And in this there is founded a certain sympathy of delight, which carries us to feel and be affected with another's joy, and makes it an object and a cause of ours; nay, almost the very form and essence

[1] Sentiments.
[2] Feelings.

of ours, when we are the authors of it. A grateful soul holds intelligence with God; as it receives His bounties, it delights in His complacencies.

The great effect of obligation and gratitude is amity and communion. A grateful soul is deeply concerned in the honour of his benefactor; in his benefactor's pleasure, life and safety; in all his successes, prosperities, advancements; in all his felicity and glory. He is afflicted in all his afflictions, he is delighted in all his enjoyments, he is crowned in all his promotions, he is wronged and injured in all his affronts, he is touched with the least displeasure that can befall him. Nay, he is more tender of his benefactor's repose that his own. The apple of his eye is the tenderest part in himself, yet he had rather have it touched than the person of his benefactor. No wounds can wound him more than those which his benefactor receiveth, and he in him. His own wounds may kill his body, but these destroy his contentment. A thousand injuries and calumnies against himself he can forgive, and is never provoked but when his friend is offended. He slights himself and prefers his benefactor. He would make his face a stepping-stone to his benefactor's glory. He exposes his body to swords and spears and arrows, for his benefactor's safety. He would rather be torn to pieces, and suffer a thousand deaths, than permit his benefactor to be slain or dishonoured. Now all this in time of trial and distress would seem disadvantageous. But besides the obligation, there is a sense of honour that compels a man thereunto; and a certain beauty in the act of gratitude, distinct from the goodness of the benefit, that is so naturally sweet to the goodness of the soul that it is better die than renounce it; and a certain baseness on the other side, an odiousness in ingratitude, in the very act, so abominable that it blasts any safety and repose that can be gotten by it.

Where the benefits are small, the virtue of gratitude is less powerful and perfect; for its strength depends upon its food and nourishment. A thin and spare diet is not very healthful for it. Though all the benefits that are done upon earth by men unto men are infinitely mean, if compared to those which the Godhead does to the least of His creatures, yet the world is full of the praise of this virtue, and an ingrateful man is the most hateful object living. Former ages afford us many rare and glorious examples of the power of gratitude, and its sacred zeal for, and tenderness of, its object. The union between the body and the soul is nothing comparable to the union of love and its beloved, though the causes are but slight upon which it is founded. The soul will often forsake its mansion to dwell with its beloved. It esteems all its beauties and members only for its beloved's sake. Yet colours and features, a little red and white, a sparkling eye, a brisk conversation and a delectable humour are all that breed it; all that produce this mighty effect, this prodigy of nature.

There is something more, where the life and honour of a man has been saved by the kindness of a benefactor; especially if he be rich and amiable that has delivered us. If he be great and honourable than was the author of the benefit, the obligation is the greater; for the worth of the person enters into the nature of the act, and enhances its value. Yet all this put together is exceeded by the gratitude of a worthy soul, because his own worth inclines him to be more generous than the cause requires, and to magnify the benefit by the mighty addition of his own goodness. It is the natural property of goodness to communicate itself; any occasion of doing it is instead of a cause. But when there is a cause, it is like a spark to powder; it enkindles a flame in his inclination. All acts of gratitude have a great deal of sweetness in their own nature, and for the sake of that beauty which is seated in themselves will not be rigorous or exact in their proportions, since it is a beautiful thing to exceed in goodness. Its own disposition prompts it to do more than is deserved by the kindness it receives and, if not to conceive itself more obliged than it is, yet to be more honourable in its returns than the mere goodness of its benefactor can exact; because it conceives itself by its own virtue obliged to be noble and munificent in all its acknowledgments.

But however slow gratitude may be in the returns which it maketh for smaller benefits, it is infinitely prone to exceed all measure, when it is infinitely obliged. Praises are not fed by mean contentments, but by sublime ones. The acknowledgment is cool, where the benefits are small, and the contentments imperfect where they are limited and restrained. Full satisfaction hath another kind of influence on the soul of man than single kindnesses or some few particular supplies. An infinite bliss produces more vigorous and joyful efforts than bare acknowledgments. Here upon earth there are disquiets and desires, and expectations and complaints, and defects and imperfections, fears and interests to be still secured, that lame and darken our contentment and gratitude. But in heaven all these admixtures of alloy are removed. The glory of the light in which our gratitude appeareth adds lustre and beauty to the increase of its perfection. In the utmost height of our satisfaction, there is such an infinite and eternal force that our gratitude breaks out in exulting and triumphing effusions. All our capacities, inclinations and desires being fully satisfied, we have nothing else to do but to love and be grateful.

An infinite and eternal kingdom given to him that was taken out of nothing, by a king that is infinite in greatness and beauty; all his joys and all his treasures! It makes the soul a fountain of delights, whose nature is to receive no more, but to overflow for ever. When the soul cometh once to love God so infinitely above itself as the cause requireth, its only delight is to magnify Him and to see Him blessed. The beauty and sweetness of its own gratitude is as rich and divine as all His gifts. It is tempted here infinitely more to exceed its causes than ever before. Amazements, admirations, affections, praises, hallelujahs, raptures, ecstasies and blessings are all its delights. The pleasure of loving is its only business; it is turned all into flame and brightness and transportation and excess. It infinitely passes light and fire in quickness and motion. All impediments are devoured, and God alone is its life and glory. The more great, the more high, the more excellent He is, the more blessed is itself, the more joyful and the more contented. Its nature is to shine and burn and admire; to offer and to sacrifice itself up to its joys; and God is its sovereign joy, its perfect happiness. To suspend its beams were to act against nature. All overtures of pleasure, beauty, glory, power, exaltation and honour it would have added to its happiness. The more He is magnified and pleased, the greater is its happiness. All the excellencies and perfections in its objective bliss, though they are not locally removed, are removed into the soul of him that enjoys it; and there express themselves far more powerfully and effectually than if they were there alone.

No joy can be like that of seeing its Creator adored; no service like that of magnifying its Beloved; no pleasure like that of delighting its Beloved, no melody like that of praising its Benefactor, no honour like that of obeying its Preserver. All worlds are its treasures, because they manifest His power and glory; all angels and men its delights, because they see and acknowledge the beauty of its sovereign and eternal perfection; all creatures the instruments of its joy, that celebrate His praises! In Him it enjoys the glory of all eternity, the infinite beauty of all immensity, the innumerable riches of all worlds, the pleasures and adorations of all the angels, the state and magnificence of all empires, the splendour and perfection of all ages; all which it has in itself, by His infinite bounty, as its own immediate and proper possessions; but far more divinely and sweetly enjoys them, by virtue of its gratitude and love to Him, whose they originally are and from whom they proceeded. For the very true reason why it enjoys itself and all its own treasures is because it loves itself; and the more it loves Him, the more it will be delighted with His fruitions. It feels more, it sees more, it tastes more, it possesses more, it rejoices more in its object than itself.

The imagination and fancy that is in love frame all the thoughts of its beloved in itself. It has an exquisite and tender sense of every change and motion in the mind of its beloved. *Stir not up nor awake my love till he please* is the song of a feeling and affectionate soul. Every prick with a needle's point in its object is a stab with a dagger to itself. Its heart bleeds in every drop of its object's finger. It loves his beloved ten thousand times more than itself, and is infinitely more pleased with its exaltation than its own. The happiness of its object is most its own.

True gratitude is crowned in its benefactor, enthroned in its benefactor, admired in its benefactor, adored in its benefactor. Nothing in all the world is so easily ravished as love; nothing is so lively as love, nothing so lovely; nothing so violent in its grief or joy, nothing so capable of pain or pleasure. All the victories and triumphs of its Saviour are its own. My joy, my life, my crown, my glory; my exceeding great reward, my love, my soul, my idol and the God of my soul! my all in all! This is the language of love in its rapture. Seraphic love! It is altar, heart and sacrifice.

Angelical love! It is priest and temple; all service, freedom, duty, reward, desire, enjoyment, honour, praise, adoration, thanksgiving, ecstasy, pleasure, bliss and happiness. It is all goodness and beauty, paradise, heaven; the life and soul of heaven!

All that is incommunicable in God—eternity, almighty power, supreme dominion, independent majesty, infinite immensity, with all the adorations and praises of all the creatures—are by such a love and gratitude enjoyed. Loving God more than itself, it is more happy in God than if it were a god. Could His deity be taken away and seated in itself, the soul of a grateful creature would be grieved at the exchange. Even God in His place is perfectly enjoyed. All envy is by perfect gratitude removed; all discontentment at anything in its object, especially at its object's blessedness, is abolished. It is carried above all thrones, dominions and powers; and still ascends eternally higher, the higher its object is exalted. Could it be miserable in itself, it would be happy in its object; but the higher it is exalted, the more is its Creator delighted. If the resentment be wholly spiritual, the soul perhaps may be transformed to gratitude, as gratitude is to contentment and praise and thanksgiving. But it will have no body, no frail and corruptible flesh, no bones or members to look after. All its operations are of one kind, all its works and concernments are the same. It has no fear or care to divert it; no impediment or danger or distraction.

Pure gratitude is so divine a thing that the soul may safely wish to be turned *all* into gratitude. Its employment and nature are all one, acknowledgment and benevolence united together. It sacrifices all worlds to the Deity, and with infinite delight desires to offer all honour and glory to Him. It is very sensible that it can never pay so much honour to God as is His due, unless it be assisted with all the tongues of men and angels. It goes along with their joys and consents to their praises. In them it adores and by them it admires; with them it conspires and takes in all their powers and divine affections. It sees with all their eyes, hears with all their ears, speaks with all their mouths, and useth all their hearts in loving and adoring. All the tendencies and operations of universal nature are subservient to its desires. It surmounts the songs of David; and yet we know how earnestly he exhorted all creatures to praise Him. *Praise ye the Lord; praise him in the sanctuary; praise him in the firmament of his power; praise him in his mighty acts; praise him according to his excellent greatness. Praise him in the heights; praise him, all ye angels; praise him, all his hosts; praise him, sun and moon; praise him, all ye stars of light; praise him, ye heaven of heavens!* And when all is done, it still confesseth that *His name is exalted far above all blessing and praise.*

He that praiseth God only for his health and food and raiment, and for His blessing on his calling, as too many only do, either is very ignorant or, upon a strict scrutiny, will be detected for upbraiding God, for the meanest of His bounty. For his love must infinitely be defective that is able to bestow gifts infinitely more, yet giveth us none but these. He that sees not more causes of joy than these is blind and cannot see afar off. The very truth of religion is obscure to him, and the cause of adoration unknown. He wanteth ten thousand demonstrations of the love of God, and as many incentives to enflame his soul in the return of love, that is unacquainted with these high and mighty bounties. No man can return more blessings than he receiveth; nor can his praises exceed the number and greatness of his joys. A house is too little, a kingdom is too narrow for a soul to move in. The world is a confinement to the power that is able to see eternity, and conceive the immensity of Almighty God! He that can look into infinite spaces must see them all full of delights, or be infinitely displeased. How like an angel doth he soar aloft, how divine is his life, how glorious and heavenly, that doth converse with infinite and eternal Wisdom, intermeddle with all the delights of God, assume the similitude of His knowledge and goodness, make all His works his riches, His laws his delights, His counsels his contemplations, His ways his joys and His attributes his perfections! He that appropriates all the world and makes it his own peculiar [1] is like unto God, meet to be His son, and fit to live in communion with Him.

The kingdom of God is made visible to him to whom all kingdoms are so many mansions of joy, and all ages but the streets of his own city. The man that sees all angels and men his fellow-

[1] Possession.

members, and the whole family of God in heaven and earth his own domestics, is fit for heaven. As he hath more encouragements to believe in God and to delight in Him, so hath he more concern to engage his fear, more allurements to provoke his desire, more incentives to enflame his love and more obligations to compel him to obedience; more arguments to strengthen his hope, more materials to feed his praises, more causes to make him humble, more fuel for charity to others, more grounds of contentment in himself; more helps to inspire him with fortitude, more rewards to quicken his industry, more engagements to circumspection and prudence; more ballast to make him stable, more lights to assist his knowledge, more sails to forward his motion; more employments in which to spend his time, more attractives to meditation, and more entertainments to enrich his solitude. He hath more aids to confirm his patience, more avocations [1] from injuries to meekness, more wings to carry him above the world and more gates to let him into heaven. He hath more withholders to keep him from sin, more aggravations to increase his guilt; more odious deformities in every vice, more waters to augment his tears, more motives to repentance and more consolations upon his reconciliation; more hopes to relieve his prayer, more bounds to secure his prosperity, more comforts in adversity, and more hallelujahs in all estates. More delights to entertain his friends, more sweetness in his conversation, more arts to conquer his enemies, more feasts in abstemious fasts, more and better sauce than other at his feasts; innumerable companions night and day, in health, in sickness, in death, in prison; at his table, in his bed, in his grove, in his garden; in the city, in the field, in his journey, in his walk; at all times and in all places. He hath more antidotes against temptation, more weapons in his spiritual warfare, more balsam for his wounds, and more preservatives against the contagion of worldly customs.

From this spring of universal fruition, all the streams of living waters flow that refresh the soul. Upon this hinge all a man's interests turn, and in this centre all his spiritual occasions meet. It is the great mystery of blessedness and glory, the sphere of all wisdom, holiness and piety, the great and ineffable circumstance

[1] Diversions, distractions.

of all grace and virtue, the magazine and store-house of all perfection.

AN APPENDIX

Of Enmity and Triumph; of Schism and Heresy, Fidelity, Devotion, Godliness; wherein is declared how gratitude and felicity inspire and perfect all the virtues

I SHOULD here have ended all my discourse on virtue, had it not been necessary to speak something of our enemies. Since there was never any man so wise but he had some, it is not to be expected that the most virtuous man living should be altogether without them. Moses and David and Elijah and Daniel had enemies; so had our Lord Jesus Christ Himself. Joseph had some in his younger days, and Solomon some in his old age. Of all the prophets, I find Samuel the most clear and exempted from them. But this I observe, that men of great and transcendent principles, of staid and well-governed passions, of meek and condescending behaviours, highly kind and serviceable in their age, free from the spots and blemishes of the world, have frequently arrived to an universal applause and honour, and moved in a sphere so high above the nation in which they lived that, as if they had been creatures of another world, they have enjoyed a veneration above their degree, and been surrounded with a repose that makes them look like angels in a kind of heaven; that that heaven which they enjoyed upon earth was the work, and the reward and crown, of virtue. Thus Moses, after his long meekness and invincible fidelity to the Jewish nation, was in the close of his life most exceedingly honoured by all the people, and lamented after his death by a million of persons, that felt the disaster of so great a loss. Joseph suffered much by the envy of his brethren in the beginning, and the lust and slander of his mistress; but after he had once been the saviour of the land of Egypt and of his father's family, his virtue being known, he enjoyed a long life of glory and honour and, of the abundance of his own peace and tranquillity, communicated a repose and prosperity to his nation. Joshua did run the hazard of being stoned for crossing the perverse humour of the Jews, when he returned from searching the land of Canaan; but from Moses' death, throughout all his life afterwards, was an absolute prince among his own people and a glorious victor over all their enemies. Samuel was from his infancy chosen of God, and from Dan even to Beersheba they knew he was established to be a prophet of the Lord. The honour of his communion with heaven, joined with his great integrity and gravity on earth, gave him a reputation that made him greater than all the elders in the land. And it is very apparent that the eminent holiness and goodness and great wisdom of these men made them to prevail, with God's blessing on their virtues, and to reign like benefactors and magnificent patriots of their country. Solomon was by his wisdom exceeding glorious, till he revolted from God; and those mischiefs which befell David after he came to the throne did spring from his fall in the matter of Uriah.

These things I note to encourage men to virtue. For though our Lord Jesus Christ and His apostles were persecuted to the death, yet two things are very considerable; first, that their glory surmounted the rage of all their enemies, and continues immortally shining throughout all kingdoms and all ages: next, that they were born to troublous times, and were to break the ice for all their followers. For their business was extraordinary; to change the state and condition of kingdoms, to alter the public rites of religion both among Jews and Gentiles, and therein to shake and dissettle the secular interests of millions, as well as to touch and offend the conscience, in defaming that for which so many ages had so great a veneration. This created all the difficulty in their lives. But where the public rites of religion are approved, and a man is born in peaceable and quiet times, I do not see but the most virtuous men inherit all the honour and esteem of the people and, whatever degree they are of, reign in the fullest and freest prosperity. Nor has the death of Christ so little prevailed upon earth but that all the world does now take notice of the glory of His doctrine, and far better understand the excellency of virtue than they did before. They feel and admire its influences, insomuch that, as some virtuous men grow contemptible by their vices, so do the most debauched and vicious men find a necessity of appearing virtuous, if they mean to be honourable. For as all errors receive their strengths from some truths professed by heretics, so do all vices and vicious persons owe their supports to the powerful strengths of those virtues on which they lean, and which they use (though in a wicked manner) for their own security. For they cannot rise and thrive in the world without some virtue, or show of virtue at least, to cover and help out their vices.

Three things I desire you to note seriously, when you have first observed that it is a very hard matter to hate an excellent man, or contemn him when he is known. The one is, that enmities and disgraces are like the pangs and throes of the new birth; they fall like storms and showers upon budding virtues in their spring and greenness. When a man first begins to be virtuous, he is despised, suspected, unknown; he may be censured and hated. But when he has made himself eminent and conspicuous, is a man of tried and approved virtue, well known for a person of honour and worth, the first envies and censures abate; and if he constantly exercise all honesty and goodness with great activity, courage and prudence, he shall conquer all his enemies, and inherit the benefit of his own virtues in the peace and tranquillity of his happy condition.

Note also that it is not so much the malignity of the world as some vice of the proficient, or some occasion that religious men give the world to blaspheme religion by some infirmity or other, that makes them to be hated. And this I note, because I would have you not cry out of other men's corruptions so much as of your own. There is a little pride, or covetousness, or laziness, or scorn, or anger or revenge, some deformity or other, that gives men advantage against us, when they deride at our profession; but under the name and notion of virtue no man was ever yet upbraided. As a fool, perhaps, and a coward, but not as a wise and gallant man, he may be scorned.

Thirdly, some secular interest may put people together by the ears; but no man is hated for being perfectly virtuous. Misapprehensions, slanders, injuries, quarrels about estates and possessions may arise; but where the land is at peace, and the true religion established, no man is hated for being wise and good, and holy and chaste, and just and liberal, and honest and merciful, and meek and courageous; but the more admired for being holy and blessed, when he joins all God's virtues together. A man may be perverse and turbulent, a schismatic and a heretic and by a rash and erroneous zeal bring many enemies and penalties on himself, while he rails against the magistrates and reviles the bishops and pastors of the church, breaks the laws and disturbs the kingdom, profanes and blasphemes God's public worship, and endeavours to overthrow the established religion and discipline among us. But all the troubles which a man brings on himself by any such means as these are not to be fathered on virtue, but rightly to be ascribed to their proper causes. Had he that suffered them been more virtuous, he had been less miserable. And truly this I may say for the glory of Christianity, where it is freely and purely professed in any nation or kingdom (as at present in ours) a man may be as divine and heavenly as an angel. And if he be liberal and kind, and humble and cheerful, especially if withal he be undaunted and courageous, most exceedingly honest and faithful in his dealings, the more holy and divine he is, the more he is commended and valued in the land; but if he have any flaw, the greater stir he makes in religion the more he is hated. He loses his credit, and undergoes the censure of a supercilious hypocrite.

As for all the enemies which strife and contention about worldly goods occasion to a virtuous man, he is no more liable to them than other persons; and yet when he meets them, he has far more advantages over his enemies than other men. For, being full of courage, he dares do anything that is fit against them, and that sparkle of the lion makes them to dread him; whereas a coward is baffled and run over in a moment. Being full of temper and humility, he is not apt to exasperate them and make them mad, as hot and angry spirits are apt to do. By kindness he obliges and wins and softens them; by prudence he knows how to manage them; and all his other virtues come in as so many strengths against them. Being just, he never quarrels but in a good cause; being good and merciful, he is not apt to make an enemy. Being wise and holy, his soul is in another world, and it is no trivial injury that can make him contend. Being liberal and magnanimous, he is prone to do heroical things, and to make himself venerable to his very adversary, and above all to tender and love his soul, and to steer all the contention to both their benefit. We rail on the world when the fault is in ourselves. The most of men professing virtue are but children in worth; very weak and very defective, and too timorous too, God knows. They neither trust God enough, nor carry virtue to the height. Virtue is base, and not virtue, while it is remiss. It never shineth gloriously and irresistibly till it be acted almost in a desperate manner. He only is the great man, that contemns danger, life and death and all the world, that he may be supremely and completely virtuous.

Enemies may sometimes spring from envy; and indeed, there alone lies the core of the matter; when some men, imperfectly virtuous, abhor others for being more excellent than themselves—at least, for being more honourable and more prosperous. Here again, temporal interest is the ground of the enmity; for thus our Saviour was hated by the scribes and pharisees. Pilate knew that they delivered Him for envy. But the main pretext and cause of His condemnation was the testimony of those that heard Him say He would destroy the temple; without which, and His imputed blasphemy, they could hardly have killed Him. But He came to die, and was the less solicitous.

Where these public cares are away, they that envy virtuous men are greatly men of equal rank and degree with themselves; but a man truly virtuous will outstrip them, as far as a swallow will a snail. All his inferiors and all his superiors that understand him, and the most also of his equals, and all they too, if he invents ways and methods to oblige them, will at last be won to confess and acknowledge him. But in the meantime he grows and thrives, and enjoys their very enmity. He never speaks ill of them behind their backs. He is not a jot discouraged nor exasperated; he pities their weakness, and is humble under the sense, perhaps, of his own. He is careful to give them no advantage against him. He confides in God, and strengthens himself in hope of divine assistance. He rejoices exceedingly that he has the opportunity of forgiving, and considers how many virtues he has to exercise upon that occasion. It makes him to exult, when he considers that these enemies are the instruments and materials of his greater glory. He foresees the victory, and delights in the triumph. And besides all this, he is obliged by Jesus Christ to forgive greater wrongs than these, and gladly yields some trials of his obedience. He has an infinite felicity in daily view, and remembers he is a pilgrim in a strange country. He is dead to the world, and alive unto God. The moon is beneath his feet, and so are all fickle and transitory things. He is clothed with the sun, and walketh in the light, environed with the beams of his own enjoyments. If his enemy be able to do him a mischief (which to a man perfectly virtuous seldom happens) he turns it into good, which a foolish and vicious man cannot do. He sinks not under it, but plunges out again, and surmounts it altogether; immediately forgives it, and can after cheerfully serve his enemy. For his part, he will be an enemy to no man in the world. He knows his duty and his Master, the value of souls and the excellency of virtue. His very gratitude to God and Jesus Christ is enough to make him go through a thousand greater and more terrible brunts than these.

I would not have men ungrateful to Jesus Christ, nor blind to themselves. I know very well that the age is full of faults, and lament it; but withal I know it is full of advantages. As sin abounds, so does grace also super-abound: never so much clear knowledge, in any age; learned ministers, multitudes of sermons, excellent books, translated bibles, studious gentlemen, multitudes of scholars, public liberty, peace and safety—all great and eminent blessings. There were many disorders in the Church at Corinth, and yet the Apostle tells them of their reigning, and wishes, would to God he could reign with them, after their city had a little flourished in peace and received religion: and makes his comparison between them and himself after such a manner that, when it is considered it would make one apt to think the reigning of the saints (which is spoken of in the Book of the Revelations) were either now present or already past. *Now ye are full,* saith he, *now ye are rich; ye have reigned as kings without us, and I would to God ye did reign, that we also might reign with you. For I think God hath sent forth us the apostles last, as it were appointed to death; for we are made a spectacle to the world, and to angels and to men. We are fools for Christ's sake, but ye are wise in Christ; we are weak, but ye are strong. Ye are honourable, but we are despised. Even to this present hour, we both hunger and thirst, and are naked and are buffeted, and have no certain dwelling place.*

A small matter will make a saint to reign, by reason of the greatness of his interior bliss. If he be not buffeted and cast out of doors, having food and raiment, with his godliness it is great gain. Especially when kings and princes yield a professed subjection to the gospel of Christ; for then *all the kingdoms of the world become the kingdoms of the Lord and of his Christ.* When the cross is exalted above the crown, and the king's palaces surmounted by the magnificence of our Saviour's temple, and there is no idolatry nor poison in the Church, but a pure public worship; when the very laws and magistrates countenance religion, and those apostles, that were once persecuted and cast out as vile, are now glorified and admired for their sanctity, men may be Christians publicly, and in the face of the sun. It is horrible ingratitude to be insensible of the advantage; to calumniate and reproach and disturb the Church, as if it were a sink of paganism. Rather we should admire and adore God Almighty, *that other men laboured and we are entered upon their labours.* We inherit the blood and toil and sweat of the martyrs; they bore the burden and heat of the day, and we enjoy the victory and peace they acquired. This is one, but not one of the least, of God's mercies for which we should be grateful.

That all the business of religion on God's part is bounty, gratitude on ours, and that this gratitude is the sphere of all virtue and felicity easily is discerned after the first intimation. Gratitude is all that is to be expressed here upon earth, and above in heaven. All our complacencies in His infinite highness, all our delights in His eternal praises, all our adorations, ecstasies and offerings, all our joys and thanksgivings, are but the feathers and the wings of that seraphim in glory. All the acknowledgment and faith and hope and repentance, all the obedience and resignation of a sinner upon earth, all his care and fear to offend, all his desire and endeavour to please, all his worship and charity, all his courage and perseverance and patience, all his fidelity, devotion and godliness, are but gratitude in several dresses, as time, place and occasion require. Sermons are to inform and assist our gratitude, sacraments to revive and exercise its virtue. Virtues themselves are our aids to bring us thereunto. Upon sabbaths it enjoys a rest that hath something in it of heaven, and it is a hard matter to be wicked in a sanctuary. But in ordinary conversation, in shops and taverns, in the camp, in the navy, at a feast or on a journey, to retain the sense of all mercies and to carry all these virtues and graces about a man is not ordinary for a common Christian. But that which does realize our gratitude and make it perfect is a true fidelity to God and ourselves, which is an acquired habit or a grace infused; by virtue of which we keep all those promises which we made to God in our holy meditations, and all those holy resolves which in our best retirements we put upon ourselves, to do His will even in the midst of all assaults and temptations. It is a virtue by which we remain constant in all persecutions and allurements; not warping or moving aside on any consideration; neither melting with pleasures, nor flinching at distresses; but continuing faithful to the death, that we may obtain the crown of life. He certainly that sees himself a king of all worlds, and brother to our Lord Jesus Christ (who hath said, *He that doth the will of my Father is my mother, sister and brother*), will not be wrought on to forsake or hazard so great a bliss. His knowledge of its perfection will animate his soul with all fidelity.

It will draw him from the world, too, and make him desire to be much alone, that he may be much with God. A covetous man will be telling his moneys, an ambitious man aspires to be always near the king's person, an epicure is for his wine, or women, or feasts continually. A virtuous man is more covetous, more ambitious, more prone to celestial epicurism, if I may so speak, than all the world besides. And so art thou, if thou art really engaged in the study of felicity. A pious man has greater treasures, higher honours, more pure pleasures, sincerer and truer delights, a more glorious Friend than all the earth beside. Why should we not enjoy Him, why should we not retire to adore Him, why not delight in devotion and communion with Him? There a man is to feed by sweet contemplation on all his felicities. He is there to pray for open eyes and a pure heart, that he may see God.

There thou art to exercise thy strengths, and acquaint thyself with Him; to look into all ages and kingdoms, to consider and know thyself, to expatiate[1] in the eternity and immensity of God, and to gain that godliness which, with real contentment, is great gain. There thou art to stir up thyself, by way of pure remembrance, to recollect thy scattered and broken thoughts, and to clothe thyself with all thy necessary perfections.

For godliness is a kind of God-likeness, a divine habit, or frame of soul, that may fitly be accounted the fullness of the stature of the inward man. In its least degree, it is an inclination to be like God, to please Him and to enjoy Him. He is God-like that is high and serious in all his thoughts, humble and condescending in all His actions, full of love and goodwill to all the creatures, and bright in the knowledge of all their natures. He delights in all the works of God, and walks in all the ways of God, and meditates on all the commandments of God, and covets all the treasures of God, and breathes after all His joys. He that hates all that God hates, and desires all that God desires, and loves all that God loves, and delights in all His delights, is Godly; he that aspires to the same end, by the same means, and forms himself wittingly to the same nature. Every like in nature draweth to its like—the beautiful, and the wise, and the good, and the aged, but especially the God-like. There is more reason why they should delight in each other. They have more attractions and incentives.

Godliness, or God-likeness, is the cement of amity between God and man. Eternity and immensity are the sphere of his activity, and are often frequented and filled with his thoughts. Nothing less than the wisdom of God will please the God-like man; nothing less content him than the blessedness and glory of his great Creator. He must enjoy God, or he cannot enjoy himself. That is, he must rest satisfied in Him, as the Creator, the Lawgiver, the Lord and Governor of the world; and for that end must be completely satisfied with the glory and perfection of all His works and laws and ways. He must delight in all His counsels, that he may enjoy Him as the great Counsellor of all nature; and see the beauty of His mind, that he may take pleasure

[1] Range freely.

in Him as the blessedness of angels, the redeemer of men, the sanctifier of His elect people and the sovereign end of all things. He must enjoy Him as his own supreme and eternal object, his King, his Father, Bridegroom, Friend, Benefactor, all in all; which he can never do, till he sees God to be the best Father, the best King, the best Benefactor, Bridegroom and Friend in all the world; nor that, till he sees the beauty of the whole creation, the great and wonderful things of His law, the marvellous glory of His all-wise dispensations, the sacred perfection of His decrees, and the nature of His essence. And all these must be as sweet and satisfactory to himself as they are to the Deity. To be God-like is a very sublime and most glorious perfection, which no man can attain that is not either curiously [1] satisfied in all these things, or humbly confident of their beauty and perfection. And for this cause have we thus written upon all the virtues, that all that need it and read the book may be elevated a little higher than the ordinary rate, have something more erect and angelical in their souls, be brought to the gates, at least, of God's kingdom, and be endued with Godliness a little more completely by their care than hitherto they have been; because they know both that *God is, and is a rewarder of them that diligently seek him.*

[1] In every particular, scrupulously.